I GOT A SONG

I GOT A SONG

A HISTORY OF THE
Newport Folk Festival

RICK MASSIMO

Wesleyan University Press ✳ Middletown, Connecticut

Wesleyan University Press
Middletown CT 06459
www.wesleyan.edu/wespress
© 2017 Richard Massimo
All rights reserved
Manufactured in the United States of America
Designed by Eric M. Brooks
Typeset in Calluna by Passumpsic Publishing

Library of Congress Cataloging-in-Publication Data
NAMES: Massimo, Richard, 1964–
TITLE: I got a song: a history of the Newport Folk Festival / Rick Massimo.
DESCRIPTION: Middletown, Connecticut: Wesleyan University Press,
    [2017] | Includes bibliographical references and index.
IDENTIFIERS: LCCN 2016038490 (print) | LCCN 2016038662 (ebook) |
    ISBN 9780819577023 (cloth: alk. paper) | ISBN 9780819577030 (pbk.:
    alk. paper) | ISBN 9780819577047 (ebook)
SUBJECTS: LCSH: Newport Folk Festival—History. | Folk music festivals—
    Rhode Island—Newport—History.
CLASSIFICATION: LCC ML38.N4 N374 2017 (print) | LCC ML38.N4 (ebook) |
    DDC 781.62/1300787457—dc23
LC record available at https://lccn.loc.gov/2016038490

5 4 3 2

FOR
CHRISTINE,
FLORENCE &
HENRY

CONTENTS

Illustrations appear after page 68

PREFACE

The Newport Folk Festival was an American musical institution almost as soon as it began in 1959, and it's been a touchstone for more than fifty years, even given a pair of interruptions during its history. This book examines how the festival came to be in the beginning, how it came to be what it is today and how it came to be what it was at each distinct stage of its history in between. At every point, the story both drives and reflects changes in individuals and the collective musical world in which they work.

In July 2009, I was planning coverage of the fiftieth-anniversary Newport Folk Festival for the *Providence Journal*. I had already written about the fiftieth-anniversary Newport Jazz Festival in 2004, so I knew there would be a lot of history to cover. I also knew that George Wein was stepping back in to take the reins of both festivals after having sold his operation to a startup that had since failed.

My editors at the *Journal* sent me to New York to spend a day with Wein; we spoke for about two hours, went to a jazz festival–related event, returned to Wein's home and spoke for about two more hours. On the train ride back that night, I plotted out a series of stories on the history of the Newport Folk Festival; by the time I got back to Providence, I knew the subject deserved a book.

Those interviews yielded valuable historical insights as well as a picture of what it was like to be in the driver's seat to one of American music's landmark events, and these are sprinkled throughout. The portion of that day recounted in chapter 11, however, comprises the heart of the interviews, and in many ways it is the heart of this book: the festival's original sense of purpose, which has been refracted but never distorted over the decades.

The festival has meant many things to many people at many times. The real meaning of individual performances, and the festival as a whole, in many ways resides in the minds of those who witnessed it live. Some aspects of this history can only be fully understood by reading books; some can only be grasped by delving into unpublished primary sources such as board minutes and sometimes-angry letters; some of it requires face-to-face talks with the people who were there in the early days and are still involved; some of it can only be learned by listening to the music. A lot of people helped with each of these aspects.

Elijah Wald's book on Bob Dylan's electric performance at Newport is loaded with important information and analysis, and he was consistently willing to help. And Benjamin Filene was not only happy to discuss his work with me but found my interpretations of it not totally laughable.

Many thanks to my old *Journal* colleagues, including Alan Rosenberg and Phil Kukielski during the reporting and writing of the original stories, and G. Wayne Miller, Mark Patinkin, Mike Stanton and especially Bill Reynolds in the early stages of this project.

I'd also like to thank all who shared their stories of Newport and the festival over the decades. I appreciate the time and attention paid by dozens of people, whom you'll find in these pages, but special mention has to be made of George Wein, who was particularly generous with his time, and Murray Lerner, who provided valuable contact information for other sources. Similarly, Carolyn McClair smoothed the way for many interviews.

Jeff Place, Cecilia Peterson, Stephanie Smith and the staff at the Ralph Rinzler Folklife Archives and Collections at the Smithsonian Institution provided a wealth of photos, as well as access to Rinzler's papers regarding Newport, including board minutes, financial records and personal correspondence. Likewise, Todd Harvey, Jennifer Cutting and the staff at the American Folklife Center at the Library of Congress provided access to tapes from the early Newport Folk Festivals, as well as Alan Lomax's papers, which included illuminating correspondence as well.

The documents in those archives, as well as other resources in the Smithsonian Institution and the Library of Congress (particularly the American Folklife Center), were invaluable in piecing together the events of the history of the Newport Folk Festival, particularly in its early days. So too were the memories of the people who created that history.

Inevitably, however, these sources sometimes clashed. Every effort has been made to reconcile people's years- and decades-old memories with accounts from primary documents and recordings. In probably one of life's more predictable ironies, some of the most confidently expressed memories were among those proven incorrect.

Preface

At other junctures in the history of the Newport Folk Festival, there's no clear-cut answer as to what actually happened, and in that case the differences of opinion and of recollection stand as testimony to the size of the event and the many angles it could be viewed from.

This appears most obviously in the structure and form of chapter 7: the recently available tapes in the Jackson/Christian Collection at the American Folklife Center settle pretty much all questions as to what happened on the stage. That's not, however, the full answer to the question "What actually happened at Bob Dylan's electric performance on July 25, 1965?" That answer lies in the minds and memories of the people who were there and in their thoughts, analyses, arguments and actions thereafter. In this context, it's not a matter of weeding through the many responses in order to find the answer; the fact that the community to and in which the performance was delivered could generate such responses is in fact the answer itself.

More people's efforts need to be mentioned and appreciated. Carole Sargent and Marcia Chatelain at Georgetown University were instrumental in putting me in touch with Wesleyan University, and thanks of course to the past and present staff of the Wesleyan University Press, including Suzanna Tamminen, Marla Zubel, Dan Cavicchi and Parker Smathers. Thanks also to John Spangler, who helped with interview transcription, and Aaron Winslow for the index.

Large portions of this book were written while tagging along on my wife's residencies at the Rockefeller Foundation's Bellagio Residency Program and the Bogliasco Foundation. While I wasn't the official resident, the hospitality, time and (especially) respect that both these institutions afforded me were instrumental in the development of this work.

Finally, special acknowledgment must go to my wife, Christine Evans, who not only was endlessly morally and emotionally supportive through the entire process but was a sharp and perceptive reader and editor throughout.

I GOT A SONG

I HAVE a song. Here it is.
PETE SEEGER

PEOPLE THINK THIS STUFF JUST HAPPENS

It's a summer afternoon in Newport, Rhode Island, a small city on Aquid-neck Island where some of the world's richest people once had their summer "cottages," and Pete Seeger takes the stage in Freebody Park, a quadrangle with baseball diamonds at opposite corners in the middle of the city.

While thirty-three-year-old George Wein, the producer of the show, busies himself with a million details backstage, the master of ceremonies, Studs Terkel, introduces Seeger by referring to his iconic status: "Whenever you see a young banjo player anywhere in the country with a banjo waist-high, head back, Adam's apple bobbing, you can say 'Like Kilroy, Pete Seeger has been there.' Here, then, is America's tuning fork—Pete Seeger."[1]

Despite the introduction, Seeger begins with a twelve-string guitar around his neck. Ever the educator as well as the entertainer, Seeger explains to the audience that the words to his first song, "The Bells of Rhymney," were written "by a man in Wales, a man who was raised as a coal miner" who adapted a nursery rhyme to depict Wales's mining towns and include a critique of the barons of the mines. Seeger adapted the song himself, adding, "Throw the vandals in court, say the bells of Newport." He begins slowly, almost arrhythmically, but then picks up the pace, ending in a speedball of energetic righteousness.

From there he hoists his trademark banjo and goes into the gentle "Grains of Sand," interrupting it halfway through to inform the audience that he used to sing the song to put his daughter to sleep—"until she realized my purpose in singing it" and asked for something "more exciting." Instead, he begins his version of the Bantu story/song "Abiyoyo" about a giant who was neutralized by a father-son team using the very musical and magical skills that had gotten them cast out of their village. He encourages the audience to sing along. The conjoined voices float over the field and sweep on the wind over the roofs of the privileged and Newport's oft-forgotten working class alike.

The show was vintage Pete Seeger; the year was 1959, and on that July weekend the Newport Folk Festival began.

On another summer afternoon in Newport, the sun begins to slant its light into the eyes of anyone to the left of the stage where Pete Seeger is playing again. Once again, it's vintage Seeger as he plunks through classics such as "Turn, Turn, Turn," "Midnight Special," and "This Little Light of Mine." He explains that "This Land Is Your Land" is a song that was "never sold in any music store, never played on the radio. But the kids liked it." And again, he gets the audience to sing: he says a couple of hours before taking the stage, "If the human race is here in a hundred years, [they] will find how important a word, in any language, is 'participation'—in all walks of life." In fact, he seems to gain energy from the voices around him.[2]

He could use the extra energy. It's 2009; Pete Seeger is ninety years old. Freebody Park is quiet; Seeger is performing at Fort Adams, a Revolutionary War–era fort overlooking Newport's harbor. More than nine thousand people are listening to Seeger in the field in front of the stage, with more taking in the concert from various boats bobbing in the water (as well as some too big to bob).

This time, Seeger isn't by himself. With him on the stage is his grandson, Tao Rodriguez Seeger, thirty-eight, who performed earlier in the day with his own band. He's not the only heir: also on stage with Seeger is Billy Bragg, the British singer and activist who has been raising a ruckus for thirty years but treats this appearance with the humility of a student. (Bragg had already given a performance in the afternoon, during which he called mocking attention to "the poor people who couldn't afford tickets so they had to come free in their yachts.") There too is Tom Morello, who performed in his solo acoustic, politically charged persona, the Nightwatchman, and earlier in the day called Seeger "the living embodiment of justice and everything that is good about America." (As guitar player with Rage Against the Machine, Morello started his musical life with the kind of electronic volume that, legend has it, sent Seeger looking for an axe to literally cut power to the sound system decades ago.)

Also with Seeger are Gillian Welch and David Rawlings, two keepers of the flame for roots-oriented, singer-songwriter-based folk music, as well as young singer-songwriters Iron and Wine and Ben Kweller and members of some of the hippest rock groups of the day: Fleet Foxes, the Decemberists, Low Anthem.

And even performers who are less than a third Seeger's age, who played to cheering throngs of their own fans earlier and had to be shown the chords to some of Seeger's songs, have spent the afternoon walking around in an anticipatory giddiness. Once on stage, they spend much of their time looking at each other in amazement that this is really happening. The next day, the scene will be repeated, with Low Anthem, Fleet Foxes and Elvis Perkins in Dearland returning to the stage—they all either got to Newport a day early or stayed a day late to participate—and Joan Baez, Levon Helm and his group, and the Preservation Hall Jazz Band among the new arrivals.

In the audience, Henry Hotkowski of Connecticut is seeing Pete Seeger for the first time. He listens raptly, stopping to explain that he learned to play the banjo from one of Seeger's books, all originally published long before Hotkowski was born. He's twenty-one.

Radiating out from the two Seeger performances lies the history of the Newport Folk Festival, which continues to play out, grow and develop. Today, many performers at Newport are unaware that they're not standing on the same stage or looking out over the same field that Seeger did in 1959 or that Bob Dylan did when he enraged Seeger by picking up an electric guitar in public for the first time. Throughout its tenure, the festival has added phases and levels with every major change in its organization.

Newport started off with the goal of presenting a form of music that was topping the charts in an era when rock 'n' roll was still establishing a foothold, and it stepped into the controversies engendered by that popularity. It continued as what one observer called "Woodstock without drugs or electric guitars"—a multiday hangout that explored the power of music to change minds and by extension the world, while at the same time, and partially by dint of, keeping alive long-forgotten musical traditions—all years before the more celebrated rock festival.

The original festival reached its cultural apogee in 1965, when it hosted the first electric performance by the already-legendary Bob Dylan—a moment that wasn't unforeseen ("Like a Rolling Stone" was the number-two single in the country at the time of the show). But it catalyzed the argument over what had happened to Dylan, to folk music and to rock music in the six years since the festival had begun. The debates, the insults and the declarations of allegiance—"It was a sad parting of the ways for many. . . . I choose Dylan. I choose art" was one critical reaction—continued for years afterward.

But the brushfire that Dylan's performance ignited didn't illuminate the Newport Folk Festival; it left scorched earth in its place. Dylan's performance was a key step in the process of rock's emergence as a music that could speak to the hearts and minds of America's young people, and over the rest of the '60s the folk festival became a symbol of a worn-out genre looking for a reason to continue to exist—an annual gathering of people in a field to wait for a second lightning strike. When the festival went down in a thicket of red tape and red ink, helped along by an incidence of violence at its big brother, the Newport Jazz Festival, it was worthy of a two-line announcement in 1971, and not many people cared.

In the mid-1980s, the festival came back to life as a different beast. Where it had been a nonprofit, utopian, determinedly egalitarian presentation onstage and backstage, in which everyone from Bob Dylan to the fiddler for the Greenbriar Boys got $50 a day, it reemerged as a sleek, commercial, corporately sponsored weekend of individual concerts. The festival's focus changed as the times around it had changed: while attendees and organizers still made efforts to effect real-world changes, the musical ethos sprang from the desire of a generation of artists and fans—most from the same generation that had propelled the initial incarnation of the festival—not to be left behind as the music industry moved on to another new sound and crowd. This version of the festival lasted longer than any of the others have so far. By the early twenty-first century, however, attendance and enthusiasm had waned once again; even the Indigo Girls, the festival's most reliable draw of the 1990s, couldn't attract an audience.

After dropping out of Wein's control for two years, the festival finished its first half century with its founder back at the helm and a reinvigorated focus. The festival presents a mix of music, much of which doesn't seem to fit into a folk festival until you hear it at one. And it thrives under a new leader handpicked by Wein and his lieutenants, whose relative youth inspires him not to ignore the festival's past but to recognize, honor and use its iconic stature among a new generation. Thanks to technological advances in communication and a youth culture that in many ways echoes that of folk's glory days, the festival participates like never before in the celebration and creation of its own history.

Today, veteran stars come to Newport to entertain knowledgeable, appreciative crowds, while young performers come to prove that they deserve to share a billing and a stage with the audience's musical heroes and their own. Indeed, some of the iconoclasts became festival mainstays themselves. The mix of experienced hands and young upstarts has always provoked conflicts—at least one of which got physical—over basic questions of what folk music is, who should play it, and how, but it has also produced what Billboard called "the longest-running and possibly the most visible example of American festival success ever."[3]

On this afternoon in 2009, eighty-three-year-old George Wein sits off to one side of the stage listening, holding hands with Pete Seeger's wife, Toshi Seeger. His image on a video introducing Pete has already received a standing ovation, and he'll get another when the final chords of "This Land Is Your Land" fade away, the sun begins to set in earnest, and he thanks the audience, his staff, the musicians ("I'm so happy to know them") and the Seegers for "never giving up hope."

The musical businessman (though he won't call himself that), who has curated jazz festivals in Newport and all over the world for more than half a century, didn't know much about folk music fifty years ago and doesn't know much about the young bands on the stage now. A few weeks before this afternoon, he summed himself up: "We all have what we do best. And my best skill is organizing things."[4] The reason he first organized a folk festival is simple—it was a commercial proposition. Why he continued it is a little less obvious.

Jazz is the music Wein grew up playing, loving and living, but he says the folk festival has given him some of the best memories of his life and remains one of his proudest achievements. Its mid-1960s era bore similarities to, though it predated, the hippie spirit. (Wein can go into a monologue about the trouble that the long-haired, rock-loving crowd brought down on his jazz festival in 1971.)

But when George Wein, a Jewish piano player, and Joyce Alexander, an African-American science major (who died in 2006) were married in 1959, their union was still illegal in nineteen states. The Newport Jazz Festival makes the case for a better, smarter, more racially integrated world tacitly and by example, but the folk festival stands up and shouts it out: over the years, it has embraced causes moving from civil rights to the anti-Vietnam War movement to the environment. While the folk festival may have begun like any other business expansion, and the tam-wearing Wein would appear to have little in common with the hacky-sackers on the Fort Adams lawn, it's no accident that he created the space, both literally and figuratively, they're inhabiting now.

"People think this stuff just happens," Wein says. "It doesn't. There's thinking behind it."[5]

Pete Seeger wrote "If I Had a Hammer," most famously made into a hit by Peter, Paul and Mary. The song's point is not only to impart the vision of "love between my brothers and my sisters / All over this land," but to point out that not only the singer but the listener has the tools to bring it about. Seeger once said, "The last verse didn't say 'But there ain't no hammer; there ain't no bell; there ain't no song, but honey, I got you.' We could have said that! The last verse says, 'I HAVE a hammer; I HAVE a bell; I HAVE a song. Here it is.'"[6] Songwriters all over the world have heeded that call, whether it be a political vision or a personal one, and for more than fifty years they've come to Newport to share the results.

Each year, through the conscious acts of gathering performers and attracting audiences, the Newport Folk Festival asks anew, and tries to answer anew, two questions: What is folk music? And what can it do? Over the decades, the debate has not only continued but grown to include related questions: Is it folk music if it's a professional musician singing it? Is it folk music if it has an electric guitar? Is it folk music if it's popular? Is it folk music if it's not popular? Is it folk music if it's presented with the help of a corporate sponsor? Is it folk music if you have to plug your ears? These questions weren't first asked at Newport, and they've never been answered —indeed, they may never be. And most of the people who ask these questions know that, but they ask anyway. John Cohen, who played at the first Newport Folk Festival with the New Lost City Ramblers, said at a panel discussion in 2015, "Maybe the festival needs controversies." Perhaps even more accurately, maybe the fans do.

Through the years, the festival, and the questions behind it, have made different sounds—the earth-moving power of Odetta in 1959; the big-dreaming, group-singing "We Shall Overcome" of 1963; the electric shock of Bob Dylan in 1965; the out-and-proud Indigo Girls, who made nine appearances in ten years in the 1990s; the radio-ready strumming and shouting of the Lumineers today—but to hear the people who were and are there tell it, it feels like one conversation stretched out over a lifetime.

2

THE AMERICAN PUBLIC
IS LIKE SLEEPING BEAUTY

George Wein's road to putting on the Newport Folk Festival was circuitous. The first music festival he ever produced was in his own house.

George Theodore Wein was born October 3, 1925, in Lynn, Massachusetts, and grew up in nearby Brookline. His parents, Barnet and Ruth, were second-generation Americans of Eastern European Jewish ancestry; his father was a doctor, and in his memoirs Wein recalls that "his clientele included people from every station in life." Both his parents also loved music and show business, and Wein was singing from an early age around the house and occasionally on children's radio shows.

Wein started playing jazz piano in school, and he and his older brother Larry spent many nights of their adolescence driving around New England—and sometimes to New York City—listening to giants of jazz such as Cab Calloway, Duke Ellington, Tommy Dorsey and others.

Sometimes they did more than listen. If a good band was playing nearby, the Wein brothers would invite the musicians back to their family home for a late dinner cooked by their mother; jam sessions invariably happened afterwards. "For whatever reason, my parents saw nothing unusual about the situation," Wein later wrote. "They welcomed these musicians into their house as close friends."[1]

Wein joined the army in 1943 and served in France, then finished his military time serving at a hospital in New Jersey, the better to make the scene on New York's 52nd Street after hours. After the army, he began playing in better and better places in the Boston area while he was supposed to be attending classes at Boston University. He loved playing the music, but the closer he looked at the life of a jazz musician, the less he liked it. Great musicians, players he knew were better than he, were living in poverty. He didn't see much of a future in an onstage life.

In 1949, he was playing with clarinetist Edmond Hall at the Savoy, in Boston. At the end of their first monthlong run, the manager wanted to re-sign them. Wein asked club manager Steve Connolly for more money—Hall was making $120 to play eight shows a week; Wein and the rest of the band were paid $60 each. Connolly, Wein remembers, was sympathetic, but no more money was forthcoming.

Wein had another suggestion: in lieu of more money, he asked for every other Saturday night off. This would allow Wein and Hall to take better-paying gigs elsewhere. Connolly agreed, and the system worked. But when March 1, 1949, loomed without an engagement, Wein and Hall rented Jordan Hall, at the New England Conservatory of Music, and put on their own show.

"I knew [the Hall-Wein group] was not enough to fill the hall," Wein writes. "We had to do something special." They put together a bill with some of the other heavyweights of Boston jazz, and "Edmond Hall and George Wein Present: From Brass Bands to Bebop" went off without a hitch and made $1,200.

Later that year, Wein ran the series Le Jazz Douxce out of a suite in the Hotel Fensgate, in Boston, with the trumpeter Frankie Newton, and he promoted an unsuccessful series of rhythm and blues shows in Maryland. Even so, the life of a promoter, even an only occasionally successful one, was making more sense than that of a freelance piano player.

Wein was still playing, but as he writes, "I had neither the confidence [nor] the desire to devote my life to being a professional jazz musician." The lack of confidence stemmed from his experiences with great pianists such as Art Tatum, Teddy Wilson and Earl "Fatha" Hines; the lack of desire came from the hard financial times he and his compatriots were experiencing.

Determined to find another way to keep music in his life, Wein opened the nightclub George Wein's Storyville in Boston's Copley Square Hotel in September 1950. That location lasted only six weeks, but a new place in the Buckminster Hotel in Kenmore Square was successful enough that by mid-1953 he was running two clubs at the Copley: Storyville and Mahogany Hall. (He would also run seasonal Storyvilles in the towns of

Gloucester and Magnolia.) The clubs ran until 1960, but in 1953 Elaine and Louis Lorillard met Wein at Storyville and proposed a jazz festival in Newport to liven up the boring society summers.

According to Burt Goldblatt's history of the jazz festival, the Lorillards helped put on two concerts by the New York Philharmonic in Newport's Casino Theatre in the summer of 1953. (Originally scheduled to be held outdoors, they were forced inside by the weather.) They didn't do well artistically or financially.

Later that summer, John Maxon, at the time the director of the Rhode Island School of Design, was at a lunch at the home of George Henry Warren and his wife in Newport. Maxon remembers telling Elaine Lorillard, "Do you really think people want to hear what they undoubtedly hear in the wintertime? They would like to hear something different. If you want to do something, why don't you put on a jazz festival? It would be a wild success. You can't fail." So the Lorillards ended up in Storyville, pitching the idea of a Newport jazz festival to owner George Wein. In 1967, he recalled thinking, "I'd never thought about Newport before then, but I figured it might work, and I knew I wanted to do more in life than own a jazz club, and so I kept saying, 'Sure, sure, but call me in a couple of days if you're really interested,' half knowing that these people wander into the club and unburden themselves of some great project and never call you back, and half hoping that she would."

The sleepy resort city seemed an unlikely choice for such a show, but then, Maxon said, the unlikely sometimes takes hold in such terrain: "Newport is a very strange place. They really are terribly unimpressed. They're bored and worldly, but they are nice people, and they're terribly grateful for something new."[2]

The first festival, entitled "The First American Jazz Festival," was held July 17 and 18, 1954, presenting the full spectrum of jazz "From J to Z." The first day's concerts featured Dizzy Gillespie, the Modern Jazz Quartet, Lee Konitz, Oscar Peterson and more. The second day included an afternoon panel discussion on "The Place of Jazz in American Culture" and performances by Billie Holiday, Lester Young, Lennie Tristano, Gerry Mulligan and Gene Krupa. A reported eleven thousand people showed up, even though it rained on the second day, and *Down Beat* magazine said that the festival "opened a new era in jazz presentation." The producers cleared $142.50.

Patrick O'Higgins—who handled festival publicity for three years and wrote the Helena Rubinstein biography *Madame*—later said, "I think what happened was they said we'll all go to this bloody Festival because it's going to be a terrible flop. Mrs. Lorillard was going to be chased out of town, and much to their surprise it had the opposite effect."[3]

For the next five years, Wein and his fellow board members made the jazz festival the preeminent showcase of the genre in America, while he also ran his nightclubs and instituted other fests, including the Midwest Jazz Festival, in French Lick, Indiana, which ran for two years. In 1958, he booked Odetta, "The Queen of Folk," to sing at Storyville in the usual format of "the eight-day week," as he describes it—a show every night and a Sunday matinee.

The nighttime performances were sparsely attended, but the Sunday-afternoon shows were sold out—packed with college kids from across the river in Cambridge, where venues such as Club 47 were incubating a seemingly incongruous boom in folk music among young people of means. It was Wein's first inkling of the folk movement and of a young generation of music fans more interested in Lead Belly than Lester Young.[4]

Wein had already decided to hold a folk afternoon during the Newport Jazz Festival of 1959 (he had held blues and gospel days in previous years) featuring Odetta, Pete Seeger and the Weavers. But it soon dawned on Wein that there was even more of a scene going on than he realized: "When I saw the young people filling the club Sunday afternoon, drinking ginger ales, a crowd I had never seen before, I realized that we had enough for a folk festival."[5]

By the time Wein was clued in, folk music was in the midst of a revival that had started much earlier and had generated the kind of controversy that in one form or another has surrounded the festival throughout its history.

While the historian Benjamin Filene writes that the first "explicitly historical collection" of folk songs was *A Collection of Old Ballads*, published in 1723, folk music was most likely identified and distinguished from popular music first by nationalist movements in Europe in the mid-nineteenth century, the folklorist Neil Rosenberg writes.[6] Between 1857 and 1858, Francis Child, a Harvard professor who collected ballads mainly through correspondence with sources in England, released the eight-volume collection *English and Scottish Ballads*. He topped himself by releasing, between 1882 and 1898, the ten-volume collection *The English and Scottish Popular Ballads*. The dispositive implication of "The" in the title was no accident.

Child's thoroughness was impressive, with more than three hundred ballads and more than thirteen thousand annotations documenting additions and evolutions, but he worked out of a conviction that no new folk songs had been created in centuries—since the invention of the printing press, really. "Like many of his predecessors," Filene writes, "Child felt that although in premodern times the ballad had been 'a common treasure' passed on orally and enjoyed by all, it was now a long-dead art."[7]

In the United States, the Library of Congress established the Archive of American Folk-Song in 1928, with Robert Winslow Gordon at the helm, the same year the performer and collector Bascom Lamar Lunsford opened the Mountain Dance and Folk Festival in Asheville, North Carolina. Gordon traveled the country in search of folk music, and when John Lomax succeeded him in 1933, Lomax, who had published books of folk songs in the early twentieth century, put in thousands of miles collecting and recording hundreds of singers and players performing songs that went back generations (later traveling with his son Alan, who continued the process on his own).

From the beginning, those who sought out folk music began to fall into two camps, identified by the historian Ronald D. Cohen. The first, the evolutionist mode, held that "folk songs belonged to an early stage of cultural development that required respect and preservation." The idea was to treat the music like a collection of artworks that required not only painstaking preservation—the way a restorer brushes away dust and debris from a recently found artwork—but a diligent watchfulness against degeneration, akin to the way paintings are displayed in rooms with carefully monitored levels of light and humidity. Lunsford, Gordon and the Lomaxes undertook their work as evolutionists, working in the cause of holding regional music and culture safe against the forces of twentieth-century modernity. This was in keeping with a personal and political conservatism: "As folk music and crafts symbolized the grassroots democracy of preindustrial America," wrote folk historian Robert Cantwell, "they also embodied the values of rootedness and authenticity characteristic of patriarchal aristocracy."[8]

Others interested in folk music comprised what Cohen calls the functionalist wing, which believed that "folk songs might have not only an ancient lineage but a dynamic present; they could serve practical purposes, energizing the folk to struggle against racism and oppression."[9] This wing came to the fore as the 1930s dawned. Almost from the beginning, labor groups and unions such as the International Workers of the World had written folk-style songs and rewritten traditional material to suit their purposes. (They began with complex, modernistic compositions, on the theory that a new age called for new music, but they soon found that it didn't make for good rallying cries.) During the Great Depression, leftist, Communist and Communist-influenced groups began to tap into the power of folk and traditional music to use as their anthems and sometimes to write their own. Logically so: If old folk songs could have a dynamic present and serve practical purposes, how much better would be a new song written specifically for the times? These lines of thought led by 1940 to the formation of the Almanac Singers, featuring Pete Seeger, Lee Hays and Millard Lampell and later described in *Time* as "young men who roam around the country in a $150 Buick and fight the class war with ballads and guitars," singing protest ballads old and new. The onset of World War II led to the dissolution of the Almanacs, but Seeger and Hays would resurface, along with Ronnie Gilbert and Fred Hellerman, as the Weavers, a group that was itself an outgrowth of People's Songs, a collective including Seeger and Woody Guthrie that issued albums of labor and leftist songs after the war.

Commercial record companies mined folk music nearly from the beginning, bringing "hillbilly" and "race" music to the masses using the same technology. Vernon Dalhart's "The Wreck of the Old 97," backed with "The Prisoner's Song," sold more than a million copies in 1924; Southern musicians began performing on the radio earlier than that. And the commercial potential of folk music only grew.

The Weavers hit it big beginning in 1950 with songs such as Lead Belly's "Goodnight, Irene" and Woody Guthrie's "So Long (It's Been Good to Know Yuh)," as well as "On Top of Old Smoky," "Wimoweh," "Midnight Special," and more. The sound was often sweetened with horns and strings from producer Gordon Jenkins' orchestra, but Lee Hays recalled later that "Jenkins never told us to change a note of anything we sang. He surrounded us with fiddles and French horns and trumpets and things, but when people sang 'Goodnight Irene,' they didn't sing the fiddles, they sang the words."[10]

Meanwhile, as the Weavers began to perform in some of the country's top nightspots, they continued to play for the benefit of leftist and Communist causes, which, combined with their People's Songs' roots, quickly brought them into the purview of the FBI and the House Un-American Activities Committee. In 1952, Harvey Matusow, a former Communist turned paid informant for the FBI, testified before Congress and a separate Ohio committee on un-American activities that the Weavers' popularity was being used by the Communist Party to drive young people into the movement.[11] After that, the bookings began to dry up, until "there was no work to be had," Gilbert has said.[12] The Weavers broke up in 1952.

Robert Cantwell's *When We Were Good*, an essential examination of the folk music revival of the late 1950s and early 1960s, details the chill that fell over the music, and much of American culture in general, thanks to anticommunist hysterics. *Sing Out!*—the folk music magazine that sprang up as part of the People's Songs' movement—"urged its readers to carry the folk gospel to schools, summer camps and other small venues."[13] Cantwell describes "a new posture of permanent alert that read subversion into almost any form of deviance," leading to "the utter starvation of political and cultural discourse."[14]

In such an atmosphere, folk music didn't stand a chance. America was remaking itself, Cantwell posits, with World War II as a wall against the past not to be looked beyond and with the marketplace and militarism at the center of the nation's field of vision. This was not the blippy, fragmented marketplace that the Weavers had managed to conquer: modern communications, particularly television, had a homogenizing impact. Moses Asch, the founder of Folkways Records, described the effect: "An American became an 'average man.' He dressed, acted, wanted and behaved in the image of what the advertiser and manufacturer and song plugger said was 'normal.'"[15]

Cantwell adds, "Participation in the market . . . had a peculiar new imperative to it, as if the very survival of the social order were at stake."[16]

There were still pockets of folk music, of course, and places to play, but the commercial success of music derived from American traditions had dried up. Performers such as Josh White, Burl Ives, Tom Glazer and many others mentioned in *Red Channels*—a publication dedicated to exposing so-called Communists in the broadcasting and entertainment fields—became better known for defending themselves, sometimes in front of the Un-American Activities Committee, than for their recordings.[17]

But in the same year the Weavers appeared finished, Asch's Folkways Records released the *Anthology of American Folk Music*, assembled by the collector Harry Smith from his vast store of 78-rpm records from the 1920s and 1930s. A collection of *Ballads*, *Social Music*, and *Songs* (as the three records were subtitled), the eighty-four tracks revived and recontextualized "what had been, to the people who originally recorded it, essentially the music of the poor, the isolated, and the uneducated . . . as a kind of avant-garde art."[18]

The *Anthology* inspired a generation of musicians, collectors and fans to rediscover the classics and, in some cases, to fan out across the country, looking for the original performers and/or their musical heirs. Interest grew in the music—no matter who performed it—among urban denizens, particularly college students. Writing in *Mademoiselle*, Susan Montgomery later pondered, "Why American college students should want to express the ideas and emotions of the downtrodden and the heartbroken . . . is in itself an interesting question. But there is certainly good reason for students today to find the world brutal and threatening."[19]

By the time the Weavers re-formed in 1955 and began to tour on a limited schedule, the Red Scare was largely over, and a renewed appreciation for folk music was back in swing. Cantwell called the Folkways *Anthology* the folk revival's "enabling document, its musical constitution."[20]

Folk and folk-derived music such as calypso (exemplified by Harry Belafonte's hits "Day-O" and "Jamaica Farewell") and to a lesser extent skiffle (such as Lonnie Donegan's cover of Lead Belly's "Rock Island Line") began to make a dent in the charts as an answer to rock 'n' roll. And singer, song collector and historian Ellen Stekert later claimed that interest in traditional material surged in the 1950s because "in this cowardly and intimidated era, the city sought expression behind the words of other—perhaps more 'natural'—folk."[21]

The new popularity of folk music changed the equation, Ronald Cohen writes. Following on from the evolutionist-functionalist split of the early collectors, the possibility of doing serious business in folk music for the first time in many years divided enthusiasts and performers in three camps: the "unadulterated commercial performers"; "those who preferred only traditional performers," including Lomax and other folklorists; and "the city revivalists, whose love for the music translated into their own performance style as they strove to duplicate or reconstruct the older sounds."[22]

In 1958, the Kingston Trio, three fresh-faced folksingers who met in college and who got early musical training from a conductor stranded in their native Hawaii during World War II, blew the ceiling off the folk music revival by topping the charts with "Tom Dooley," a murder ballad from North Carolina that they learned from a book. But as we can see, by then the stage had been set for them by decades of conscious effort and cultural forces. And so the unadulterated commercial performers, in Cohen's words, had their day: they saw a new kind of music to be made and a new kind of record to be sold, while considerations of where the music came from and what purpose it served were placed varying degrees of distance down the list of important considerations.

Cantwell writes, "It was precisely this momentary obscurity that opened the immense resources of folksong to the young and made it, by virtue of their recovery of it in the postwar period, their own. When folksong re-emerged into the light of popular culture in 1958, with its ideological and cultural connections largely suppressed, abandoned, forgotten, or lost, it welled up with all the vitality of a cultural symbol eager for rediscovery."[23]

Given the history of folk music so far, a record such as the Kingston Trio's chart-topping "Tom Dooley" posed questions. The ballad of the hanging of the murderer Tom Dula in Wilkes County, North Carolina, shortly after the Civil War, was recorded many times over the decades, beginning in 1928 and most prominently in 1934 by Frank Proffitt of Tennessee. His version was collected and recorded by the folklorist Frank Warner in 1952 and saw several more incarnations before the Trio recorded it.

A listen to the Proffitt and Kingston Trio versions side by side shows the effects and the causes of the late 1950s folk boom all at once: Proffitt's rendition sounds like a musical version of a local news report on a murder. His voice is low, somber and matter-of-fact, whether he's addressing the murderer or speaking in his voice. He's backed by his own speedy banjo (Proffitt was also a maker of fretless banjos) and leaves plenty of room in his vocal interpretation for the mystery of man's inhumanity to man and to woman. The Kingston Trio's version, on the other hand, is slow, as in a clichéd take on a momentous event, but the lead and background vocals, with their whispery quality and stagey enunciation, give the impression that a favorable opinion of the Trio's vocal qualities is as important a goal for the record as telling the story. And the finger-snapping groove and jaunty syncopation is pure city—a non-English speaker could easily guess that it's a song of romantic contentment. Cantwell described the difference as that between "a kind of sober, almost a pious duty, like planting a tree" and "an articulation and phrasing perceptibly polite and bookish."[24]

Were these differences worth the benefits to the genre of having a folk song at the top of the charts? Activist Todd Gitlin would later write that in the early 1950s, "folk was the living prayer of a defunct movement, the consolation and penumbra of its children, gingerly holding the place of a Left in American culture."[25] Susan Montgomery claimed later that the new fans of folk were "young people who are desperately hungry for a small, safe taste of an unslick, underground world."[26] Was the clean, collegiate background of the Trio—or for that matter the music-theatre backgrounds of folk song performers such as Theo Bikel and Harry Belafonte—an evolutionary step from the bona fides of Lunsford or Proffitt or even the Weavers? Or was the process more of an appropriation—or even a straightforward theft? As folk music became bigger and bigger business, the debate around these questions became more and more heated, helping start and bring purpose to magazines such as *Gardyloo*, the *Little Sandy Review* and *Caravan* as well as the already legendary *Sing Out!* By the early 1960s, mainstream magazines such as *Seventeen* and *Mademoiselle* were covering and analyzing the folk scene. And the Newport Folk Festival, with the Kingston Trio headlining, jumped into the middle of the argument.

There were precedents to Wein and Grossman's Newport idea: along with Lunsford's Mountain Dance and Folk Festival, the Pinewoods Camp, a Massachusetts-based outgrowth of the Country Dance and Song Society, had proven that people would gather in the summer to listen to a variety of folk performers (many of whom went on to play at Newport), albeit in an instructional, residency-based setting; and the National Folk Festival, begun in 1934, brought folk performers together for multiday series of concerts in different cities each year. Several folk festivals had sprung up on college campuses, including at the University of California at Berkeley, whose festival featured many performers in common with Newport and began one year before, in 1958. But the specific idea for Newport was new.

Robert Shelton, writing in the *New York Times* after the first festival, said that "there have been regional events for many years, but the program that sailed into Newport was a full-masted craft with a cargo from all over the country."[27] John Cohen, of the New Lost City Ramblers, remembers, "It was a strange strategy—Newport grabbed the center and said 'We are important; we will deem what's to be considered important.'"[28]

Wein knew from his experience with Odetta at Storyville that folk music could be good business. He also knew that the music's activist tradition suited the integrated life that Wein had and the integrated world he wanted to see. What he didn't know about folk music was pretty much everything else. Joe Boyd, who worked for Wein during the 1960s and was at the center of some of the most controversial moments in the folk festival's history, says that Wein "knows what he likes, but he also has the bigger vision, which is so rare and so valuable, that can step back and say 'I don't know about this stuff,' or 'I'm not the right person to do this—let's let so-and-so do it.' And that's what he did with the folk festival, I think brilliantly."[29]

Throughout the history of the Newport Folk Festival, Wein has employed four men to act as native guides to the world of folk music. Each of these guides has stamped the festival with his ideas of what folk is and should be and in so doing has helped define the genre each step of the way.

Wein's first native guide showed up on his doorstep when he booked Odetta at Storyville. Albert Grossman was born in Chicago in 1927 and had a degree in economics from Roosevelt University. In 1956, he too opened a nightclub—a Chicago folk spot called the Gate of Horn ("the inside place for inside people")—in the basement of the Rice Hotel on Chicago Avenue and Dearborn Street. He hosted performers such as Odetta, Bob Gibson and a then-unknown Joan Baez, all of whom would figure prominently in the first Newport festival, and soon began managing some of the acts who played there.

Grossman would go on to become one of the most important and best-known managers in musical history, spanning the folk and rock worlds and with a client list that included Bob Dylan, Joan Baez, Peter, Paul and Mary, the Band and Janis Joplin. He was a big man with a big, deep voice, and he was considered a businessman in a world where business wasn't supposed to matter. A lot of people in the folk world considered him an anomaly. In *The Bob Dylan Encyclopedia*, Michael Gray wrote of Grossman,

"In a milieu of New Left reformers and folkie idealists campaigning for a better world, Albert Grossman was a breadhead, seen to move serenely and with deadly purpose like a barracuda circling shoals of fish." David Braun, a lawyer who worked for both Dylan and Grossman, said, "He was the first person to realize that there was real money to be made in the music business."[30] Grossman was no stranger to lawsuits, including from Dylan, who would eventually call him, in the documentary *No Direction Home*, a "Colonel Tom Parker figure . . . you could smell him coming."

But not everyone felt that way. Indeed, Grossman carried with him many of the conflicts and contradictions of the folk revival itself. Peter Yarrow, of Peter, Paul and Mary, calls Grossman "a person who was misunderstood and resented by some people, because of his bellicose nature. But frankly, I think he made as great a contribution to folk music as any of we artists, with the exception of Pete Seeger." Yarrow also claimed that Grossman

> believed in Bob Dylan, and he protected Bob, so Bob could be what he was. Bobby was allowed to make those decisions for himself, as were Peter, Paul and Mary, because Albert protected him. And made contracts that allowed him to sing the songs he wanted, rather than having an A&R person tell him what to do. And record them the way he wanted, with the producers and the engineers he wanted; to decide what the record album would look like, and entirely be free to be an artist. Albert was a genius in that, and he changed the field to make that happen. And he made that happen for all his artists."[31]

After Grossman's death in 1986, Yarrow told *Musician* magazine's Rory O'Conner that Grossman "was concerned first and foremost with authenticity," but that he "realized that it wasn't enough just to write and perform songs, that there was a multitude of ways to be successful and to happen, to become important, to be wanted by that public. It was necessary to couple artistic success with enormous economic success in order for that to take place."

Wein recalls sitting up with Grossman until 3 a.m. every night of Odetta's Storyville engagement. "I found out that he knew the entire world of folk music, and he was a brilliant guy, and we became very close friends."[32] They also became partners, forming Production Artists and Management Associates. Their first project was the Newport Folk Festival. Wein remembers that the idea of a separate festival was an easy sell to the board of directors of the Newport Jazz Festival and the city. "We were riding high at that time. The festival was doing well, and we didn't have any problems. . . . Everybody wasn't excited about folk music per se, but the concept of doing a second festival met with unanimous approval."

The first festival was held Saturday and Sunday afternoon and night, July 11 and 12, 1959, in Freebody Park. Studs Terkel was the MC for the first day, Oscar Brand for the second. Billy Faier, editor of the folk music magazine *Caravan*, welcomed festivalgoers in the program by writing, "The Scholars, the city-bred folksingers, and the 'authentic' singers are here to give you what is probably the very first representative picture of American Folk Music ever held on the concert stage."

John Cohen of the New Lost City Ramblers, a group of young players reviving old-time American music, recalls that they "were odd birds there. . . . Everybody else was a pretty smooth, professional act, so to speak, and we were just musicians dressed in our everyday clothes. And there was nothing like us there. And somehow we were well received."[33]

Frederic Ramsey Jr., writing in the *Saturday Review* of July 25, said that there was no "consistent mood that was established early and maintained . . . there were slumps, swells, wallows and heights."[34] Still, he found plenty of heights, including John Jacob Niles and Cohen's Ramblers. In the *New York Times* of July 19, Robert Shelton called the festival "perhaps the most ambitious attempt ever made at delineating a cross-section of the nation's folk music. . . . The range of the programs . . . stressed the American idiom, and within that framework it was far-reaching, if not encyclopedic." He added that Odetta's performance was "the crowning performance of the week-end. . . . Here was folk music identification married to theatrical vocal artistry at its very best."[35]

Shelton was a little more conflicted about the festival in private. In a letter to folklorist Archie Green, he wrote that "I rather consciously held back on negative criticism at Newport in both my Times piece and Nation piece. I may be wrong, but I think a new venture like this needs public support now. There'll be time enough to tear into it after it is old enough to stand on its own feet."[36]

On Sunday morning, a panel discussion was held at Rogers High School on the topic "What Is American Folk Music?" The panel, moderated by critic and musicologist Marshall Stearns, took on some of the questions that had been swirling around the folk revival, debating whether indigenous regional folk music would survive in an increasingly commercialized musical world. Folklorist Alan Lomax argued, according to the *Providence Journal*'s account, that "the very essence of folk music and style is rooted in particular localities and warned that the destruction of local traditions and cultures in a mass-communication age would make a 'gray world.'"[37]

After an afternoon program including Seeger and the duo of Tom Makem and Paddy Clancy that drew 2,500 people, 5,500 turned out for an evening bill that included Jimmie Driftwood (including his hit, "The Battle of New Orleans"); Leon Bibb, whose volcanic voice set spirituals ablaze; the country blues of Barbara Dane; the bluegrass of the Stanley Brothers and more.

John Cohen remembers the Stanley Brothers, which of course featured the seemingly immortal bluegrass pioneer Ralph Stanley, for two reasons. He says the rest of the band was a sight to behold as well: "One guy, Bill Napier, the mandolin player—he was dressed up like Grandpa Jones, with a big old funky mustache. And then Chubby Anthony, the fiddler, was in overalls. And the bass player was this crazy Cousin Mort, who . . . did these crazy imitations of sounds, like a hog eating garbage, and he made you aware of a tomato going down his throat. Or starting an old Ford. Weird stuff!"[38]

Second, Cohen saw the Stanley Brothers with a young girl who had seen the Ramblers rehearsing on the back of a truck: she was "barefoot, looking at us with a rose in her hair. I was immediately attracted to her, and she started asking about us, and she and I walked around, this and that, and when the Stanley Brothers played . . . she and I were right next to the stage, and she'd never heard this kind of music. . . . And the next evening, she and I were standing around, and suddenly she says, 'I've got to go on the stage; this guy's inviting me up.'"[39]

The guy was Bob Gibson, a frequent performer at Grossman's Gate of Horn and a lower-tier star through the early 1960s. The girl who had attracted Cohen's attention was Joan Baez (or, as the *Providence Journal* mangled her name, "Joan Byers"), whose spectral soprano rose out of "Virgin Mary Had a Son" like a revelation. Gibson once described Baez as "bare feet, three chords, and a terrified attitude!"[40] But years later, Oscar Brand would recall other members of the Ramblers, as well as would-be headliners the Kingston Trio, running out into the audience to see the teenager's first major public performance, and Dave Van Ronk would remember immediately recognizing her performance as "the start of something big for all of us."[41] For Gibson's part, he later eschewed any credit for having helped bring Baez to the limelight: "It was like 'discovering' the Grand Canyon. I may have introduced her to her first large audience, but do you think that girl was going to stay unknown in Cambridge?"[42]

Fifty years later, Baez told the Associated Press, "Looking back, I barely know that child who stepped onto that stage. That child . . . was 18 years old and had a high, high soprano and was as neurotic as anybody could possibly be—and was high, high maintenance. . . . I didn't faint; I sang, and that was the beginning of a very long career."[43]

In her autobiography, Baez writes of singing the song with Gibson:

> He played the twelve-string, and with eighteen strings and two voices we sounded pretty impressive. I had a solo part next, and my voice came out just fine. . . . An exorbitant amount of fuss was made over me when we descended from the stage. Into one tent and out the other. Newspapers, student press, foreign correspondents, and, of course, *Time* magazine. I gave *Time* a long-winded explanation of the pronunciation of my name which came out wrong, was printed wrong in *Time* magazine, and has been pronounced wrong ever since.[44]

The next day, Baez sang with Gibson at a party in Newport, pocketing $120 for the performance. She wrote that that "impressed me more than anything else that year at Newport, aside from realizing in the back of my mind and the center of my heart that in the book of my destiny the first page had been turned, and that this book could no longer be exchanged for any other."[45]

That Sunday evening, the very conflict between popularity and local tradition discussed at the morning panel played out under rainy skies in Freebody Park.

The Kingston Trio was supposed to close the show, befitting their run on the pop charts: "Tom Dooley" reached number one the previous year, and they hit the Top 20 three times that year with "MTA," "A Worried Man," and "The Tijuana Jail." They also put out three chart-topping albums in 1959 and 1960.

While their set included the hard-driving "Saro Jane" and Woody Guthrie's "Hard Ain't It Hard," the jingoistic lyrics and fresh-scrubbed harmonies of "Remember the Alamo," the leering drunken joke of "Scotch and Soda," and the pseudotragedy of "South Coast" were jarring in contrast with, say, the possessed howling of John Jacob Niles on "The Hangman, Or the Maid Freed from the Gallows," the acoustic protometal of Sonny Terry and Brownie McGhee, or Jean Ritchie's gorgeous, reedy "Pretty Saro." John Patterson wrote that the Kingston Trio's songs were "not a record of traditions, but what a mass audience wishes to accept as traditions."[46]

Still, the crowd loved every minute. And as one listens to the live recording fade out, the cheers audibly turn to dismay as the crowd realizes that it's over. But real conflict would soon unfold: in his memoirs, Wein recalls that throughout the day members of the audience had been asking Louis Lorillard to put the Kingston Trio on in the penultimate slot, which had been reserved for bluegrass banjo king Earl Scruggs. The show was running late, and many young people and parents of young children needed to get home. Eventually, Lorillard talked Wein into flipping the two acts' time slots. It was a mistake.

When the Kingston Trio finished, the audience wasn't ready to let them go. Brand tried to quiet the crowd so as to let Scruggs come on stage to perform, but to no avail. Scruggs "just stood backstage, patiently, patiently, watching what was going on," Cohen remembers. Dave Guard, of the Kingston Trio, also came out to beseech the crowd to pay Scruggs the respect due him. It eventually became clear that the only way to convince the crowd to give Scruggs a chance was to essentially promise that he would be only a minor annoyance: "They kind of had to plead with the audience, 'Let Earl Scruggs go on; then you can have the Kingston Trio again,'" Cohen says. "It was bizarre; it was painful."[47]

It worked for a while. But Scruggs played only a brief set before the Kingston Trio returned and finished the show. It's no surprise that the popularizers had won a popularity contest, but they had done so in the worst way possible.

"I lost a lot of friends in the folk world because of that slipup," Wein writes,[48] adding later that it took years to earn back a sense of trust that he was more than a huckster. Scruggs was one of the kings of regional American folk music, and he'd been treated like a distraction from the real deal.

Bob Shane, the last surviving original member of the Kingston Trio, doesn't recall the evening happening like that. "If I did [hear any commotion regarding Scruggs]," he says, "I didn't pay any attention to it," though he allows that the group played about 280 shows a year at that time, and that memories tend to run together after a while. (The Trio had even played at the previous week's Newport Jazz Festival: "We were used in various situations because of the fact that we were honest to God a perfect anything-you-wanted live act," Shane says.)

Shane argues that the Kingston Trio's pop-tinged success helped the larger folk revival that eventually led to the careers of Bob Dylan, Joan Baez, Peter, Paul and Mary, and more, as well as making possible a festival that would allow "genuine" performers such as Scruggs the chance to play in front of large audiences. "Everyone we met in the business was very happy that we had our success," he says, "because it made them have success,"[49] and he recalls Joan Baez and sister Mimi Fariña coming to see them at Storyville and asking for advice on breaking into the business.

But on this night, it simply looked like the real folk music got snubbed. One critic who loved Scruggs but hated the performances by the Trio, Odetta, Gibson and others wrote, "On the whole, Newport was a great disappointment to me. 'Folk' is such a debased and misused word, given far too wide an interpretation by some of its worst perpetrators."[50]

The triumph of the commercial performers in Newport as well as the commercial world left critics feeling conflicted. In *Gardyloo*, Mark Morris wrote, "What connection these frenetic tinselly showmen [the Kingston Trio] have with a folk festival eludes me, except that it is mainly folk songs they choose to vulgarize." He grudgingly admitted, however, that if the crowds such groups brought in would enable the festival to present roots performers, "I shall grit my teeth and welcome them." In the end, he said, "It's undeniably thrilling to see everyone gathered and jumbled up like a deck of playing cards and thrown together in a string of concerts, come rain or come shine. I'm for it."

By the organizers' lights, the festival was a success. Grossman told Shelton, "The American public is like Sleeping Beauty, waiting to be kissed awake by the prince of Folk music." Shelton wrote that Louis Lorillard told the *Providence Journal* that the inaugural festival was "great," and that "number two is coming up."

"Number two" was held in Freebody Park, June 24–26, 1960, and featured a more diverse lineup in terms of pedigree as well as geography: seven nations were represented, including the clarinets of the Oranim

Zabar Israeli Troupe and the flamenco of the Spanish Romany guitarist Sabicas.

Earlier in the year, Seeger, his wife Toshi, his half-sister Peggy and her husband, Ewan MacColl, wrote to Wein about the festival. In the documentary *Pete Seeger: The Power of Song*, Seeger says that "the first folk festival was mainly well-known performers. So we sat down and wrote a long letter to George and said 'George, do you realize you could have . . . a real folk festival next summer? Because you could have old-timers from the country contrasted with the young-timers from the colleges.'"

That's just what happened. "I always admired Pete Seeger," Wein recalls, remembering their early encounters at a Seeger concert at Boston's Symphony Hall and a Seeger booking at Storyville. "I always respected his idealism and his feeling about people, and so when I got letters from them I paid attention."[51]

Along with the Brothers Four, a quartet of actual fraternity brothers who had reached number two on the pop charts earlier in the year with "Greenfields," the essential hard-and-heavy bluesman John Lee Hooker performed, as did the Louisiana fiddle-and-guitar duo of Butch Cage and Willie B. Thomas, who had recently been discovered by the traveling folklorist Harry Oster. The field also included the Weavers (who had replaced Seeger with Erik Darling in 1958) and Joan Baez (or Boez, as the *Providence Journal* continued to err[52]).

And on Sunday afternoon, Freebody Park hosted a hootenanny—an opportunity for amateur musicians among the attendees to strut their stuff for one song each. Shelton, of the Times, wrote that the amateurs' songs ranged in subject matter from the recently downed U-2 spy plane to the discipline of psychoanalysis, and while he danced around the question of how good any of them were, he called the hoot "a welcome idea. . . . Folk music is more than an art for spectators. It is a participation sport."[53]

In 2009, Seeger remembered the performance of the eighty-eight-year-old retired Canadian lumberjack, O. J. Abbott:

He came down with his daughter, and sang a song she didn't approve of:

An old man come a courtin' me
Fa la la loodle
An old man come a courtin' me
Hi-diree-down

An old man come a courtin' me
Offered to marry me
Maids, when you're young, never wed an old man
He has no fa loodle
Fa la la loodle
He has no fa loodle
The divil a-one
He has no fa loodle
He's lost his ding-doodle
So maids, when you're young, never wed an old man.

Oh, the audience loved it! But his middle-aged daughter was a little embarrassed."[54]

The festival drew about 10,000 people, down from the previous year's 12,000 to 14,000, Shelton estimated in the *Times*. But already the festival was serving as a focal point for the youth culture that drove, and took sustenance from, folk music's commercial revival. Susan Montgomery, in *Mademoiselle*, described the scene in terms befitting the transmission of sacred texts:

> Each night the music continued long after the regular performances were over, when it became the property not of professionals but of small groups of students who carried their sleeping bags and instruments down to the beach.
>
> There, around fires built in holes scooped out of the sand to keep off the fog . . . [they] sang and clapped to songs like "It Takes a Worried Man". . . . Before the morning was over students would be playing and singing again —on the beaches, on the narrow strip of grass dividing the main boulevard. Inevitably students sat huddled in little groups as if drawing warmth from one another. Their faces were solemn, almost expressionless, while they were singing, and they moved quickly from song to song without talking very much.[55]

While the attendance had slid, the organizers had said that it was good enough to keep the festival going. But they didn't get the chance. The 1960 Newport Jazz Festival, held the next weekend, started off strongly, with performers including Eubie Blake, Willie "the Lion" Smith, Dizzy Gillespie, Louis Armstrong and their bands and an estimated 8,500 people at the evening show. The next night, however, was nearly the end of music in Newport.

About 16,000 people packed Freebody Park the night of Saturday, July 2, for the bill, which included the Oscar Peterson Trio, the Horace Silver Quintet, the Ray Charles Orchestra, and Lambert, Hendricks & Ross. But outside, thousands of young people roaming around the periphery of the park tried to break down the gates of the park and climb its stone wall. After they were repelled by the police, they roamed through downtown Newport, throwing bottles and beer cans at police officers and vandalizing shops. City Manager George A. Bisson was quoted in the *New York Times* as saying, "We simply don't have the manpower to cope with the situation."[56] The state police and the Rhode Island National Guard were called out; tear gas and fire hoses were used to clear youths from the gates of the park, while the Newport police shuttled arrestees into holding cells.

Inside the park, the festival continued relatively normally. Indeed, the police asked Wein to keep the music going—and concertgoers inside the park—while the security forces tried to clear things up. The show lasted until 2:15 a.m., after which, Wein writes, "the musicians left in a phalanx of cars, with a police escort, the fans streaming out onto streets littered with broken glass, beer cans, overturned cars, smashed windows, and the lingering, diffuse odor of tear gas."[57] In all, 182 people were arrested, plus another 27 the next day on the city's beaches, which were then closed.

Later that day, the Newport City Council voted to cancel the rest of the festival, save a blues show scheduled for that afternoon featuring Jimmy Rushing, Otis Spann, John Lee Hooker, Muddy Waters and more. The city's taverns were also shut down for two days. Afterward, Louis Lorillard announced his intention to sue: "The audience was well behaved and enjoying the performances. It was only the unruly element outside of the jazz festival park that created the disturbances. . . . City officials publicly claimed they could handle any situation arising which proved to be completely untrue and they took the unnecessary step of canceling our remaining performances even though the jazz festival itself was entirely blameless."[58]

Not everyone in Newport agreed with the council's decision. Leonard Scalzi, board president of the Newport Chamber of Commerce and manager of the Viking Hotel, was opposed to the action, as were at least several concertgoers, who told the *Times* that the police had at least as much to do with the violence as anyone else.

As befitting the era, Harold Boxer, music director of the Voice of America, called the decision "food for the Communists."[59] His colleague Willis Conover added, "The Russians are going to pick up on this incident. They will say that this proves that jazz bands are hoodlums."[60] But it didn't matter.

While the council didn't explicitly rule out future jazz or folk festivals, Bisson was adamant: "As far as I am concerned that's the last jazz festival of a similar nature that will ever come to Newport."[61] When Lorillard tried to get a license for a 1961 festival, the council voted down his request.

It only took a few months to prove Bisson's words wrong: A new group, called Music at Newport and comprising city businessmen and fans, acquired a license to put on a festival in Freebody Park. They hired concert promoter Sid Bernstein (who later brought the Beatles to America for the first time) to produce the festival, to be held June 30 through July 3, 1961, and the bill included Bob Hope, Judy Garland, Dave Brubeck, Oscar Peterson, George Shearing and Julie Wilson. Crowds were decent, and the festival passed peacefully: "as sedately as a Tanglewood concert," the *Times* reported.[62] Newport police chief Joseph A. Radice agreed that "Newport has regained its good name and can produce a successful jazz festival without riots."

But the festival lost a reported $70,000. (Hope canceling probably didn't help.)

Wein says he was driving with Joyce one day and heard Bernstein being interviewed on the radio. Asked whether he'd be returning to Newport, Wein remembers Bernstein saying, "No. I can't make any money there. No one can make any money there except George Wein." Wein turned to his wife and said, "He's right."[63]

Wein applied for a license for a 1962 Newport Jazz Festival. Louis Lorillard had been the liaison with the city, but Wein says that the Lorillards were in the process of splitting up—"she sued him for divorce three separate times," Wein says. Louis was out of the country, not to be found; all the other investors dropped out, convinced that Newport had gone cold as a music venue. The license was granted with a few conditions: the festival was limited to three days; capacity was set at ten thousand; the shows had to be over by 12:15 a.m. Wein, speaking today, is fairly certain that he had to put up some money for possible security expenses (as had the Bernstein group). The festival included Louis Armstrong, Count Basie, Duke Ellington, and a program that exhibited the relationship between tap dancing and jazz.

The folk festival would return to Newport the next year, but there would be changes on the producers' side as well—Grossman was out. He had already become one of the busiest and hardest-working managers in the music business, and the company he'd formed with Wein was dissolved ("a huge financial mistake on my part," Wein writes, "and Grossman never failed to remind me that I had ended the association, not he"[64]).

So Wein needed a new native guide—someone whose name would open doors in the folk world and whose life and work would keep them open. That's where Pete Seeger came in.

Seeger was already the dean of American folk music by this point. Born in New York and the product of prep schools and a stint at Harvard, he changed tracks dramatically after first hearing folk music while traveling with his father, musicologist Charles Seeger, at Lunsford's Mountain Dance and Folk Festival in Asheville, North Carolina. After dropping out of Harvard in 1938, he'd worked with Alan Lomax and ridden the rails with Woody Guthrie himself. He'd performed with Paul Robeson in a 1949 concert that ended in a hail of rocks thrown by anticommunists claiming to be defending American freedom. (The concert was the second of two planned shows; the first was canceled thanks to a similar outbreak of freedom-loving violence.)

He'd toured the country with Guthrie and the Almanac Singers, singing labor songs from coast to coast, and cofounded the Weavers, whose political message may have been sweetened by the state-of-the-art (for 1950) arrangements but was never muted. Even after their hit with "Goodnight Irene," Seeger had been hauled before the House Un-American Activities Committee and sentenced to a year in prison for contempt of Congress for refusing to say whether he had ever been a Communist. (The sentence and conviction were overturned in 1962.)

The Weavers' reunion concerts at Carnegie Hall were sold-out affairs, but Seeger later left the group—over their decision, he said, to record a jingle for a cigarette commercial. And while his conviction was overturned in 1962, he "mysteriously" didn't appear on TV or radio for seventeen years, as he continued to be tailed by the FBI. Unaccountably for someone who was considered a dangerous subversive, he was allowed to continue performing for children and teaching the banjo. Many of the figures of the folk revival credited him with inspiring them and creating their audience from the children he had taught and performed for. Not for nothing was he called "the Johnny Appleseed of folk music."

In short, he'd walked the walk. He'd earned his credibility. Wein had listened to Seeger back in 1960, when he wrote about having a more diverse, authentic folk festival, and he was the man Wein turned to when he needed another key to presenting—and helping to create—the folk world.

*It was a very nice dream,
I think. All in all it worked
quite well.*

JOYCE WEIN

UTOPIA

In the fall of 1962, the Weins drove to Beacon, New York, where Pete Seeger and his wife Toshi were building their log-cabin house. There, George Wein asked Pete for his help in reviving the Newport Folk Festival. Seeger agreed, but he had ideas of his own.

Most importantly, the folk festival, unlike its commercial brother, the jazz festival, would be run as a nonprofit entity. That wouldn't free the festival from the responsibility of taking in at least as much money as it paid out, but it meant that everyone's compensation would be set by the board of a Newport Folk Foundation, unlike in a for-profit business, where an owner or a group of shareholders gets whatever is left after expenses. In the nonprofit model, whatever is left after expenses and salaries goes to the furtherance of the organization's mission.

That mission was laid out in a manifesto billed as the result of discussion among Seeger, Wein and Theo Bikel. It foresaw a seven-member board that would "be representative of every branch of the folk world." They also proposed using the net income of the festival "to underwrite research of ethnic material . . . to the benefit of the entire field of folk music."[1]

The proposal envisioned three nighttime concerts with bills led by star performers but also giving a chance to lesser-known acts, along with a slew of themed daytime workshops that would offer a chance for "fans of one particular performer or idiom to really soak up all they want, and for the performer to really give more than a superficial glance at what they can do."

It also said that performers' fees would be set—no individual negotiating. Seeger said the fee should be union scale—$50 a day, no matter how many concerts or workshops a performer did in that time. The idea originally came from Toshi Seeger, inspired by Pete Seeger's having donated his Newport fee in order to bring Quebecois fiddler Jean Carignan to perform.

Then as now, performers and managers were wary of any promoter who asked an artist to take much less than their normal fee for the good of the organization putting on the show and who swore that no one would pocket the money the performer was leaving on the table. Businessman George Wein would likely have a hard time asking someone used to getting hundreds or thousands of dollars a night to play for $50 to help keep alive the American folk tradition. But if Pete Seeger asked, that was different.

"There was only one Pete Seeger," Wein remembered in 2009. "You need to have somebody whose integrity could not be challenged. And no one ever challenged Pete's integrity. He had the respect, and he still does have it."[2]

Joyce Wein told historian Carol Brauner in 1982, "Pete gives the whole folk field a conscience and an attitude and a dignity, and all the youngsters follow his lead. There are things they wouldn't think of doing, because of Pete. And there are things they naturally do, because of Pete."[3]

Members of the first board of directors of the Newport Folk Foundation would have curatorial responsibilities in a given musical field. There was Seeger; Bikel; Bill Clifton of the bluegrass kings, the Dixie Mountain Boys; gospel singer Clarence Cooper of the Tarriers; Erik Darling of the Rooftop Singers, who had succeeded Seeger in the Weavers; Jean Ritchie, an expert in Appalachian music; and Peter Yarrow of Peter, Paul and Mary, who represented the young performers of the urban coffeehouse scene. Wein was designated nonvoting chairman.[4]

This began a phase in the festival's history that Wein described as "Utopia." It was the high point of the melding of traditional music, popular folk artists and the conscience that ran through both, and Wein called it probably his proudest achievement in a lifetime of producing musical events. Each year, traditional performers opened young concertgoers' ears to enduring musical traditions, while chart-topping singer-songwriters purported to give voice to contemporary concerns such as the Vietnam War and nuclear proliferation.

"From '63 to '69 was seven years of the most beautiful relationship of artists with each other that I have ever seen," Wein remembers.[5] Yarrow says of the structure, "Something happens when you make it a nonprofit. Nobody's getting paid anything really. The spirit is that you're doing it for a cause—in this case, something that was near and dear to our hearts, which was what folk music embodied. . . . In its intent and in its performance, it was accessible; it was inclusive, and it was joyous."[6]

In *How Can I Keep From Singing*, his biography of Seeger, David King Dunaway describes the Newport festivals of the early and mid-'60s as the realization of Seeger's dream to make folk music America's favorite music. "People parked ungrumblingly in vast lots and carried in instruments and picnic coolers. Campgrounds filled with singing teenagers and sleeping bags. When a downpour threatened an outdoor concert, performers and audience only laughed and sang rain songs. This was more than a concert; it was a gathering, Woodstock before drugs and electric guitars."[7]

Yarrow agrees, saying that despite the obvious aesthetic differences, "the consciousness of Newport fed the impulse of Woodstock. . . . There were people who said, 'We want morality; we want legitimacy; we want an ethical country; we want fairness. But also, we reject the restraints of conventional society, and we are going to live that way here for this one moment.'"[8]

Robert Cantwell said the festival "provided for the eruption into daylit social space the hidden underground life of an emergent youth culture."[9] Murray Lerner's film *Festival!*—a documentary about the 1963–1966 Newport Folk Festivals—shows the continuation and the growth of the youth scene Susan Montgomery had described in 1960: Crowds of young people dash into the fields of Newport for afternoon and evening workshops and concerts;[10] young people on motorcycles roar past the staid mansions before bunkering down in parks, beaches and sidewalks; "fresh" from such rough accommodations, they gather anew in and around the festival site to hear the music again.

Lerner says his original intention in shooting was merely to provide footage for the Foundation's archive. He was inspired to turn his material into a film after seeing that do-it-yourself attitude among youthful folk devotees—not just in regards to music: "I thought, 'Wait a minute; there's something going on here that's beyond entertainment.' . . . It was growing in popularity . . . and it was being used to create a philosophy and a cultural movement. I thought I could make a very broad film about the meaning of that movement."[11]

"Why are we doing this?" Pete Seeger asks and answers in the film. "Because we believe in the idea that the average man and woman can make his own music in this machine age. It doesn't all have to come out of a loudspeaker. You can make it yourself. . . . And it can be your own music."

At the main venue, as well as at St. Michael's School and Touro Field, there was room for workshops and small concerts in various styles: "You have 1,000 people over here, listening to fiddlers," Seeger said in 2009, "and 500 people over there listening to some blues singers, and another 500 over there listening to Irish ballads."[12]

In Jim Rooney and Eric Von Schmidt's *Baby Let Me Follow You Down: An Illustrated Story of the Cambridge Folk Years*, Everett Alan Lilly, bassist of the young bluegrass hotshots, the Charles River Valley Boys, described the mosaic of workshop stages as "like taking an alcoholic to a picnic":

> Over in one field you had genuine Southern Comfort; over here you had Ballantine Ale; over there you had Seagram's; then you had very fine, old wine somewhere else—maybe too many people wouldn't go over there, but the ones who did really understood it.
>
> I was tireless. I didn't want to miss anything. Whenever we weren't playing, I was out in the field going to hear Maybelle Carter or Doc Watson or Bill Monroe or Bob Dylan or Joan Baez. As young as I was, I was impressed by the range of music and styles and also the quality of the music. And then there were the parties in those mansions! Where else could you go and walk among so many truly great musicians?[13]

A lot of what Seeger envisioned for the nonprofit festival came to pass. The 1963 festival, held July 26–28, included recent rediscoveries such as Appalachian singers and songwriters Dock Boggs, Jim Garland and Dorsey Dixon, a North Carolinian who had spent more of his life as a millworker than as a musician; country bluesmen Sonny Terry and Brownie McGhee; Maybelle Carter; and Tony Saletan, a former Shaker-camp folksong leader who adapted the modern version of "Michael Row the Boat Ashore."

Festivalgoers could learn from a workshop on music of the Kiowa tribe or pick up on the fine points of autoharp technique from Mother Maybelle Carter and Mike Seeger (including a Carter version of "Never On a Sunday"). Bob Davenport performed the unexpurgated version of the ballad "Seven Nights Drunk" ("Bollocks upon a rolling pin I never saw before"). John Lee Hooker told the crowd, "We are here to pay our dues to the natural facts," while seagulls cawed around his introduction to the haunting "Freight Train Be My Friend."

The Georgia Sea Island Singers contributed by chanting story-songs, overcoming a condescending introduction from Alan Lomax ("You probably won't understand all the words"), who also saw fit to introduce each song. And the Freedom Singers brought raw, righteous power with "Fighting for My Rights" (to the tune of "Lonely Avenue") and "I Love Your Dog," a gospel-based chant of racial harmony.

The discovery of the festival, however, was bluesman Mississippi John Hurt. His distinctively honeyed voice made him a connoisseur's favorite; his scarce recorded output—twelve sides for Okeh Records—made him a collector's prize; and his mysterious whereabouts—no one knew where he lived, and many presumed he had died—made him a larger-than-life figure. So when he came to perform at Newport, rediscovered by blues historian and collector Tom Hoskins, it was more than a musical moment.

Jim Rooney later wrote of that appearance, "It was unreal. John Hurt was dead. Had to be. All those guys on that Harry Smith Anthology were dead. They'd all recorded back in the twenties and thirties. They'd never been seen or heard from since. But there was no denying that the man singing so sweet and playing so beautifully was the John Hurt. He had a face—and what a face. He had a hat that he wore like a halo. In another place, in another time, Eric might well have got on his knees, but he didn't."[14]

But people weren't sleeping on Second Beach to hear Tony Saletan. The bill also included Seeger; Peter, Paul and Mary (a Grossman creation who had already had hits with Dylan's "Blowin' in the Wind" and Seeger's "If I Had a Hammer"); Baez; and Del McCoury and Bill Monroe. Baez was her usual incandescent, powerful self, including her by-then-routine Bob Dylan cover ("Don't Think Twice, It's All Right"), while Dylan himself slew the audience with the unapologetic "Masters of War" and joined Seeger in an afternoon-workshop version of "You Playboys and Playgirls Ain't Gonna Run My World."

More than 46,000 people attended the three-day festival, and the foundation cleared more than $70,000. Shelton exulted that "integrity in folk music had a field day at the box office."[15] To an extent it was true, but as Wein notes, it was always the case that the best-known artists, working for union scale, paid the way for the Dorsey Dixons. "When you look over the list of people we brought here, it's amazing. And it was all paid for by the fact that the Peter, Paul and Marys and the Joan Baezes were popular. It was an idealistic situation, and it really worked. And it was great to be part of it."[16]

In keeping with the activist tradition, some saw the musical alternatives presented at Newport and were inspired to provide alternatives to other aspects of mainstream American life. The civil rights movement was always a part of the Newport festival in the 1960s. Before the passage of the Civil Rights and Voting Rights Acts in 1964 and 1965, respectively, the presence of the Congress of Racial Equality and the Student Nonviolent Coordinating Committee (SNCC), which had literature and information tables at the festival site, as well as performances by the SNCC–aligned Freedom Singers, lent an extra sense of purpose to the proceedings.

The cultural highlight of that year's festival came at the finale, when Dylan led Baez, the Freedom Singers, Peter, Paul and Mary, Seeger and Bikel in his "Blowin' in the Wind," and Seeger's reworking of the spiritual "We Shall Overcome," an anthem for the civil rights movement.

Great songs or great politically charged anthems can't be written on command; indeed, it takes more than a songwriter and a performer to create them. The original "We Shall Overcome" had been around for years. The 1963 festival finale wasn't even the first time that someone had sung it at Newport—Guy Carawan did the honors in 1960. But in July 1963—the year that Governor George Wallace tried to block the integration of the University of Alabama; the year that Dr. Martin Luther King wrote his "Letter from Birmingham Jail"; a month before the March on Washington and King's "I Have a Dream" speech (an event at which Peter, Paul and Mary, Baez, and Dylan performed); and the summer that four girls in Birmingham, Alabama, were killed when the Ku Klux Klan bombed their church—the song rang out far past Newport.

Bikel later called it "the apogee of the folk movement. There was no point more suffused with hope for the future." Robert Cantwell called it

the supreme moment in this national seance, in which the summons of
folksong to the cultural dead populated the stage with a reunited family
of heroes and heroines of the past. . . . It was a moment in which, like
a celestial syzygy, many independent forces of tradition and culture,
wandering at large in time, some of them in historical deep space and others

only transient displays in the contemporary cultural atmosphere, briefly converged to reveal, though inscrutably, the truth of our national life.[17]

Yarrow says that "not everybody was on board" with making such a direct political statement, "but for me, that was where we were. To the degree possible, we were walking the walk on stage."[18] He adds that an assessment of the performance and the era has to take into account the continued legacy of the blacklist, most notably in its treatment of Seeger, who was in the middle of his long ban from the nation's airwaves—including from the *Hootenanny* TV show, which kept him off even though virtually every performer it showcased was a disciple of Seeger's and was profiting off the boom he did so much to create:

> We were living a perspective that would have been abhorrent to those
> people who had blacklisted Pete. Remember that Pete was a huge enemies-
> list guy, and . . . here we were, jubilantly celebrating this amazing legacy,
> and saying that we are doing exactly what the blacklist would have
> abominated. And at that very time, he was under surveillance, and we knew
> that. We're talking about not just music here; we're talking about really
> living something that was in the avant-garde of building a better nation.
> And that's what we felt. . . . We felt we were speaking to the aspirations of
> our country to be a moral nation. And for that reason, it was a very precious
> experience.[19]

The ethic of the folk festival—imagined by Seeger, championed by the board, and exemplified by the volunteers, the underpaid musicians and the stunning musicological finds—didn't stop when the concerts were over. Many of the performers lived together for the duration of the festival, put up in dormitories at Mount Vernon Junior College, sleeping on navy surplus sheets and blankets, eating food cooked by local chefs—all arranged for by Joyce Wein, with an army of helpers.

In 1982, Joyce Wein, speaking with historian Carol Brauner, remembered the logistical challenges behind the scenes as an integral part of what the folk festival was all about. While the jazz festival largely featured professional musicians, she said, "Under the structure of the folk festival, the folk foundation, we agreed to put the people up, to pay their transportation, whether it was by car, or bus or airplane. And we were dealing with people who, in many cases, were not professionals. So it became a horrendous thing, because we had these mimeographed contracts that we sent out—sometimes we got answers, sometimes we didn't; we tried to track them down."[20]

Thanks to the complexity of the logistics and the fact that the Weins had just moved to New York and Joyce Wein hadn't found a job in her field yet, she said, "I started taking over. . . . We used to put up, oh, anywhere from three to five hundred people, I think, and then I used to put up a big tent behind one of the houses and there was a cook that was very nice to work with. . . . And we used to feed everybody three times a day. . . . And then in addition, we ran a party every night, at one of the houses."[21]

Betsy Siggins was the doyenne of the Cambridge folk venue Club 47, where for eight years in the 1960s she handled the bookings and offered her couch to any musicians who needed a place to stay—and in the Boston area in the early and mid-1960s, most of the black players did. She volunteered at the Newport Folk Festival during those years and often booked the touring musicians who played the festival at Club 47 a few days after Newport was over. She recalls the festival as "one of the most startlingly important things that ever happened to any of us who cared about the music. Because right then and there we could be exposed to about fifteen kinds of American music."[22]

And as a volunteer, she got up close with many of the legends. Ralph Rinzler introduced her to Louisiana bluesman Robert Pete Williams, who when he was discovered had been serving a life sentence for a murder he said was in self-defense and was released into "servitude parole," an arrangement which saw him work eighty hours a week without pay. Siggins recalls, "I remember taking his hand and breaking into tears. I could cry now. [It was] that immediate connection I got with (a) people who are being oppressed, and (b) the way we had treated people in this country for way too long—and that he had a kind of music I had never experienced before."[23]

And when the nighttime shows were over, the artists got together at the dorms or the houses Wein had rented in town for the festival and played yet more. Wein, in his memoirs, recalls a night when Hurt was playing in the backyard to a group of enthralled kids, Odetta was singing in the living room, a bluegrass band was picking on the front lawn, and Dylan and Baez were in a room by themselves, trading songs.

Bob Jones, who began as a festival volunteer in 1963 and rose to become producer in 1985, recalls a night in 1964 talking with Bill Monroe and Muddy Waters on the steps of the Blues House (a house in the center of town where the blues musicians would be quartered together).[24] "Monroe asked Muddy, 'Do you even play in the South?' And Muddy said, 'Not really.'"[25]

"When it came down to it," Jones says, "everybody sang with everybody else. Everybody played with everybody else. The blues players were very happy to hear Bill play."[26]

"Moments like these," Wein writes, "were what the Folk Festival was really all about."[27]

Jim Kweskin played at Newport with his seminal jug band (including Geoff and the future Maria Muldaur) and solo for five years in a row. While playing Newport carried with it a certain degree of validation, he says, "I would have gone to Newport whether I was on the bill or not. . . . I went to Newport because I wanted to see those great musicians," such as Hurt, Skip James, Son House and Bukka White, as well as exotic fare such as the fife-and-drum of Ed Young and the penny whistling of Spokes Mashiyane. "And not just the older guys; I got to see these musicians I didn't get to see that much, like Spider John Koerner, or Mavis Staples, Dick and Mimi Fariña, the Paul Butterfield Blues Band—much as they were my contemporaries, we didn't get to see each other that often. So it's an opportunity to hang out with all these great musicians who were my age."[28]

Judy Collins, the singer-songwriter and activist best known for Joni Mitchell's "Both Sides, Now," whose Newport career has ranged from 1963 to 2009 and who served on the board of directors, remembers the festival similarly as "a gathering place. An old boys—and young girls—convention, where you could get together and hang out and sing songs and stay up late." Her favorite Newport moments don't involve her own performances or her years on the board—they all involve seeing and meeting other performers. To her, Newport meant hearing Pops Staples and his Singers, the Charles River Valley Boys, the Chambers Brothers and more. "I did my part," she says—"I certainly sang and performed. But it was so important to be at midnight around a campfire listening to Son House and Mississippi John Hurt—I mean, those were the days."[29]

The 1964 festival was the most successful one yet and the first to outdraw the jazz festival, with a total of seventy thousand people streaming into Newport over three days and four nights (July 23–26). With 4,500 in attendance, acts ranged from Bikel, Collins, Peter, Paul and Mary, Baez and Dylan to Seamus Ennis, Bessie Jones and the Georgia Sea Island Singers, Kentucky's Dewey Shepherd and a Jean Ritchie–led demonstration of a "Play-Party," a mix of a cappella singing and children's game-style movements that early settlers used to get around prohibitions on music and dancing.

It was also the year Skip James, Son House, Sleepy John Estes, Muddy Waters and others made appearances at Newport, which the blues writer and photographer Dick Waterman later called "the greatest collection of country blues singers" assembled to that point.[30] There was also a performance of Cajun music by a band including Dewey Balfa, and while it went largely unremarked at the time, it had a seismic effect, in both Rhode Island and the Cajun homeland of Louisiana. These performances were the first fruit of the Newport Folk Foundation's efforts to promote and foster the development of folk music not just one weekend per year at Newport but year-round and across the country.

Ralph and I would say,
"OK; we'll find them."
BOB JONES

TEXAS WAS THE WORST

When Mississippi John Hurt, who had been living in obscurity for many years, came to the 1963 Newport Folk Festival, his reemergence was seen as an example of the long-lost and forgotten talent that could still be found living in North America's backwaters. George Wein wrote in his memoirs, "If John Hurt could live in obscurity for 35 years, how many other hidden treasures were scattered across American soil? His presence at the Folk Festival was a confirmation of every impulse that ran through the folk collector's psyche."[1] The discovery, preservation and promotion of those treasures comprised an important part of the mission of the Newport Folk Foundation.

In January 1964, the foundation made its first cash grants to institutions —$250 each to schools in Brasstown and Pine Mountain, North Carolina, and Hindman, Kentucky; the folk publications *Little Sandy Review* and *Broadside* (both of which had been and would continue to be critical of the Newport Folk Festival in their pages); and the Cooperative Recreation Service of Delaware, Ohio, to print five thousand books of folk songs for members of the Peace Corps. Five hundred dollars each were granted to the Old Town School of Folk Music in Willmette, Illinois; the Council of Southern Mountains in Berea, Kentucky, and Boston's WGBH. Two hundred dollars went to the Institute of American Indian Arts in Santa Fe, New Mexico. They also gave performers Dorsey Dixon and Hurt a tape recorder and a guitar, respectively.

In the program for the 1964 festival, folklorist and historian Ralph Rinzler wrote that grants were "an obvious point of departure," but he added, "unlike some Socialist countries, where the government assumes responsibility for the collection, stimulation and preservation of folk creation and culture, we live in a situation where the product of folk culture nets millions of dollars annually in the entertainment industry but neither the industry nor the government has sought to conserve its natural resources in this area."

Toward that end, the foundation gave Guy Carawan two $500 grants for the production of a folk music festival on John's Island, South Carolina, home of Bessie Jones and the Georgia Sea Island Singers, who had performed at Newport in 1963, and a place many of whose natives ended up at Newport in the next few years.

And on the recommendation of board members Alan Lomax and Mike Seeger (half brother of Pete Seeger), the foundation hired Rinzler to scour the country looking for little-known local talent and to sign them up to play at Newport, as well as to find areas of the country where a Newport-supported festival would bring traditional cultures to light. In their memo to the board, Lomax and Seeger said that "if Newport interests itself professionally in the destiny of American folk artists themselves, through trained personnel such as this scout, the Foundation can greatly benefit the whole field."

A former member of bluegrass revivalists the Greenbriar Boys and a fixture on the New York folk scene when Bob Dylan was still getting his feet wet there, Rinzler had already traveled many miles in pursuit of folk music by the time he signed on with the Newport Folk Foundation. In 1961, while on the road with the Greenbriar Boys in North Carolina, he found Clarence Ashley, a performer whose music was on the *Folkways Anthology* but had long been assumed dead; on a subsequent trip to record Ashley, Rinzler was introduced to the guitarist and singer Doc Watson. He became Watson's manager (others he managed included Bill Monroe) and encouraged him to pursue traditional music rather than rockabilly. Along with John Cohen and Izzy Young, Rinzler founded the Friends of Old-Time Music, presenting and producing concerts with veterans such as Ashley, Watson and Monroe, thus spreading the gospel of American music through its great purveyors as well as playing it himself.

As a scout for the Newport Folk Festival, Rinzler's main purview, according to Lomax and Seeger, would include Canada's maritime provinces, as well as French Quebec, "the foreign minority neighborhoods of Detroit,

Chicago and Pittsburgh," Mexico's southwest, rural Alabama and the Cajun areas of Louisiana. On many of these trips, Rinzler, who died in 1994, went with Mike Seeger, who died in 2009; on others, he went with Bob Jones.

Jones had spent the 1963 festival working as a volunteer with Joyce Wein. But starting after that festival, he and Rinzler traveled through the South and in Texas, in later years heading up to Canada. He began working for the festival full-time in 1965—"I didn't have anything else to do"[2]—and was named producer of the festival in 1985, a title he holds to this day.

This was part of the point of becoming a nonprofit: the proceeds of the festival, after expenses, were to be spent on finding talent that met Seeger's definition of "old-timers" and indigenous musicians. That meant beating the bush for interesting, traditional, yet overlooked players and singers, so that the Newport Folk Festival would truly represent America's musical traditions and materially support them where they were based.

In those days, that required a lot of driving and searching, without many clues to guide them. "Alan would say, 'I know there are some black Cajun players,'" Jones says, "and Ralph and I would say, 'OK; we'll find them.'" And off they went.

Sometimes they didn't even have that much to go on: "We'd go to the last remembered town" of a musician they had their eye on, Jones says, and start asking questions. When Jones and Rinzler found someone who piqued their interest, they'd let them know they were interested in having them come up to Newport. "And for those who could—well, who could read, number one—we had stories and pictures of the festival, to show what we do. And we told them that everything would be paid for." They'd then make a quick recording of the musician or group to play for the festival board, who would have ultimate say over their choices.

Jones says he and Rinzler didn't have any sort of quota; they simply signed up whomever they liked. Often, the person they were scouting wasn't necessarily the person they signed.

The duo had local contacts and scouts: Mack McCormack, in Texas, would hip them to blues players; Paul Tate, president of the Louisiana Folk Foundation, was good for lots of names and locations, as well as staying in contact with musicians when the board approved one of Rinzler and Jones's choices. "You know the white Southerner in the white linen suit?" Jones says of Tate. "This guy was the picture-perfect [representation] of that. He was right out of a movie script. But he was an incredible fan of the music—black, white, everything." Jones would call Tate and send him bus tickets for performers they wanted; Tate would find the musicians, give them the tickets and get them on the bus.

But Rinzler, Jones and Mike Seeger were the ones who put in the miles. In the pre–civil rights South, this could carry some dangers. "We ran into a little bit of ill will in Florida," Jones remembers, "as far as being white guys going into the black communities in 1963 and 1964. We were a little bit crazy."

It wasn't just Florida. "Louisiana was not that difficult. Texas was the worst, and Alabama was fairly reasonable, in that they'd stop us and ask what we were doing, and we had the pictures of the festival. But then Elliot Hoffman, the lawyer for Festival Productions, got nervous. . . . From then on we had to call every night."

The stories, not surprisingly, are endless.

Alan Lomax once sent the pair to Dothan, Alabama, the self-styled Peanut Capital of the World. "We heard of this guy who sang a song about Kennedy's death," Jones remembers, "and someone recorded it for a TV news thing." But while they were there, they heard someone playing, with children singing along. They walked in the direction of the sound, "and there was a black guy playing the pan pipes!" This wasn't much more common in mid-'60s Alabama than it is now, but Joe Patterson was an uncommon player. Jones remembers that Patterson had a steel plate that he would beat to keep the rhythm, and he would hoot when the song got to a note that he didn't have on the pipes.

Rinzler and Jones signed him up for the festival, but in the process they ran into the Patterson family dynamic: "I remember the family was upset because we didn't take them. I wouldn't say [Patterson] was retarded, but he might have been a little slow. The family pushed him out in the back, and he was living in this little shack. He was part of the family, but not really." Instead, Patterson came to the festival accompanied by guitarist Willie Doss, who worked in the mill there.

Jones remembers himself and Rinzler driving in the Florida Panhandle heading into Louisiana. It was about 6 p.m. and pouring rain, and they saw someone hitchhiking while carrying a caseless guitar. They stopped and picked him up. He was headed to a small town to play in a bar that Jones describes as one of three or four shacks that pretty much constituted the downtown. But even from outside, they could tell a great harmonica player when they heard one. "So we go in, and there's a whole bunch of people milling around, some dancing. They were all black. Everyone's looking at us. So the guy we picked up goes to this bar—not really a bar, more like a shelf—and he's standing there, and this harmonica player is playing there with one microphone."

The band consisted of their passenger, the harmonica player, and a drummer with a makeshift kit—"a bass drum, a cymbal stand, a snare, a hi-hat, and some device which looked like a drum but wasn't really a drum—you could bang on it." But the harmonica player was good enough, Jones says, to continue hanging around.

The good time didn't last long. "Suddenly, we see this scuffle. And the guy we had brought in was involved in this scuffle. So the harmonica player says into the microphone, 'GET OUT!' And he's looking right at us.

"We're out of there. So we go out, across the street and get into the car. And it's still pouring. And these guys come out and they're throwing bottles."

They escaped, but Jones says, "We were intrigued, so we didn't go far." They stopped for the night at a motel about twenty minutes away, then drove back the next day, still hoping to make contact with the harmonica player. Not only was the player gone; so was the bar. "The place was over with." The bar was itself attached to a food store, and Rinzler went in to inquire about the situation, and came out saying, "The guy we brought in was a real badass guy. And he was the one who started the fight!"

No one knew who the harmonica player was—Rinzler learned he wasn't from that town and had just blown in for the night—and the duo lost their quarry. There's regret in Jones's voice to this day as he remembers the lost opportunity. "We never found out who the hell he was. And I tell you, this harmonica player was unbelievable."

He shrugs his shoulders: "Those are the risks."

In Texas, they found the preacher/singer Doc Reese and surprised him on moving day: "We were helping him and talking with his wife and his kids." Rinzler and Jones were familiar to Reese, an ex-convict, because Lomax had recorded him during his incarceration. Later, Reese's lawyer drove up and advised the two to come over to his house to talk about groups and musicians to check out.

The police followed them to the lawyer's house. But when Rinzler and Jones got to the lawyer's house, the police stopped at the end of the driveway. "So the lawyer's telling us about the choir they had, and he says, 'Now, don't worry about this police car. He will not move until you start moving. He will not come onto my property, because if he does I will shoot him.' And we thought, 'Oh, very interesting.'"

From there they headed to the Huntsville prison to scout singers, but they were pulled over. According to Jones, the officer invented a law that required all white people to notify him personally if they wanted to speak to a black resident, and he made them empty the car, looking for guns, pamphlets, tapes of Martin Luther King, or any other dangerous weapons. But thanks to Rinzler's association with bluegrass king Bill Monroe, the search turned out to be the break the two scouts needed:

> So [the cop] comes across this file box of Bill Monroe photos and letters to mail out. So he pulls them out and says, "What's this?" Ralph says, "That's photos of Bill Monroe." "I know who that is; why do you have these photos?" So Ralph says, "I'm his manager." The cop says, "I don't believe this. Pack the car up. I happen to be a big fan of Bill Monroe's." So we pack the car up and he says, "I am gonna drive you to the line. You're not going back to the lawyer; you have to go directly out."
>
> So we get beyond the town, and the car stopped. And he stopped because this is now state property, and a state police car is flagging us down. . . . The state police officer came over, who was white, and admonished the sheriff—"These people have an appointment with the superintendent of the prison; why are you bothering them?" So we got back in the car and followed this guy for an hour.[3]

In 1964, they were in Tennessee, looking for a black Sacred Harp singing group to balance the thirty-member white group from Georgia they had already signed up. They headed to a church where the occasion, known as a "singing," followed the norm: hours of singing in the afternoon, then a big meal afterwards. The minister introduced them to the group and the congregation, saying they were the first white people to ever come to their church. After the singing, "which was great," Rinzler and Jones joined the meal. "And this woman said, 'I never sat beside anyone white. And I wouldn't be able to touch that chicken after you touched it.'

"Pretty amazing. Those were the things that happened," Jones said.

Usually, Jones says, it wasn't difficult to find the people they were look-ing for: "Most of these people we found were stalwarts in their own community. Even if their community was a rough black section of town, they were all well known." It also wasn't too hard to get people to agree to come to Newport, particularly after the festival had been around for a few years. (Even in the Southern towns where they'd gotten hassled by the police, things would go more smoothly the next time, especially since they made a habit of sending clippings of the residents' Newport exploits.)

There were exceptions, though. Jones remembers looking for the self-proclaimed "World's Greatest Fiddle Player." They found him digging a ditch outside his house, but he rebuffed their advances—"I don't play the fiddle anymore," Jones recalls him saying. "Because I have religion—my wife and me. It's not a good instrument to play."

Jones says that he and Rinzler spent two days trying to change his mind. He never relented on his claim of being the world's greatest fiddle player. But he also never agreed to come to Newport and play.

DeFord Bailey ("the Harmonica Wizard") was the first black man to play at the Grand Old Opry. He'd been playing "Pan American Blues" in 1927 and was a regular on the Opry in 1928, one of its charter members. While reportedly his race was no obstacle to the radio and touring audiences loving him, he was required to use separate accommodations and restaurants on the road.

By 1941, however, he was getting phased out of the Opry, not least because of the Opry's licensing disagreement with ASCAP (the American Society of Composers, Artists and Producers), which led in part to the founding of BMI (Broadcast Music Incorporated). Bailey's music was controlled by ASCAP, and he was told he'd have to learn new material. No one else had to do that, Bailey replied, and ignored the request. He was let go in May 1941, and in 1946, Opry founder George Hay's history of the venue referred to him as "a little crippled colored boy who was a bright feature of our show for about fifteen years. Like some members of his race and other races, DeFord was lazy. . . . He was our mascot and is still loved by the entire company. We gave him a whole year's notice to learn some more tunes, but he would not. When we were forced to give him his final notice, DeFord said, without malice, 'I knowed it waz comin', Judge, I knowed it waz comin'.'" Bailey, not surprisingly, saw it differently, claiming that he'd wanted to do different songs and was told to stick with what the audiences liked. "They seen the day was coming when they'd have to pay me right . . . and they used the excuse about me playing the same old tunes."[4]

When Rinzler and Jones found him in Nashville, he was shining shoes. They asked him to come to Newport and play, but Jones says Bailey's response was categorical: "He did not want to play for white people." The pair would call on Bailey every time they came through Nashville, and it took three or four times to convince him to play.

It took three tries to get Pete Forge as well, Jones says. In that case, Rinzler's Opry connections worked against them: "He felt that he had never been given his due. So he held it slightly against Ralph; he felt he'd be taken again."

To this day, Jones kicks himself for not finding any good musicians in the Canadian Maritimes in the 1960s. He reasons that the generation that brought the region's traditional music to the fore in the 1980s, such as Natalie MacMaster, the Rankins, Barra MacNeil and others, must have had parents and uncles who played and sang—although they got canned salmon, a sweater and a commitment from one singer.

Overall, Jones says his days on the road were "a little terrifying at times. [But] I loved it. I think that's where I found out that I was very comfortable with musicians, in general. I never was awed by any musician on a star basis or anything like that. And I think these were humbling experiences, to see these guys who were great musicians in their own right and were just being musicians. I just got along very easily."

And he was struck by the fact that virtually none of the artists whom he and Rinzler pulled out of rural backwaters and back porches had any problem suddenly playing or singing into a microphone miles away from home to thousands of strangers: "They never really were awed themselves by the idea that they were going to play in front of ten thousand people. They just went out and played. You would have thought they'd be terrified. But they just went out and played. I found that to be stunning."

While the traditional musicians may not have been awed by the venue, Rinzler writes of helping to polish his discoveries' live-performance techniques. More importantly, though, he sometimes also had to explain to them that their most traditional songs were what the Newport organizers and audiences wanted.

A craftsperson can make something that looks like something he's just seen in a newspaper, thinking that that's what's the latest thing. So he'll copy a crockpot that's mass produced and sold at K-Mart because that's what he sees in the paper. . . . Doc Watson wanted to play Eddie Arnold songs and Chet Atkins songs because he knew that Nashville was a symbol of success and he figured that for him to be successful he had to sing what was popular. . . .

Doc, being an imitation of a Nashville performer, would never have been as successful as he was being himself. And that took time and fieldwork . . . to take out the deepest cut of tradition that they were in contact with through their family or community and encourage them not to imitate pop Nashville or pop Cajun or rock musicians but to play the grassroots stuff that was unique and distinctive regionally and familially.[5]

The efforts by the Newport Folk Foundation to foster and develop folk art and traditions, as well as their appreciation, had plenty of successes during the 1960s. In 1968, a grant to high school English teacher Eliot Wigginton and a group of his students at the Rabun Gap-Nacoochee School helped sustain and expand the Foxfire Project, which became a magazine and series of books on the oral history and traditions of Appalachian culture that continues to this day.

Local and regional music benefited from the exposure and efforts of Newport, of course: Ralph Rinzler wrote in a memo to the board in 1965 that Jimmie Driftwood organized a small festival in Mountain View, Arkansas, and "found that once the event had passed the singers and pickers had gotten so accustomed to coming to Friday night rehearsals that they just kept showing up at the courthouse every Friday night throughout the year. Several years have passed and now they come by the hundreds rather than the dozens." The Moving Star Hall Singers, from the Georgia Sea Islands, made their public debut at the Newport Folk Festival in 1964 and by the next year had played two engagements in Los Angeles.

The greatest accomplishment of the Newport Folk Foundation, however, is probably the beginning of the revitalization of Cajun and zydeco music.

It's been said that the performance by an ad-hoc Cajun band at Newport in 1964 was the first large-audience performance of Cajun music outside of Louisiana. Contemporary Cajun king Steve Riley, leader of Steve Riley and the Mamou Playboys, and his former bandmate David Greely agree that the show was critical for the cultural flowering of Cajun music—and that the appreciation worked in both directions.

In the 1960s, Cajun culture in Louisiana was generally considered an embarrassment. Burton Grindstaff wrote in the *Opelousas Daily World*, "I contend there is no more music coming from a fiddle, accordion and triangle when three Cajuns get together than seeps through the cracks in your house when crickets feel an urge to make themselves heard. Cajuns brought some mighty fine things down from Novia [*sic*] Scotia with them, including their jolly selves, but their so-called music is one thing I wish they hadn't. . . . All we can do is sit back and wait for the verdict from Newport, scared stiff."[6]

In the 1965 Newport Folk Festival program, Paul Tate of the Louisiana Folk Foundation wrote that the disdain for Cajun music came from the circumstances of the Acadians' arrival in Louisiana: having been expelled from Nova Scotia in 1755 and spent ten years wandering down the coast of the United States, "the Acadian sought in Louisiana not a new life but the old life in a new location."

This led to a lack of integration between the Cajuns and the rest of Louisiana, leaving most Cajuns with the choice between standing seemingly aloof from their immediate surroundings or renouncing their heritage. Cajun music, Tate wrote, "lay captive, isolated and dying, hedged in by a 'sub-tradition' of mediocre imitation of country or Western or popular music."

While Dewey Balfa's performance at Newport put the lie to Grindstaff's fears and turned the New England region on to the beauty of the Cajun music and culture, David Greely, a former student of the late master's, says that the reaction to that performance had a similar effect on Balfa.

In Newport, Balfa said he would "bring home the echo of the standing ovation" he received there to Louisiana. Greely says Balfa returned to Lafayette, Louisiana, determined that his music would no longer get second-class treatment. Balfa himself later said, "My culture is not better than anyone else's culture. My people were no better than anyone else. And yet, I will not accept it was a second-class culture."[7]

In 1965, Tate wrote to the board that the music was on its way back. Just in the year since the Newport performance, Tate related examples of Cajun music being played at official and quasi-official Louisiana events, including the first-ever performance of Cajun music in the governor's mansion.

The foundation, he wrote, sponsored music competitions at such Louisiana institutions as the Dairy Festival in Abbeville, the Cotton Festival in Ville Platte, the Rice festival in Crowley, the Yambilee Festival in Opelousas and the Acadian-style Mardi Gras activities in Church Point, Kaplan and Mamou:

> We had been greatly concerned about the rapid loss of status of Acadian
> music in favor of western and country music, rock and roll, and popular
> music. . . .
> The invitation of the Cajun band to Newport had the desired effect
> of giving stature to traditional Acadian music played on traditional
> instruments. Directly related to this recognition of authentic Cajun music,
> there has occurred a revival of interest in such music far beyond anyone's
> expectations.[8]

In the 1966 festival program, Tate wrote that Cajuns had lit out for Minneapolis, Houston, Boston and Denver, as well as going on a four-week tour of Europe. "The Newport Folk Foundation is principally responsible for what is happening to Cajun music today," he added, concluding that the promulgation of the music was resulting in "a greater appreciation and understanding of Acadian culture and the Cajun soul—by the Cajun as well as by those with whom he comes in contact."

By 1968, the state formed the Council for the Development of French in Louisiana. In 1977, several small festivals united to form what we now know as the Festival de Musique Acadienne, which has run ever since. Thanks to the tireless efforts of musicians, folklorists and fans alike, Cajun culture is now recognized as one of the distinct American cultures.

Alongside the foundation's fieldwork, many of the blues players who came to Newport in the first years of the nonprofit era were discovered by record collectors. Inspired by the Folkways *Anthology of American Folk Music*, these aficionados began to look for the men behind the songs, figuring that at least some would still be alive—the original recordings had been cut in the 1920s and 1930s, which wasn't so far in the past.

Indeed, Dick Spotswood's introduction of Mississippi John Hurt at the 1963 festival was an entertaining example of the process: "This spring, Tom Hoskins, my friend, went down to Avalon, Mississippi, after we had decided that there was a good chance that John might be there. He heard his old record of Avalon Blues and on there was a line, 'Avalon's my home town, always on my mind.' Putting two and two together, we decided there must be an Avalon, Mississippi. We went there; the first person we asked knew where he was, he played a few notes for us, and we said, 'That's all.' "[9]

(Hurt, speaking from the stage, remembered it a little differently: "Spotswood discovered me down in Avalon, Mississippi. I thought it was real funny. I said 'Why? What have I did? Is the FBI looking for me? I ain't did nothing' ").

It was a transcendent moment. Dave Van Ronk, who followed Hurt onto the stage, told the crowd, "I feel like fainting." Many artists were plucked from obscurity and given a chance to see and feel the appreciation that people had for their long-ago work.

But the process didn't always work like it was supposed to. Folklorist Phil Spiro said, "I'm half inclined today to say that if I had to do it all over again, I wouldn't do it." Some of these artists were only part-time musicians even in their prime, Spiro explained, and bringing them into the entertainment business thirty years later was a shock.

> We . . . consciously or unconsciously tried to shape the music they
> played on stage. The same statement could be made for the guys running
> Paramount during the thirties, but at least their motive was simple profit,
> which motive the artist shared. Our motivation was a strange combination
> of ego, scholasticism and power. I wonder now what would have happened
> if we had just left them alone instead of telling them what songs to sing and
> what instrument to play them on. . . .
>
> Worst of all, aside from a couple of people like Chris Strachwitz and
> Dick Waterman, the rediscoverers all too often didn't see the old guys as
> real, breathing, feeling, intelligent people. In general, we were collectors of
> people, who we tended to treat as if they were the very rarest of records—
> only one copy known to exist.[10]

And Jack Landron, who performed as Jackie Washington in the Club 47 scene and at Newport in the mid-1960s, says that as with so many other processes, the experience of musical integration was very different for white and nonwhite players and fans:

> For the white kids, they were put into contact with black musicians [about
> whom] they said, "Oooh; I admire what they're doing, and I wanna learn
> how to do it, and these people aren't what Daddy told me they were." They

were having a sense of discovery, whereas I think nonwhite people were having a sense of a lessening of tension. Which is a different experience.

And one enters an experience like that with a certain level of apprehension or distrust; "How far is this gonna go?" . . . The white kids were discovering something that the nonwhite people knew. So [for us] there wasn't a sense of excitement about it.[11]

Still, the rediscovery by the Newport Folk Festival and Foundation in the 1960s of long-forgotten artists and the unearthing, development and encouragement of traditional performers tucked away in America's hollows and highlands had effects that spread across the nation and outlasted the first incarnation of the festival itself.

During his travels, including those for the Newport Folk Foundation, Rinzler began to notice that music wasn't the only old-time tradition that fascinated him. "Often while listening to people sing," he later said, "I'd sit down on a folk chair or put my foot on a folk basket, or kick over a folk table."[12]

That appreciation for folk art, craft and story led Rinzler to start collecting items from the places he'd been and eventually to present them at the folk festival, both as exhibits and for sale. It didn't work out very well; later, he said, "At Newport I persuaded the board to do traditional craft and found to my chagrin that Newport was the wrong venue. I personally paid for the inventory and I shudder to think now the enormous physical effort and danger that was involved with hauling a 15-foot U-Haul with a bumper hitch behind an old station wagon, loading, unloading and repacking it at every stop with pots and rugs which weighed a ton."[13]

But Rinzler opened a store in Cambridge, Massachusetts, with the leftovers that didn't sell at Newport. He eventually left the Newport board to join the Smithsonian Institution, producing the Smithsonian Folklife Festival, which began in 1967 and runs to this day (he died in 1994). "My experience at Newport, where a disinterested public had walked right by the crafts demonstrations and sales, prepared me to rise to the occasion," he cracked.[14] A celebration of all aspects of traditional life, the festival has drawn up to a million people to the National Mall each year, in some way certifying Rinzler's vision.

One more story, told by Jones to Kate Rinzler in 1995, illustrates the effect that Ralph Rinzler and Jones could have on the people they encountered. Jones and Rinzler, along with folklorist Revon Reed and a few other Cajuns, were driving down a road in Louisiana when they happened across an old man whom some of their group knew. As they talked, Rinzler spoke to the old man in Cajun French.

The old man asked Rinzler how he knew the language—according to Jones, Rinzler was skilled but obviously not a native speaker. As Rinzler explained that he had studied the language, Jones said, "It came out that this guy thought his language was only oral." He couldn't understand that his language had been written down somewhere, so that someone who hadn't grown up there could learn it. Rinzler wrote something down in French on paper and handed it to the man. "He never realized that the language that he was speaking was legitimized. . . . His face lit up," Jones remembers. He didn't know written French existed. Jones characterized the old man's reaction as, "'Wow! I'm part of this bigger thing that's happening.' . . . Those were the kinds of things that happened there."[15]

You're dealing with something where the terms change, and the definition of the terms change, and the times change.

JOHN COHEN

A REAL FOLK FESTIVAL

In 2009, Pete Seeger recalled the "very serious letter" he and his wife Toshi, along with his half-sister Peggy Seeger and her husband Ewan MacColl, wrote to George Wein after the first Newport Folk Festival: "You had some very good performers, like the Kingston Trio," Seeger remembers them writing, "but you didn't have any old-timers. And without old-timers, this isn't a real folk festival."[1]

Is Newport a real folk festival? The question was asked on a panel during the second day of the first festival, and it's been asked ever since: Will next year's festival be a real folk festival? Has it ever been? What's a real folk festival, anyway? For that matter, what is real folk music? Attempts to define the genre have generally led to more questions.

Writing in the 1960 Newport Folk Festival program book, Seeger defined the criteria of the festival negatively: "No bel canto voices, no orchestra, no reading of notes from paper, practically no singing of songs simply because they were 'hits.'" How to positively define folk music—to list what it does include rather than what it doesn't—has proven considerably more difficult. Despite those difficulties, Benjamin Filene writes, "Twentieth-century Americans have been consistently searching for the latest incarnation of 'old-time' and 'authentic' music. Such terms may have lost their referents, but their cultural power has remained undiminished."[2] And during the commercial boom in folk music in the late 1950s and early 1960s, the question of what constituted real folk music was never fiercer, perhaps because the stakes were never higher. "The movement's rhetoric significantly brought the concept of tradition in a modernizing society into a public forum," Simon Bronner wrote. "The meaning of tradition as a visceral, hazy category of authenticity came to the fore."[3]

Ronald Cohen, who observed the three-way split among commercial performers, traditional performers and "city revivalists" at the beginning of the folk revival, called this division "often a tempest in a teapot but vital to those involved," and at no time was it fiercer than during the period when the Newport Folk Festival was getting up and running.[4]

Some of these debates were probably inevitable and were likely brought on by the efforts of preservationists such as the Lomaxes themselves. As folk scholar Neil Rosenberg points out, their efforts led to the enshrinement of the recording, rather than the printed text, as the standard of the authentic.[5] That meant that a particular version or arrangement was the coin of the realm, and the performer and performance gained equal billing with the song itself. Filene writes that audiences

> could embrace not just specific folk songs but the folk themselves. . . . The Lomaxes began to promote not just the songs they gathered but the singers who sang them. In doing so they produced a web of criteria for determining what a "true" folk singer looked and sounded like and a set of assumptions about the importance of *being* a "true" folk singer. In short, they created a "cult of authenticity," a thicket of expectations and valuations that American roots musicians and their audiences have been negotiating ever since.[6]

But the interests of the musician/fan aren't the same as those of the preservationist (although Bascom Lamar Lunsford and Alan Lomax were both), and in hindsight it seems naïve for those who recorded prison singers, field hollerers, square-dance players and the like not to see that their recording devices were supplanting the oral traditions they were trying to preserve and producing a similar modernizing effect to the dreaded automobile and radio. Musicologist Charles Seeger, Pete Seeger's father, wrote that such technological efforts "kept nineteenth-century music romanticism artificially alive beyond its day."[7]

It's not known what Lomax and company thought would happen when a musician in New York or Hawaii or California got the chance to hear a Smoky Mountain ballad or an Appalachian play-party song, but what in fact did happen, in retrospect at least, seems obvious: new people heard old music—"like many revivals," folklorist Bruce Jackson wrote, "it appealed primarily to individuals who celebrated traditions not their own"—and did what they wanted with it.[8] While the early method of collecting folk songs, in books with or without sheet music, might seem to encourage even more experimentation and change, the wider dissemination of records seems to have more than made up for it.

Folk music, or at least the popularization of old folk songs as hit records, became big business. The Kingston Trio's "Tom Dooley" sold 4 million copies, and the group made between $8,000 and $12,000 per performance and $300,000 a year from their records. Other folk-derived performers, such as the actor/singer Harry Belafonte with his mix of pop and calypso, were hitting the top of the charts in the pre-Beatles days. The word "hootenanny," descriptive of folk-music get-togethers of varying degrees of inclusion and informality, began showing up on merchandise such as sweatshirts, shoes, candy bars, bath mitts and pinball machines. It was also the title of a magazine and a television show that ran for two seasons on ABC, which as mentioned before issued increasingly implausible denials that the exclusion of Pete Seeger from its airwaves had anything to do with his politics.[9]

Almost immediately, sides were taken over whether commercial recordings of old-time folk music were exploitative hijackings of traditional culture meant to make a few bucks, or sincere attempts to give America's truest culture the kind of wide appeal and financial reward it deserved. Jeff Todd Titon writes that "among enthusiasts in the folk revival, debates were held about 'authenticity' and 'selling out.' Who was 'more ethnic' (as the saying went) than whom?"[10]

As the singing of folk songs became a profession and the performance of folk songs became something to be put on stage and on record, with admission or purchase price charged, the relationship between performers and audiences changed. In a 1963 article, Ewan MacColl, a folk historian who produced a hit BBC folk song radio program with Alan Lomax and A. B. Lloyd, explained it this way:

> In the past, the folksinger was a member of a small community and
> shared identical interests, accent, vocabulary with every member of that
> community. Surrounded by familiar faces and familiar objects, he would

find it a comparative [*sic*] simple matter to communicate his most intimate thoughts and feelings. The modern urban folksinger, on the other hand, is rarely a member of a community in that sense. His audience is made up of strangers or of casual acquaintances about whom he knows little or nothing and whose experiences, accent and social outlook may be very different from his own. They have paid their money to hear him sing, in exactly the same way that an audience pays to see a play or a film.[11]

Though the debates rarely produced any definitive answers, the effect of the popularization of folk music led to the spilling of gallons of ink in the folk music press for years. Every issue of *Sing Out!*, *Gardyloo*, the *Little Sandy Review*—even the *Hootenanny* magazine published in connection with the TV show—included or effectively constituted a symposium on what was happening to folk music and where it was going. But almost all the arguments and many of their major proponents, including Lomax, Oscar Brand and Irwin Silber, were gathered under one roof in 1963 at a literal symposium convened by the New York Folklore Society.

Brand explained that an unscientific survey by the society did little to clear up the question of how to define genuine folk music: "Each one of these reasons was usually accompanied by a word—'meaningful' or 'had meaning' or 'they meant something,' or 'they mean more.' The word 'mean' seemed to come out in 80 percent of the replies. Now, the question was, What did they mean by the word 'meaning'?"[12]

Lomax didn't see the popular revival in the United States as a good or even neutral thing, warning that it threatened to stamp out, not enhance, other forms of folk: "In Pakistan today, they are singing 'Careless Love.' . . . This is not just some sweet and affable folk process going on here. This is a great big money-making machine, and we are all in it."[13]

Singer, song collector and folk historian Ellen Stekert replied that the folk process was more durable than that. She recalled sitting in a miner's shack in Kentucky watching a TV show, "and it is a totally different show from when I watch it in my urban, middle-class apartment. People will take this show off television, the mass-produced show, and they will start talking about the cowboy show as if it is a folktale. They have their traditions, and they have their ways of expressing themselves, and they are always going to last in spite of the mass media."[14] Meanwhile, Irwin Silber argued that the process had never been pure: while early scholars went out to collect folksongs from traditional singers, "they had decided in advance what folksongs were. They did not collect everything that they heard."[15]

Indeed, Cecil Sharp's disappointment when he found an insufficiently rustic town—or, for that matter, his complete disregard for African-American music as a kind of American folk—speaks to the point. Filene writes that "there was a racial undertone beneath the earliest self-conscious efforts to define America's folk-song heritage."[16] And the fact that Francis Child—an early preservationist of British folk songs—was American, and Sharp—an early preservationist of American folk songs—was British suggests a search for a mythic purity that could be idealized from a distance; it certainly seems plausible in Sharp's case.

The arguments continued in successive issues of *Sing Out!* in 1962 and 1963: Stephen Fiott argued that the Kingston Trio, for example, had not received sufficient credit from hardcore folk fans for doing "what should have been done years before, reached an intelligent audience with intelligent music. . . . Today's tradition in folk music is commercialization; the folk want it that way."[17]

He was rebutted in the next issue of the same magazine by Dan Armstrong, who responded, "I doubt the 'folk' would have it any other way. It would be too uncomfortable, too close to the fears that drive them obsessively to seek security. . . . If these 'folk' would accept John Lee Hooker for 25 min. on the Ed Sullivan show, as they do Belafonte, I would have a little faith in what they want."[18]

He was joined by the duo of Jon Pankake and Paul Nelson, founders of the *Little Sandy Review*, who used a derisive nickname for Harry Belafonte: "Many's the time we've played an aspiring folk-singer the source material for a song popularized by Belaphony (or some such), only to have the singer turn up his nose at it and proclaim that B. does it much better, more smoothly, etc. Here progress toward the appreciation of the traditional seems to be permanently stifled, not heightened."[19]

Across the water, MacColl wrote that Fiott's conflation of folk music with popular tastes "implies that there was once a time when everybody knew all the songs and every other person could sing them. There is not one shred of evidence to support this assumption. It is true that in the past there were probably many more country singers than there are today but this doesn't necessarily mean that the traditional repertoire had the wide currency of today's 'pops.'"[20] British A&R man Nathan Joseph fired back against "The folk music puritan," who, he argued, "cannot abide thousands enjoying a popular form of his own material because like all puritans, he is not interested in what others enjoy . . . his only interest is his own academic indulgence."[21]

As a vehicle for popularizing folk music—especially in the earliest days, when groups such as the Kingston Trio and the Brothers Four occupied prominent spots on the bill—the Newport Folk Festival was one of the major battlefields for these arguments. Joyce Wein said that her husband always placed great value on "showing a more complete side or aspect of the music than can just be shown on a commercial basis." But at the same time, the folk festival board was up against a show-business truth: the single-malt stuff doesn't sell. Joyce Wein described it as "that conflict of whether things are . . . commercial enough to do what you want." This was more of an issue with the folk festival than the jazz festival, she added. Jazz, she said, "has always been a minority music. . . . There has never been anything in jazz to compare to the folk revival and the number of records sold by people like the Kingston Trio and Peter, Paul and Mary, and all like that. So . . . that's one aspect of saying how people were attracted." In both festivals, she added, "the audience was swelled by people who liked the music and (also) liked the event."[22] Less euphemistically, Susan Montgomery wrote in "The Folk Furor," her examination of the scene as it stood in 1960, "It must be admitted that along with the high priests and faithful disciples it also harbors its share of hangers-on."[23]

Alan Lomax was blunter, calling the first Newport Folk Festival "a publicity stunt."[24] But Jerry Silverman, who wrote for and was music editor of *Sing Out!* from 1951 through the 1960s, describes Lomax's interests as "Folk Music with a capital F and a capital M. . . . He would have called [anyone] that didn't have him up there in the front row some kind of a usurper."[25]

Pete Seeger was legendarily so upset with Bob Dylan's 1965 electric performance that he threatened to cut the power lines to the public-address system with an ax; on the other hand, his own recorded works included "You Are My Sunshine," "TB Blues," and banjo-and-whistling arrangements of Beethoven's Ninth, Bach's "Jesu, Joy of Man's Desiring," Grieg's *Peer Gynt* suite and Stravinsky's *Petrouchka*. In 2009, Seeger credited the younger Lomax as "chiefly responsible for the revival of folk music," but rebutted the "publicity stunt" argument by citing *Cowboy Songs and Other Ballads*, the 1910 book collected and edited by John Lomax:

> You could collect [such music], but if you tried to sing it you could not be authentic. But Alan's father, John Lomax, he didn't give a shit for authenticity. He just said, "These are good songs; people ought to sing 'em." . . .
>
> My father put it this way: "Don't waste your time arguing about the definition of folk music. Just know that the folk process has been going on for thousands of years, in all endeavors." Cooks rearrange old recipes for new stomachs; lawyers rearrange old laws for new citizens; and it's quite normal for people to put new words to old melodies, or new melodies to old words.[26]

The question of authenticity often reduced to a question of the right of a certain type of person to play a certain type of music. Many such questions were being debated in the blues community, including at Newport: Could a white kid who grew up middle class, or better, sing and play the blues? Could a professional musician play and sing the music that farmers and craftsmen picked when they came in from work at the end of the day? The pages of the 1963 Newport Folk Festival program book were one of many places these questions were hashed out. Under the title, "Whose Blues?" Lightnin' Hopkins led off by writing, "The white boys just don't have the voices for blues. They can play it but they can't sing it. . . . He can feel it but he just don't know where it's at. . . . They haven't been through it, only get it from records and concerts and don't live it out."

Eric Von Schmidt responded that there was not much to be done about being white and that there was only so much that could be done about the inherent differences between a sharecropper's kid and a millionaire's kid (which Michael Bloomfield, for one, was). He conceded that there were some essential differences between black and white blues players—"Too many white guys come to the blues like it was a baton-twirling contest. Zip-zip up and down that guitar like it was a drag race." But, he maintained, the key to getting around these circumstances was to create rather than re-create: "Robert Johnson and Bukka White were talking about *their* times, *their* women. . . . Got to get with this NOW. Jet planes not Terraplanes, outer space instead of mules. . . . Some of the younger guys are starting to do it. And when it happens it isn't going to sound like the Delta or the Southside, it's going to sound like them."

The quest for authenticity could drive promoters to ridiculous lengths: Titon writes of concert organizers who would ask blues artists such as Lightnin' Hopkins and John Lee Hooker, who had been playing and recording with electric instruments since the late 1940s, to play acoustic guitars for audiences of young, white revivalists. They'd switch back to electric instruments—for them, their truly traditional tools—to play for the next round of revivalists during the electric blues revival in the late '60s.[27]

The question wasn't settled, only modulated. It soon became clear (thanks to the careers of a host or performers, including Von Schmidt himself) that a middle-class-or-higher white kid could listen to blues, learn blues from unquestionably authentic bluesmen, and play music based on the songs and styles he had learned that had genuine feeling, made a genuine statement and had to be respected as music with roots and original value. But a corollary of the original questions remained: Could you call it blues? Hopkins didn't think so: "Up here they call almost everything the blues. But it isn't the blues. They're just making a mess of it."

Something similar happened with folk music as the years went by. As the 1960s began, a new class of artist emerged under the broad definition of folk: the urban singer-songwriter. To use Seeger's terms, they put new words to new melodies. And if the answers to questions posed in the late 1950s were unclear, the rise of singer-songwriters such as Joan Baez and Bob Dylan made the questions even messier. "Folk music became so ill-defined once *Time* magazine put Joan Baez on the cover in 1962," John Cohen says; "it became a very slippery deal."[28]

No one could argue that at least some, if a disputable fraction, of the new singer-songwriters' music was genuine and valuable. But was it folk?

It may have been only logical that performers such as Baez and Dylan would begin to look for, or write, songs that dealt with contemporary questions and concerns, but as they incorporated more original songs or works by contemporary writers into their live sets and records, others followed suit. And when songwriters such as Dylan took to more esoterically worded songs with more personal viewpoints, the folk audience who came for, say, "Mary Hamilton" or "House of the Rising Sun" stayed for "Farewell Angelina" or "My Back Pages."

Silber, at the 1963 symposium, said that young people turn to many other sources of music, including folk, because of the "negative values" of Tin Pan Alley and the desire to make something of their own, even from elements that had been handed down to them: "There are some who can fall in love with the traditional music the way they hear it from traditional singers and want to continue that. But, in most cases, it is not their own. It does not express their feeling or their emotion. So they want to change it in some way to fit their tempo and spirit. They do not care that it is a folksong they are changing or a popular song that they are changing or a new song that they are writing because that is what they need."[29]

Consequently, the importance and weight of tradition took a back seat to self-expression. Josh Dunson wrote that "it was in the years 1960 and 1961 that the pronoun 'I' replaced 'we' in topical songs, and that a new group of songwriters emerged, influenced by, yet very different from, their less spiritual fathers."[30]

In *The American Folk Scene*, a book of essays dedicated to exploring the changes in what was still being called folk music, David A. DeTurk and A. Poulin Jr. address this issue: "Antiquarians will debate the point, but it is they who will have to prove that preservation and 'survival' were more important than the creation of new songs and modification of old songs to meet the ends of social expression. The evidence in the mid-sixties seems clearly to point in other directions. Folk music and song are no longer 'other-directed' by tradition, but have become 'inner-directed' extensions of the search for a palatable and viable future."[31]

Stekert added that the new generation of singer-songwriters "had known neither the intimidation of the 1950s nor the Guthries and Aunt Mollys of the 1930s and 1940s. Seeger was winning his battle with the courts, and young people were feeling very different from the mountain folk who sang of corn liquor and distant murders."[32]

When the Newport Folk Festival revived in 1963, it expanded its defi-nition of folk to incorporate the new breed. George Wein and Seeger envisioned a mix of performers, where the young, popular singers would bring in the kids, who would then be inspired by the old masters—or, as MacColl, Pankake and Nelson might argue, not.

"Even at the Newport Folk Festival," Titon writes, "where southern black bluesmen such as Sleepy John Estes and Mississippi John Hurt, or mountain balladeers such as Sara Gunning or Almeda Riddle, were regarded with admiration, reverence and even awe, it was nevertheless the young white revivalist such as Joan Baez or Bob Dylan who attracted the enormous crowds and inspired the most calculated musical and personal imitation."[33]

John Cohen argues that the rising stars created an unhealthy attitude toward traditional music. His band, the New Lost City Ramblers, began because rather than hear Burl Ives, John Jacob Niles, or Pete Seeger reinterpret a song from the hills of Kentucky, "I wanted to hear the guy from Kentucky"—or, failing that, as accurate a representation as possible. At Newport, however, "The prevalent feeling was, 'Something new might happen this year; what's it gonna be?'"[34]

It wasn't always a matter of the oldest performers being the most authentic, however: "Folksingers like Oscar Brand and Theodore Bikel were suspect: Chatty and sophisticated actors on stage, they tried to entertain, sometimes at the expense of their material," Titon writes. "But Joan Baez was praised for her self-effacing stage manner, which let the songs 'speak for themselves.'"[35]

Silverman says that the conflict over authenticity stepped up a notch with Bob Dylan's emergence, and that he himself has been on both sides of it:

> It was hard for the traditionalists like Alan [Lomax], and even to some extent like me, to see where the young singer-songwriters fit into the continuum of what we like to call traditional music. Of course, I was dead wrong, and I'm glad to admit it now.
>
> Folk songs didn't just get born; somebody had to write them. The fact that we don't know the names of the composers of "On Top of Old Smokey" doesn't mean that someone didn't actually sit down and write it. So when other people came along, like—well, Bob Dylan for example, but many, many others—to write their own songs, us old-timers [said], "How can they call this folk music?" But of course it was as folky a music as anyone else had contributed over the years.
>
> I think it was Louis Armstrong—it was attributed to him anyhow—when he was asked about folk music, said, "Well, I never heard a horse sing," so to him, everything was folk music.[36]

That sense has only gotten stronger as the years have gone on. Seeger's grandson, Tao Rodriguez Seeger, who has played at many Newport Folk

Festivals accompanying his grandfather, as a member of RIG (with Sarah Lee Guthrie and Johnny Irion) and with his own group, the Mammals, puts it this way: "The idea that folk music is supposed to be this precious thing that you put on a mantelpiece, that gets preserved in amber, is absurd. . . . I don't think they should call themselves folk festivals if all they're gonna do is white string-band music. That's white folk music, or white New England folk music—[and] there are a lot of white people who don't dig on string-band music. So the racial lines have blurred; the cultural lines have blurred."[37]

At Newport, the arguments over whether singer-songwriters constituted folk music seemed to never really resolve so much as peter out over the lack of territory to fight over as rock and roll grew in popularity, particularly when the Beatles took over the charts—or perhaps the two camps realized that they had more in common than not, and their mutual survival was most important.

But the impossible questions, it seems, will always be asked, whether answers can or ever will be found. "We've always stretched the limits, and there are always people saying, 'What are these people doing here?'" Bob Jones told the *Boston Globe*'s Joan Anderman in 2008.

"Drop all your worries about authenticity," Jack White said from the stage during his set at the 2014 Newport Folk Festival. "Authenticity is a phantom. It'll suck the blood out of you. It's about the music [artists] play, is it not?"

At the 2013 festival, one longtime observer assessed the direction the festival had taken over the previous few years and approvingly noted the musicianship and songwriting skills of several of the younger, louder, more rock-oriented acts. He noted the festival's burgeoning popularity and credited the producers with having made a good philosophical decision.

"Or," he said, "they could go in the other direction, and have a real folk festival."[38]

KEEP ME COMPANY AND
HOLD MY HAND (A PRELUDE)

If the 1963 finale of "We Shall Overcome" was the apogee of the folk movement, as Theo Bikel called it, at the 1965 Newport Folk Festival the various opposing forces in folk music that had been building for nearly ten years came to a full-on confrontation. Both Pete Seeger's Utopia and the creeping professionalism he feared went on display and head-to-head on Festival Field July 22–25.

John Cohen of the New Lost City Ramblers calls the 1965 festival "astounding. If you just looked at the traditional music . . . you would have a major, major statement about American traditional music."[1] Performers included Eck Robertson, who had first recorded in 1922, Roscoe Holcomb, whom Cohen discovered in Kentucky, Doc Watson, Clarence Ashley, Bill Monroe, the Osborne Brothers, a return appearance by the Cajun Band, the Kweskin Jug Band and more. Great bluesmen who had made such an impact at the 1964 festival were back, joined by the recently rediscovered Son House. The Chambers Brothers electrified soul and gospel. The young singer-songwriter crowd was out in force as well, led by Bob Dylan, back for his third appearance in a row; Joan Baez; Donovan, hailed as "the British Dylan"; the duo of Richard and Mimi Fariña, Baez's sister; Peter, Paul and Mary; Gordon Lightfoot; Ian and Sylvia; Odetta; and many more. The total number of performers hit 175, and a staggering 74,000 people turned out for the four-day festival.

A riotous workshop performance on Sunday, July 25, by Baez and the Fariñas didn't pause—on either side of the stage—for a torrential rainstorm. The sight of the audience dancing with abandon in the downpour —captured briefly in Lerner's *Festival!*—wasn't the first time or the first respect in which Newport anticipated the hallowed Woodstock. Their performance was later described, in the wake of Richard Fariña's death in a motorcycle accident the next spring, as "grand theft of the 1965 Newport Folk Festival." Pete Seeger opened the Sunday-night show by playing a tape of Cohen's newborn baby crying and asked the audience and the performers to ponder what kind of world was being created for that infant to grow up in: "What kind of bombs have we got hanging over its head? What kind of pollution are we putting in its water?"

Yet despite—or perhaps because of—the massive scale and importance of the Newport festival, many took note of the bad vibes that seemed to be on display.

Irwin Silber later wrote in *Sing Out!* that at Newport '65, "The era of Folk-Music-as-Show-Business reached what may prove to be its ultimate peak." Phil Ochs reportedly seethed in the audience as Ronnie Gilbert and Theo Bikel sang two of his songs while he himself was not invited to play and was even denied a backstage pass. He later called it "The Newport Fuzz Festival," a reference to what he considered an overbearing police presence.[2]

Paul Nelson, in a critique he was invited to write for the 1965 festival program, detested the previous year's "babyish, namby-pamby, good-goody, totally phony atmosphere" and said the festival, overrun with "fraternity folkorists and record-company desperados," had become "an out-of-control Sunday School class taught by its talentless topical in-mates" and "a dizzying blur of faces and styles in a comic pageant of . . . nothing, nothing at all."

During an afternoon workshop that presented a panoply of blues artists, Alan Lomax was tasked with introducing the Paul Butterfield Blues Band, a young band that played electric instruments and had as much to do with rock and pop as with folk and blues music. He evidently wasn't thrilled about the job. Wein remembers him saying, "Now here we've got these guys, and they need all of this fancy hardware to play the blues. Today you've heard some of the greatest blues players in the world playing their simple music on simple instruments. Let's find out if these guys can play it at all."[3] Elijah Wald's recounting of Murray Lerner's unreleased audio has Lomax saying, "I understand that this present combination has not only caught up but passed the rest. That's what I hear—I'm anxious to find out whether it's true or not."[4] When Lomax got backstage and the Butterfield band started playing, manager Albert Grossman, George Wein's former partner in the festival, was waiting for him. As Joe Boyd remembers it, Grossman said, "That was a real chickenshit introduction, Alan." Lomax responded, "Out of my way." They immediately began to tangle.[5]

Barbara Dane later wrote that "we saw the 'stars' climb all over each other in blind opportunism, rushing to the stage to be photographed in the right 'scene' . . . some of our finest folklorists raging at each other in the sun, collars rumpled and sweat rolling . . . fist fights breaking out back stage. Yes, the festival is a vital force."[6]

A week later, Mary Travers of Peter, Paul and Mary wrote to folklorist Archie Green, saying, "Somehow the concerts themselves didn't quite pull together and there was an air of tension and agitation that ran through the city singers. I separate them here and now, because the country singers were, as always, friendly and open. . . . So that was Newport, and I won't go next year—if you don't come. Besides, if it is like this year, I want somebody to document the madness and keep me company and hold my hand."[7]

Any number of moments—including the Fariñas' ragged glory, Seeger's introduction, or even the Grossman-Lomax bout—could have become the iconic moment of that year's edition and of the Newport festival and the youth-driven folk movement in general. But they were all overshadowed on Sunday night, when Bob Dylan performed.

To this day, if the average music fan remembers one thing in the more than half-century history of the Newport Folk Festival, it's Dylan's show on Sunday, July 25. Dylan had made a splash at Newport beginning in 1963 with plain talking, plain singing and a social conscience in songs such as "North Country Blues," "With God on Our Side" and, of course, the "We Shall Overcome" finale. The next year, he thrilled the crowd but puzzled some elders when his songs veered toward the poetic, such as on "Mr. Tambourine Man" (Pete Seeger's confused-yet-polite reaction, as filmed by Lerner, is striking). In 1965, he had the number-two record in the country with "Like a Rolling Stone," which teamed him with a band full of drums and electric instruments. As such, the content of his Sunday-night show couldn't have come as a complete surprise, but the varying reactions to his performance—indeed, memories of what actually happened on the stage and in Festival Field—have been locked in dispute ever since.

Joan Baez at Newport in 1964. Her Newport debut, as a teenager making an unbilled appearance with Bob Gibson, was a launching pad: "I didn't faint," she later said; "I sang, and that was the beginning of a very long career." (Photograph by Diana Davies, Ralph Rinzler Folklife Archives and Collections, Smithsonian Institution)

The Newport performance by an ad hoc Cajun band in 1964, brought about by the scouting efforts of the Newport Folk Foundation, is said to be the first performance of the music outside Louisiana and a key in the renaissance of the music and the culture in its home state. Pictured are Adam Landreneau, Cyprien Landreneau and Jerry Devillier at the 1965 festival. (Photograph by Diana Davies, Ralph Rinzler Folklife Archives and Collections, Smithsonian Institution)

Bob Dylan's first-ever electric performance, at the 1965 Newport Folk Festival. "He can't come back. Please don't make it more difficult than it is." (Photograph by Diana Davies, Ralph Rinzler Folklife Archives and Collections, Smithsonian Institution)

The finale of the 1967 Newport Folk Festival, at which Arlo Guthrie (at the microphone) debuted the hit "Alice's Restaurant." With him are Judy Collins, Theo Bikel, Mimi Fariña, Joan Baez, Jim Kweskin, Maria Muldaur and festival impresario George Wein, looking somewhat out of place amidst the late-'60s fabulousness. (Photograph by Diana Davies, Ralph Rinzler Folklife Archives and Collections, Smithsonian Institution)

Ralph Rinzler was the tireless scout for the Newport Folk Foundation, fulfilling the non-profit's mission by driving all over the continent looking for talent hidden in North America's disappearing byways. He eventually left the Newport organization and spearheaded the Folklife Festival on the National Mall; he felt that folk crafts and stories needed to be promoted and preserved as well as music. (Photograph by Diana Davies, Ralph Rinzler Folklife Archives and Collections, Smithsonian Institution)

The reemergence of forgotten bluesmen such as Son House, Bukka White and Mississippi John Hurt was one of the 1960s Newport Folk Festival's greatest legacies. Pictured is Elizabeth Cotten. (Photograph by Diana Davies, Ralph Rinzler Folklife Archives and Collections, Smithsonian Institution)

George Wein pronounced the folk scene "dead" when the Newport Folk Festival folded up shop in 1971, but a series of Boston concerts in the '70s and '80s by Tom Rush, shown here at Newport in 1994, convinced him and the rest of the organizers that an audience could still be found. (Photo © Ken Franckling)

Bob Jones at Fort Adams in 2002. He started as a volunteer in 1963; when he and George Wein decided to revive the Newport Folk Festival in 1985, Jones rose to the rank of producer. (Photo by Bob Thayer, courtesy of the *Providence Journal*)

After a tumultuous 1987 festival with a controversial corporate sponsor, the Ben and Jerry's Newport Folk Festival (pictured are Ben Cohen and Jerry Greenfield) combined music with the activism of the '60s generation brought into the new era. (Photo © Ken Franckling)

Dar Williams was one of the most popular performers of the festival in the 1990s. Her inner-directed songs were symbolic of the era and, she says, put her "in the crosshairs" of those who preferred folk music with a more traditional sound and functionalist message. (Photo © Ken Franckling)

opposite:
Peter, Paul and Mary, along with Theo Bikel, Joan Baez, Pete Seeger and the Freedom Singers, were part of the "We Shall Overcome" finale at the 1963 Newport Folk Festival, which one observer called "the apogee of the folk movement" of the time; by the 1990s, Peter Yarrow, at left, said Newport was "a commercial gig. Wonderful in some ways—a lot of ways. But it was a gig." (Photo © Ken Franckling)

Pete Seeger played at the first Newport Folk Festival and at its fiftieth anniversary. He and his wife, Toshi, made the blueprint for its Utopia; he was and remains the touchstone of what the festival aims to be. After his death, organizers still make choices at least partly based on what he would have wanted. (Photo © Ken Franckling)

Bob Jones first heard the Indigo Girls—Amy Ray, left, and Emily Saliers—because his daughter Nalini and her friends were listening to them. They played at Newport eight times in nine years. Newport "was so formative for us," Ray says, but the sense of community was the thing she remembers most. (Photograph by Diana Davies, Ralph Rinzler Folklife Archives and Collections, Smithsonian Institution)

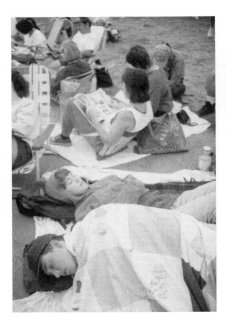

By the mid-'90s, the frenzy that had attended the Newport Folk Festival had settled down. Soon, the attendance numbers would as well. (Photograph by Diana Davies, Ralph Rinzler Folklife Archives and Collections, Smithsonian Institution)

Joyce Wein, second from left, and George Wein, second from right, with the Staples Singers at Newport. When the Weins were married in 1959, their union was illegal in nineteen states. George Wein says the realities they faced and the hopes they shared informed his life's work. (Photo © Ken Franckling)

George Wein, the leader of the Newport folk and jazz festivals, in 1999. "The folk world . . . just thought I was a businessman. The fact that maybe I was doing something I loved never entered their head." (Photo by Sandor Bodo, courtesy of the *Providence Journal*)

Judy Collins's career at Newport began in 1963; she last performed there in 2009. In between, she sang many times and served on the board during one of the festival's most tumultuous periods—the late 1960s, when it struggled for a sense of purpose in the wake of the rise of rock as America's dominant musical force. (Photo © Ken Franckling)

Scott Avett of the Avett Brothers at Newport in 2009. Their riotous, well-received show the previous year, across from Jimmy Buffett's performance, helped send a message that a new generation of musicians and fans was ready to take over. (Photo by Kathy Borchers, courtesy of the *Providence Journal*)

above:
The 2015 Newport Folk Festival finale, a tribute to the fiftieth anniversary of Bob Dylan's electric performance, including Robyn Hitchcock, Taylor Goldsmith of Dawes, Hozier, Joe Fletcher and David Rawlings (at the microphone), J. P. Harris (between Fletcher and Rawlings), Stephen Weinheimer of Spirit Family Reunion, a member of the Preservation Hall Jazz Band, Maggie Carson of Spirit Family Reunion, and Gillian Welch. (Photo by Ben Kaye)

below:
When Jay Sweet assumed responsibilities for the Newport Folk Festival, he brought an expanded definition of what folk music should sound like but relied heavily on the history of the festival as a guiding principle and a selling point to audiences and artists. (Photo by Ben Kaye)

*In the beginning, there
was rock and it was fun.
Then Bob Dylan plugged in at
the Newport Folk Festival in
1965, and the music fractured.*

JOE KLEIN[1]

A LIMITED AMOUNT OF TIME

What happened when Bob Dylan took the stage on the night of July 25, 1965, at the closing concert of the Newport Folk Festival? On the simplest level, that's now an easy question to answer: thanks to the donation of the Bruce Jackson/Diane Christian Collection to the American Folklife Center at the Library of Congress and the library's digitization work, anyone can hear what Bob Dylan, Michael Bloomfield, Sam Lay, Barry Goldberg, Al Kooper and Jerome Arnold played that night.

But what happened in the audience? In the larger folk-music world? That's much more difficult, perhaps impossible, to pin down.

This chapter takes the taped evidence, the recollections of participants and audience members, both in the moment and decades later, and the heated debates in the folk music magazines of the time and the sober histories many years down the road and lays them end to end without commentary (except, of course, for the judgment that's implicit in the juxtapositions). In the course of this chapter, different peoples' memories collide—sometimes, the same person's memories collide.

Because in the larger sense, the question "What happened that night?" has many answers. Everyone who is asked that question, everyone who talked and wrote about it then and later, has a different one. And those differences are based on experience, age, the fleeting quality of memory, changing and evolving musical contexts and any combination of the

above. All of this is a reflection of the steadfast, knowledgeable yet conflicted community that Dylan and crew performed to, both in the immediate and larger contexts.

In the final analysis, those differences themselves comprise the answer.

Some of the principals of the 1965 Newport Folk Festival had fuzzy, often
self-serving recollections and interpretations of what had taken place.

RONALD COHEN[2]

The truth is a rabbit in a bramble patch. One can rarely put one's hand
upon it. One can only circle around and point, saying, "It's somewhere
in there."

CHARLES SEEGER, AS QUOTED BY PETE SEEGER[3]

That summer, while "Like a Rolling Stone" was blaring from the
jukeboxes, rolling to the top of the charts as Dylan's first popular hit,
the singer was fulfilling a long-standing commitment to perform once
more at the Newport Folk Festival.

DANIEL MARK EPSTEIN[4]

I joined Paul [Rothchild] at the control board as they started the sound
check. Grossman sat with us as they played through the three numbers
they had rehearsed: "Maggie's Farm," "It Takes a Lot to Laugh, It Takes a
Train to Cry" and "Like a Rolling Stone." Nothing was said; we knew this
was momentous.

JOE BOYD[5]

I would like to say that he has his finger on the pulse of our generation.
Bob Dylan.

INTRODUCTION TO DYLAN'S 1963 NEWPORT FOLK FESTIVAL
MAINSTAGE ACOUSTIC PERFORMANCE[6]

We have had our great social poets, and I think when Bob's work is fully
evaluated he will number among them.

JOSH DUNSON[7]

A roughneck rebel poet and dreamer named Bob Dylan. . . . His particular
concerns are war, discrimination, capital punishment and exploitation,
and his poems and songs reflect implacable anger. . . . Clad in worn boots,
rough black trousers and a rumpled work shirt, Dylan's slight frame

presents itself as a challenge to all that is comfortable and complacent in American life.

JACK A. SMITH[8]

I get mad when I see friends of mine sitting in Southern jails, getting their heads beat in. What comes out in my music is a call to action.

BOB DYLAN[9]

I handed Paul a flourescent pink pen which he used to mark the levels of each channel and the equalization dials above the faders. Other artists' details were noted down on Paul's clipboard but Dylan's were in ink you could read in the dark.

JOE BOYD[10]

We think he's the best songwriter of the age.

JOHNNY CASH[11]

The transition from 1963 to 1964 was really quite startling, because not only was it quite obvious that he thought of himself and recognized that he was now a star, together with Joan, but some of the songs were really quite intense. Like "Chimes of Freedom" . . . a shiver runs up my spine whenever I hear it.

MURRAY LERNER[12]

Dylan himself has said that in 1964 and 1965 his consciousness was changing significantly. The crowd at the Newport Folk Festival in 1964 was dismayed that he played songs like "It Ain't Me, Babe" and "Mr. Tambourine Man" instead of the Brechtian dramas of social protest.

DANIEL MARK EPSTEIN[13]

You seem to be in a different kind of bag now, Bob—and I'm worried about it. I saw at Newport how you had somehow lost contact with people. . . . You travel with an entourage now—with good buddies who are going to laugh when you need laughing and drink wine with you and insure your privacy—and never challenge you to face everyone else's reality again. . . .

Your new songs seem to be all inner-directed now, inner-probing, self-conscious—maybe even a little maudlin or a little cruel on occasion. And it's happening on stage, too. You seem to be relating to a handful of cronies behind the scenes now—rather than to the rest of us out front. Now, all that's okay—if that's the way you want it, Bob. But then you're a different Dylan from the one we knew. The old one never wasted our precious time.

IRWIN SILBER[14]

I outlined the positions of amps and microphones and the settings of the dials with the pink marker. The sound we rehearsed had to be there from the first note. When the stage was cleared and the gates opened to the public, none of us left in search of food: we were too charged up with adrenalin to be hungry.

JOE BOYD[15]

Everybody sees themselves walkin' around with no one else.

BOB DYLAN, "TALKIN' WORLD WAR III BLUES," 1963[16]

The presence of drums, electric guitars and Al Kooper's Hammond organ on his new LP alarmed the purists who thought that once they had crowned him he would stay on the throne. Dylan's new songs were not about politics. His former mentors could barely understand WHAT they were about.

JOE BOYD[17]

The twenty-two-year-old was treated like royalty, with as much deference and reverence as any man could summon in that sentimental, left-leaning community. In public, he affected a charming, shuffling, blushing humility, gracefully offsetting the adoration.

Backstage—to the amusement of some and the horror of others—he practiced cracking a twenty-foot bullwhip, cutting the air over the lawn of Freebody Park, making little explosions as the leather tip broke the speed of sound. For a little while he was in command.

DANIEL MARK EPSTEIN[18]

We had no way of knowing what he actually had in store.

GEORGE WEIN[19]

At the Festival, Kooper was strolling about when Albert [Grossman] said Bob was looking for him and gave him some backstage passes.

ROBERT SHELTON[20]

Bob said, "I want to play Sunday night and try and reproduce what we did on the album." And I said, "OK. Sounds great."

AL KOOPER[21]

Three members of the Butterfield Band were recruited: guitarist Mike Bloomfield, drummer Sam Lay and bassist Jerome Arnold. At a party in Newport, Dylan completed his band with pianist Barry Goldberg, and Dylan rehearsed this instant group until dawn at a nearby mansion.
ROBERT SHELTON[22]

By Saturday, we knew that Dylan had rehearsed with his new stable-mates, the Butterfield Band. The gauntlet would be thrown.
JOE BOYD[23]

This could have been either a shrewd business move or a genuine musical statement. In Dylan's case, I believe it was a little of both.
GEORGE WEIN[24]

This is a young man who grew out of a need. . . . I don't have to tell you—you know him; he's yours. Bob Dylan.
INTRODUCTION TO BOB DYLAN'S ACOUSTIC PERFORMANCE, NEWPORT FOLK FESTIVAL, JULY 1964[25]

Dylan surfaced on Saturday for the Songwriting Workshop in his familiar guise of troubadour with acoustic guitar. In years past he would have worn a denim work shirt and jeans but he and Kooper turned up in bizarre puff-sleeved polka-dot "dueling shirts" . . . they served as advance notice of provocation. He played his allotted half hour and left to roars from a gigantic crowd in front of the tiny stage. This was the Folk Festival: no encores, the timetable had to be kept, and the Appalachian Fiddlers had to start on time.
JOE BOYD[26]

Even before the Sunday night, Dylan seemed under some strange new duress. Typically, he told few people about his plans, relishing the shock, the dramatic departure. He couldn't envision a backfire. Since January, his two electric singles and an album had done fabulously well. At Newport, the Butterfield Blues band and the Chambers Brothers this year, and Muddy Waters the year before, had shown that electric instrumentation and heavy rhythm were not taboo.
ROBERT SHELTON[27]

But that was thought of as, idiomatically, something that had emerged legitimately in the history.
PETER YARROW[28]

Dylan was scheduled for forty-five minutes near the end of the first half, but we knew he had only three songs rehearsed.

JOE BOYD[29]

The practice was to save the performers who had really drawn the crowd [for] the end of the show. . . . When I went to Bobby and told him that he was not being programmed in that way, he was really insulted. And he said, "They're gonna be really upset. I'm just gonna get on stage and do three songs and get off." And I said . . . "Do a song or two acoustically, tell them this is something you're experimenting with and then launch into [the electric material]." Well, he didn't do that. That wasn't his way in any event, ever.

PETER YARROW[30]

He felt that he could better express himself and reach more people by going electric; and he felt it necessary to tap into the pulse of popular culture.

GEORGE WEIN[31]

Plugging in, going electric, was tantamount to going commercial—to abandoning the intimacy of the kind of communication that was the essence of folk music, that was shared acoustically.

PETER YARROW[32]

We rushed onstage in the dark. I went from amp to amp, checking the pink marks.

JOE BOYD[33]

The person who's coming up now—

PETER YARROW[34]

[Yarrow is interrupted by a single note from each string of an electric guitar struck by someone evidently checking the tuning.]
Please don't play right now, gentlemen, for this second. Thank you.

PETER YARROW[35]

[Three more guitar notes are heard.]
The person who's coming up now is a person who has in a sense [two brief bursts of feedback hum] changed the face of folk music.

PETER YARROW[36]

When the musicians were ready, I signalled with my flashlight.

JOE BOYD[37]

Ladies and gentlemen, the person that's going to come up now has a limited amount of time. His name is Bob Dylan.

PETER YARROW[38]

The crowd was taken by surprise, wondering if it was a joke, but they weren't given much time to wonder.

DANIEL MARK EPSTEIN[39]

The introduction was made, the lights came up and "Maggie's Farm" blasted out into the night air.

JOE BOYD[40]

I just remember Michael counting it off and saying, "Let's go!" and it was like POW!!—we went into this whirlwind.

BARRY GOLDBERG[41]

. . .

I ain't gonna work on Maggie's farm no more.

BOB DYLAN, "MAGGIE'S FARM"[42]

I said, "Hey, lookit! He's taken that old 'Penny's Farm' and [he's] putting it somewhere else. That's terrific."

JOHN COHEN[43]

I thought it was a new world, and it was almost frightening when you saw it—the black leather jacket; it was almost ominous, in a way, that he was becoming the high priest of this culture.

MURRAY LERNER[44]

Wearing an Audie Murphy black jacket, playing a Chuck Berry guitar and performing his electrified alienation with passionate indifference, he assassinated the audience.

PHIL OCHS[45]

I got a head full of ideas that are driving me insane.

BOB DYLAN, "MAGGIE'S FARM"[46]

I ran straight out to the press enclosure. By today's standards, the volume wasn't particularly high, but in 1965 it was probably the loudest thing anyone in the audience had ever heard.

JOE BOYD[47]

From the moment the group swung into a rocking electric version of "Maggie's Farm," the Newport audience registered shock.

ROBERT SHELTON[48]

But the volume of the blues band was kind of wild. You couldn't get the words too clearly.

JOHN COHEN[49]

It was not possible to share the kind of intimacy that we were sharing with folk music when you've got those electric instruments going. The moment you've got drums there, everything's gotta come up in level.

PETER YARROW[50]

The sound was a bit harsh, but we thought it was way cool.

MARIA MULDAUR[51]

Pete Seeger, Theo Bikel, Peter Yarrow, Albert Grossman and I were standing on the far left side of the stage when Dylan's band began playing. At the sound of the first amplified chords, a crimson color rose in Pete's face, and he ran off.

GEORGE WEIN[52]

You could not understand the words. And I was frantic. I said, "Get that distortion out." It was so raspy, you could not understand a word. And I ran over to the sound system, "Get that distortion out of Bob's voice." "No, this is the way they want to have it."

PETE SEEGER[53]

Someone tapped me on the shoulder. "They're looking for you backstage." Alan Lomax, Pete Seeger and Theo Bikel were standing by the stairs, furious.

JOE BOYD[54]

Then he fines you every time you slam the door
I ain't gonna work for Maggie's brother no more.

BOB DYLAN, "MAGGIE'S FARM"[55]

"Where are the controls? How do you get there?" Bikel demanded. I told him to walk out to the parking lot, turn left, follow the fence to the main entrance, come back down the center aisle and he would see it there around Row G—a journey of almost a quarter-mile. They looked daggers at me. "I know you can get there quicker than that," said Lomax. I admitted that I usually climbed the fence. For a brief moment we all contemplated the notion of one of these dignified and, barring Seeger, portly men doing the same.

Then Lomax snarled, "You go out there right now and you tell them the sound has got to be turned down. That's an order from the board." OK, I said, and ran to the pile of milk crates by the lighting trailer. In a few seconds I was standing beside the sound board.

JOE BOYD[56]

I try my best to be just like I am, but everybody wants you to be just like them. They say "Sing while you slave," and I just get bored.

BOB DYLAN, "MAGGIE'S FARM"[57]

What happened next depended on where you were.

ROBERT SHELTON[58]

It was like being in the eye of a hurricane. All around us, people were standing up, waving their arms. Some were cheering, some booing, some arguing, some grinning like madmen.

JOE BOYD[59]

The audience, which was shocked into silence for a moment, quickly began to register its disapproval. People began booing; there were cries of "Sellout!" Others shouted about the sound quality, which was poor, since the sound system was designed for acoustic performers.

GEORGE WEIN[60]

The microphones and speakers were all out of balance, the sound poor and lopsided. For even the most ardent fan of the new music, the performance was unpersuasive.

ROBERT SHELTON[61]

Joe Boyd was running the sound board, and he sent one sound to the audience and another sound to the recording unit. So the recording is absolutely clear, but what the audience heard was definitely overloaded.

JOHN COHEN[62]

Tonight Bob was in a mess. He's really very good. People just don't understand his writing.

JOAN BAEZ[63]

I couldn't make out the sounds . . . we didn't have appropriate monitors at the time . . . and the microphones were not the kind with a tight pattern, so there was a huge amount of leakage. So it was a blurry sound aesthetically, more so toward the front.

PETER YARROW[64]

I was in about the twelfth row . . . you couldn't hear Dylan even from where I was. And immediately several people, including me, started to holler, "We can't hear Dylan! Turn up the mike!"

ERIC VON SCHMIDT[65]

There were shouts of delight and triumph and also of derision and outrage.

JOE BOYD[66]

Bob Dylan was booed for linking rhythm and blues to the paranoid nightmares of his vision.

ARTHUR KRETSCHMER[67]

This is the most hostile audience I've ever seen.

CAROL ADLER[68]

There might have been a few jaws that dropped open, but it's not much of a reach beyond what the blues players were playing at Newport.

NOEL STOOKEY[69]

Grossman, Yarrow and Rothchild were sitting behind the board, grinning like cats. I leaned over to convey the message from Lomax.

"Tell Alan the board is adequately represented at the sound controls and the board member here thinks the sound level is just right," said Yarrow. Then he looked up at me, smiled and said, "And tell him . . ." and he raised the middle finger of his left hand. Grossman and Rothchild laughed as I ran back to the fence.

JOE BOYD[70]

At the first sound of the amplified instruments, Pete Seeger had turned a bright purple and begun kicking his feet and flailing his arms. (A Festival official later said: "I had never seen any trace of violence in Pete, except at that moment. He was furious with Dylan!")

ROBERT SHELTON[71]

After a few excruciating minutes, someone tapped me on the shoulder. "Pete's really upset. Maybe you should talk to him."

I found Pete sitting in a parked car in the field behind the stage.

"That noise is terrible!" he cried. "Make it stop."

I said: "Pete, it's too late. There's nothing we can do."

GEORGE WEIN[72]

I wasn't standing backstage; I was out in the audience. But I hear that Pete was incensed by Dylan's electric performance, which doesn't strike me as logical at all, because he certainly was supportive of Mississippi blues singers—go figure.

NOEL STOOKEY[73]

We ran backstage and there was mayhem going on. . . . I understand Pete Seeger had an axe and was gonna go cut the electric cables and had to be, you know, subdued.

MARIA MULDAUR[74]

Several accounts of this fateful night have suggested that Pete threatened to cut the power cables with an ax. This wasn't the case.

GEORGE WEIN[75]

I said, "God damn it, it's terrible. You can't understand it. If I had an axe, I'd chop the mike cable right now."

PETE SEEGER[76]

"Pete Seeger towered over us [soundmen] by a foot, easily, just screaming and threatening," Paul Rothchild in the soundbooth recalled.

"Lomax . . . charged the soundbooth with Pete Seeger nipping at his heels. . . . Seeger tried several times to yank Rothchild's hands off the board, until Peter Yarrow declared, 'Pete, if you touch him again, I'll press charges for battery.' It was the loudest sound ever heard at Newport."

DAVID KING DUNAWAY[77]

Seeger, from all reports, was very, very upset by this. And I had heard that he tried to cut the wires, and that he'd gone into a car and wouldn't come out after this whole thing.

PAUL NELSON[78]

That's not my interpretation. You see, Peter's father was there, Charlie Seeger. And he had a hearing aid, and Charlie was very distressed when he couldn't hear things clearly. And with all this sound coming from the speakers, Charlie Seeger was quite upset, and I think that affected Pete.

JOHN COHEN[79]

Reportedly, one board member—probably Seeger—was so upset that he threatened to pull out the entire electrical wiring system. Cooler heads cautioned that plunging the audience into darkness might cause a real riot.

ROBERT SHELTON[80]

When they finished "Maggie's Farm" they played "Like a Rolling Stone" and Pete Seeger had to be restrained—he threatened to cut the wires with an ax.

DANIEL MARK EPSTEIN[81]

Actually, there were axes there. Because we had these prisoners from Texas who were doing a thing, chopping wood and singing. So there were axes available if he'd wanted one.

GEORGE WEIN[82]

A half-hearted cheer and a few hecklers' boos. Bob Dylan cared not. Characteristically it was Bobby.

MICHAEL J. CARABETTA[83]

I heard enormous vocal hostility all around me. As the group finished "Farm," there was some reserved applause and a flurry of boos.

ROBERT SHELTON[84]

People were shouting, "Turn it up!" "Turn it down!" Half the audience was going, "Yea," and half were going, "Boo." It was the great split.

PAUL ROTHCHILD[85]

And what we noticed was, about a third of the audience was booing, which was unheard of.

MARIA MULDAUR[86]

I was thinking that somebody was shouting, "Are you with us? Are you with us?" And . . . what was that supposed to mean?

BOB DYLAN[87]

Most . . . erupted into silence at the conclusion of Dylan's songs, while a few booed their once-and-former idol. Others cheered and demanded encores, finding in the "new Dylan" an expression of themselves, just as teenaged social activists of 1963 had found themselves summed up in the angry young poet's vision.

  IRWIN SILBER[88]

I was caught up in filming, so I didn't really hear too much of what the crowd was doing, to be honest with you. But I didn't hear a massive boo. I heard a combination of a lot of things.

  MURRAY LERNER[89]

I had no idea why they were booing. I don't think anybody was there having a negative response to those songs, though. I mean, whatever it was about, it wasn't about anything that they were hearing.

  BOB DYLAN[90]

As Dylan led his band into "Rolling Stone," the audience grew shriller: "Play folk music! Sell out! This is a folk festival! Get rid of that band!"

  ROBERT SHELTON[91]

The musicians didn't wait around to interpret it, they just plunged straight into the second song.

  JOE BOYD[92]

People'd call, say "Beware doll, you're bound to fall."

  BOB DYLAN, "LIKE A ROLLING STONE"[93]

It was one of the most powerful experiences of my life, to really hear "Maggie's Farm" and "Rolling Stone." I really thought it was the wave of the future, Butterfield and him. And it was.

  MURRAY LERNER[94]

He defies everyone else to have the courage to be as alone, as unconnected . . . as he. He screams through organ and drums and electric guitar, "How does it feel to be on your own?" And there is no mistaking the hostility, the defiance, the contempt for all those thousands sitting before him who aren't on their own. Who can't make it. And they seemed to understand that night for the first time what Dylan had been trying to say for over a year—that he is not theirs or anyone else's—and they didn't like what they heard and booed. . . . He had fooled them before when they thought he was theirs.

JIM ROONEY[95]

The prevailing feeling among the crowd was a sense that they had been betrayed. The rest of us were just as shocked and upset—except, perhaps, for Grossman, who must have relished the moment. This was a sacrilege, as far as the folk world was concerned.

GEORGE WEIN[96]

You shouldn't let other people get your kicks for you.

BOB DYLAN, "LIKE A ROLLING STONE"[97]

Theodore Bikel was saying, "This is what the young people want! We have to go with the change; this is what's happening now."

MARIA MULDAUR[98]

I remember saying to Pete [Seeger] that I was sure this kind of music had a place somewhere, but that the place was not here.

THEO BIKEL[99]

Nobody there that night had ever heard anything like it, not live at least.

TOM PIAZZA[100]

"Like a Rolling Stone" elicited some scattered applause, along with the heckling.

GEORGE WEIN[101]

Bobby was considered to be the bard of our times, in terms of expressing the ideology and the dreams that were embodied in what Newport was all about. Which was authenticity of expression, whether it was in a love song or a political song, or anything else. When he went electric, that act in and of itself was astonishing to the vast majority of the audience, that felt betrayed: How could you abandon your principles?

PETER YARROW[102]

Ain't it hard when you discover that
He really wasn't where it's at.

BOB DYLAN, "LIKE A ROLLING STONE"[103]

As I arrived at the foot of the stairway, Bikel and Lomax were watching Seeger's back as he strode off toward the parking lot. He couldn't stand to listen any longer. His wife Toshi was weeping and being comforted by George. I gave Bikel and Lomax the message from Yarrow, minus the finger. They cursed and turned away and I went back to the press enclosure to hear the last song.

JOE BOYD[104]

Dylan began ["Phantom Engineer"], and the applause diminished as the heckling increased.

ROBERT SHELTON[105]

A Bloomfield guitar solo screamed through the night air. Dylan's voice took up the last verse, hurling his words out into the night air.

JOE BOYD[106]

I wanna be your lover, baby; I don't wanna be your boss.

BOB DYLAN, "PHANTOM ENGINEER"[107]

Pete already knew what he wanted others to sing. They were going to sing that it was a world of pollution, bombs, hunger, and injustice, but that PEOPLE would OVERCOME. . . . (But) can there be no songs as violent as the age? Must a folk song be of mountains, valleys, and love between my brother and my sister all over this land? Do we allow for despair only in the blues? . . . Maybe, maybe not. But we should ask the question. And the only one in the entire festival who questioned our position was Bob Dylan. Maybe he didn't put it in the best way. Maybe he was rude. But he shook us. And that is why we have poets and artists.

JIM ROONEY[108]

Dylan and the group disappeared offstage, and there was a long, clumsy silence.

ROBERT SHELTON[109]

There are many accounts of what happened next. Dylan left the stage with a shrug as the crowd roared.

JOE BOYD[110]

That's it?

MICHAEL BLOOMFIELD[111]

I thought he would go out and play some other stuff by himself and then we'd come out and play these three songs. But we just came out and played these three songs and then he said "Good night." And we'd been out there for a total of fifteen minutes. And everybody else had played for an hour. So that was pretty weird.

AL KOOPER[112]

They chose to boo Dylan off the stage for something as superficially silly as an electric guitar or something as stagnatingly sickening as their idea of owning an artist. They chose the safety of wishful thinking rather than the painful, always difficult stab of art.

PAUL NELSON[113]

No explanation like "those were the only two tunes we worked out; I'm going to go back and get my acoustic guitar now," or anything like that. Just turned around and left the stage. That's when the booing started. That was, "Hey! We paid our bucks; we looked forward to hearing you sing and you give us one and a half, one and three-quarter tunes? C'mon man!" For a long time, the shortcut was, "Dylan went electric and everybody booed him."

NOEL STOOKEY[114]

Having heard only three songs, they wanted "mooooooooore," and some, certainly, were booing. They had been taken by surprise by the volume and aggression of the music. Some loved it, some hated it, most were amazed, astonished and energized by it.

JOE BOYD[115]

Clapping was void. Boos and hecklers' cries rang clear throughout the field.

MICHAEL J. CARABETTA[116]

Everybody else said, "Dylan got booed off the stage," and that was not how it happened in my recall. . . . I think it's been shown now through Scorsese's film that the audience's response, at least if he edited it chronologically correctly, was very positive.

NOEL STOOKEY[117]

Bobby Dillon [sic] came on stage all in motorcycle black, in front of a very bad, very loud, electronic r-r band. 16,000 people had come to hear him. He walked off the stage after four numbers, no word of which could be understood, to one single hand-clap of applause. The audience sat there terrified and silent. He walked off slumped like a dead man. . . . He more or less killed the festival. Pete resigned from the board. That boy is really destructive.

ALAN LOMAX[118]

Dylan and his band evacuated the stage, and then the menacing rumble of thousands of fans could be heard. When Dylan came off the stage, I confronted him.

GEORGE WEIN[119]

He walked off the stage and said, "What have you done to me?" I was responsible for interfacing with Bob Dylan, with Peter, Paul and Mary, with Joan Baez, with Judy Collins, as a board member. And I said, "Go back on stage and perform some songs." And he did, but the moment had occurred. And became the subject matter of our discussion fifty years later.

PETER YARROW[120]

"You have to go back," I told him, "You've got to play something acoustic."
   "I don't want to. I can't go back." He spoke stubbornly.
   "Bob, we're going to have a riot on our hands if you don't."
   "I don't have a guitar."
   I turned to the assembled folksingers backstage. "Does anyone have a guitar?" About twenty acoustic guitars went up in the air. This was the Newport Folk Festival; it was a sea of guitars. Peter Yarrow grabbed one and handed it to Bob. We ushered him back onto the stage.

GEORGE WEIN[121]

Bobby, can you do another song, please? He's going to get his axe. He's coming. . . . He's gonna get an acoustic guitar.

PETER YARROW[122]

And everybody [went], "YAY!"

MARIA MULDAUR[123]

However, some of these so-called "folk music" fans did not know the meaning of the word "acoustic." Some ignorant jeerers were still yelling for Dylan to get his "folk" guitar. Enough said.

MICHAEL J. CARABETTA[124]

Tell him to get a wooden box!

UNIDENTIFIED AUDIENCE MEMBER[125]

Bring back Cousin Emmy!

UNIDENTIFIED AUDIENCE MEMBER[126]

We paid for this!

UNIDENTIFIED AUDIENCE MEMBER[127]

Peter Yarrow urged Bob to return and gave him his acoustic guitar. As Bob returned to the stage alone, he discovered he didn't have the right harmonica. "What are you doing to me?" Dylan demanded of Yarrow.

GEORGE WEIN[128]

Shocked and somewhat disoriented by the mixed reaction of the crowd, a tearful Dylan returned to the stage unelectrified and strained to communicate his sense of unexpected displacement through the words and music of a song he made fearfully appropriate, "It's All Over Now, Baby Blue."

IRWIN SILBER[129]

. . . the words taking on a new meaning, as if he were singing adieu to Newport, goodbye to the folk purists.

ROBERT SHELTON[130]

But whatever you wish to keep, you better grab it fast.

BOB DYLAN, "IT'S ALL OVER NOW, BABY BLUE"[131]

I don't care what Bob Dylan says, he was shaken. I had a telephoto lens on his face, and he was shaken.

RICK STAFFORD[132]

It was a farewell to the idealism and purity of the folk revival. There was no turning back—not for Dylan, not for anyone.

GEORGE WEIN[133]

The empty-handed painter from your streets
Is drawing crazy patterns on your sheets.

BOB DYLAN, "IT'S ALL OVER NOW, BABY BLUE"[134]

I was busy taking care of Cousin Emmy! And she was a handful. She was a crazy woman from the Grand Ol' Opry days. And in those days you could buy a drink backstage. And that's why I never saw Dylan—I was shepherding her around! She was a wild woman at that point.

BOB JONES[135]

The carpet, too, is moving under you.

BOB DYLAN, "IT'S ALL OVER NOW, BABY BLUE"[136]

. . . prompting his first unequivocal applause of the night.

GEORGE WEIN[137]

Tambourine, Bobby!

UNIDENTIFIED AUDIENCE MEMBER[138]

All right, I'll do this one for you.

BOB DYLAN[139]

My weariness amazes me, I'm branded on my feet
I have no one to meet.

BOB DYLAN, "MR. TAMBOURINE MAN"[140]

He left the stage having vanquished the hostility of those who wouldn't accept his electric music.

ROBERT SHELTON[141]

He can't come back. Please don't make it more difficult than it is.

PETER YARROW[142]

There were a lot of people there who were very pleased that I got booed. I saw them afterward. I do resent somewhat, though, that everybody that booed said they did it because they were old fans.

BOB DYLAN[143]

"'Why were you booing Bob?'" Seeger reflected in 2006. "That's what I should have said at intermission. 'You didn't boo Muddy Waters—he was using electric instruments!'"

But at the time Seeger dictated a "memo to myself," which differs significantly from his account above: "Last week in Newport I ran to hide my eyes and ears because I could not bear either the screaming of the crowd nor some of the most destructive music this side of Hell. . . .

"Who knows, but I am one of the fangs that sucked Bob dry? It is in the hope that I can learn that I write these words: asking questions I need help to answer; using language I never intended; hoping perhaps I'm wrong. But if I'm right, hoping that it won't happen again."

DAVID KING DUNAWAY[144]

After the intermission, fate and poor scheduling conspired to ensure that a sequence of tired, hackneyed representatives of the "New York school" was paraded before the exhausted audience: Oscar Brand, Ronnie Gilbert, Len Chandler, and finally Peter, Paul and Mary. Even PP&M's fans seemed to sense they were watching something whose time has passed.

Backstage the atmosphere was sombre and silent, older performers in one area, younger ones in another. The significance of many watershed events is apparent only in retrospect; this was clear at the time. The old guard hung their heads in defeat while the young, far from being triumphant, were chastened. They realized that in their victory lay the death of something wonderful. The rebels were like children who had been looking for something to break and realized, as they looked at the pieces, what a beautiful thing it had been.

JOE BOYD[145]

A double finale (presumably a Newport tradition by now) saw hordes of singers, musicians, self-appointed participants and temporary freaks take over the stage in a tasteless exhibition of frenzied incest that seemed taken from a Hollywood set. One singer called it a "nightmare of pop art," which was one of the more apt and gentle comments heard in the audience.

IRWIN SILBER[146]

The two camps could not even bear to discuss an alternative finale to "We Shall Overcome," so George had to come up with something. He played piano while an odd mixture of singers tackled "When the Saints Go Marching In." Spokes Mashiyane took a penny-whistle solo. Backstage security had dissolved: on one side of the stage was a fat Providence disc jockey doing the jerk with Joan Baez. It looked horrible, a parody of the moving finales of previous years. I spotted Pete Seeger in unlikely conversation with Mel Lyman, the first real contact between the factions. Seeger asked me to ensure that the stage lights would be turned off at the end and one mic left live on stage.

The lights went down, work lights came on at the exits and people started to file out. Mel [Lyman] came out and sat on the edge of the stage and in the dark, pulled out a harmonica and started to play "Rock of Ages." It echoed out over the emptying arena without anyone being able to see where it was coming from.

JOE BOYD[147]

This plaintive, beseeching sound came through the loudspeakers, gently wafting over the masses. He played the old spiritual over and over again, with hardly any variation.

GEORGE WEIN[148]

After about ten minutes, he brought it to a close, put the mic down on the edge of the stage, got up and walked off. No one clapped. People embraced, comforting one another, then slowly gathered their belongings and went off into the night.

JOE BOYD[149]

It was a plea, a hymn, a dirge, a lullaby. Twenty times, thirty, more, and always the same beseeching, stroking, praying, pleading; then slower, softer, and as the supplication trailed away, the park was empty and people were on their way home.

ROBERT J. LURTSEMA[150]

I'd heard a rumor that Pete was gonna cut the cable. I heard it later, and it was like, it didn't make sense to me. Pete Seeger, someone whose music I cherish, you know. Someone I highly respect is going to cut the cable. It was like "Oh God!" It was like a dagger, you know? Just the thought of it was, you know, made me go out and get drunk.

BOB DYLAN[151]

I remember seeing Bob later on that evening, looking kind of blue, as though he hadn't made the point that he wanted to make properly. He didn't want to feel that he was limited here or limited there. He wanted to do something with the Butterfield Blues Band. And it was great.

PETE SEEGER[152]

The story would be de-emotionalized in Seeger's autobiography: "When Bob Dylan switched to an electric guitar at Newport I was not upset with him," Seeger wrote, his "little eraser" twanging. "I was furious at the sound system . . . you couldn't understand a word because of the distortion."

DAVID KING DUNAWAY[153]

At a party later that night, the Chambers Brothers played rock for dancing, and a discotheque ambience descended on Newport. I asked George Wein, the Festival's technical producer, why he didn't like folk-rock. He countered: "You've been brainwashed by the recording industry." Off in a corner, a sullen Dylan sat on the lap of Betsy Siggins, of Cambridge's Club 47. He looked stunned, shaken and disappointed.

ROBERT SHELTON[154]

He did not say one word. . . . He seemed to be exhausted, kind of overwhelmed, and it was just like I was his chair.

BETSY SIGGINS[155]

Bob was sitting in the corner, I guess thinking about what had happened. I said, "Hey Bob, do you wanna dance?" And he looked up at me and said, "I'd dance with you, Maria, but my hands are on fire." And it's sort of like, that was a cryptic remark, but I kind of knew exactly what he meant, you know? So I said "OK man," and I just left him alone.

MARIA MULDAUR[156]

Like a bold child who has deliberately put his hand on the steam iron, he was blistered and astonished by the heat that made no exceptions, not even for him.

ROBERT SHELTON[157]

As people began to dance, the sombre atmosphere evaporated. The beer flowed, the party got wilder, the dancing more frenetic, and Sam and Jerome never flagged as different singers came and went. When I left near dawn, it was still going strong. I drove back to my mansion maid's room, thinking sadly about Pete Seeger. I doubted he would ever come to sympathize with what had happened. There was no point wondering whether it was for the better. All we could do was to ride its ramifications into the future.

JOE BOYD[158]

It was a sad parting of the ways for many, myself included. I choose Dylan. I choose art. I will stand behind Dylan and his "new" songs, and I'll bet my critical reputation (such as it is) that I'm right.

PAUL NELSON[159]

I saw Dylan twice in New York the week after the Festival. He still seemed stunned and distressed that he had sparked such animosity. He was shaken that people had yelled "Get rid of that electric guitar!" But he refused to enter squabbles. Of his introducing electric music at Newport and the years of controversy that ensued, Dylan said, over and over again, "It was honest. It was honest."

ROBERT SHELTON[160]

It was never the same after that. By '66, I knew that we were having problems.

GEORGE WEIN[161]

*I think we are only
headed for chaos.*
GEORGE WEIN

IT IS BEGINNING TO BOG DOWN

The program for the 1969 Newport Folk Festival (July 16–20) detailed five days of performances illustrating the wide range of music that had come to be defined as folk. The bill included a Children's Day and a nighttime blues program featuring Taj Mahal, Sleepy John Estes, Big Mama Thornton and Son House. Friday night's show was headlined by the already immortal Johnny Cash; at the same time, a workshop at Rogers High School celebrated "Fiddle Around the World." The weekend promised a bluegrass workshop and an open hootenanny. The Young Performers Concert included future stars such as James Taylor and Van Morrison; Joni Mitchell was on Saturday night's bill.

The program also had two pages on Pete Seeger's project to build the sloop *Clearwater*, a project that would "serve as a Hudson River Museum afloat" and inspire and aid conservation efforts as "a symbol of a time when the river was clean, when its natural beauty was not marred by its usefulness, and when the river banks were a source of pleasure to those who lived on them."

And Newport Folk Foundation secretary Elliot Hoffman detailed the foundation's work helping those who propagated and preserved old-time folk music, with a list of grant recipients that included cowboy folk historian Glenn Ohrlin, several Native American projects, folklore departments at the University of Pennsylvania and UCLA and more.

Hoffman also described the foundation's "deliberate effort to increase the proportion of ethnic traditional performers to urban performers" and added that "the concept of the Newport Folk Foundation, in short, has worked. More than that, it has grown and promises to be stronger and more productive each year."

After that weekend, there wouldn't be another Newport Folk Festival for sixteen years.

No good idea falls apart all at once, but the Utopia phase of the Newport Folk Festival disintegrated with remarkable speed. Between its aesthetic, commercial and (seemingly) communal zenith in 1965 and the death knell of 1970, when putting up any kind of festival at all proved impossible, the festival was beset by tensions on all these fronts, from within and without—tensions between organizers, between artists and the festival and between competing factions in society itself over what music can be for. Facing only one of these problems, the festival might have survived; the combination, however, left the festival and the Newport Folk Foundation off balance and unable to recover from one last stroke of bad luck.

As the organizers of the festival began to figure out how to follow up the landmark 1965 edition, the future, to outward appearances, looked bright. The 1966 festival was headed into its second year at Festival Field, off Connell Highway, which satisfied the City Council's 1964 demand that festivals not contribute to traffic or parking problems in central Newport. Attendance had grown in the past three years from 45,000 to 64,000 to 74,000. Wein told the *New York Times* that he planned not only the folk and jazz festivals but also an opera festival for the next July. And in 1967, festivals of pop music and of readings of drama, prose and poetry would be added; the future might hold an American history pageant.

But there were cracks in (literally and figuratively) the foundation: the signs were already there that the Newport Folk Festival had grown into something its organizers couldn't quite control. At the same time, Dylan was gone, and he wasn't coming back. The planning and organizing of the 1966 festival, which would determine Newport's direction after the biggest event in its history, needed cohesion and cooperation; instead, it was done in an atmosphere loaded with conflict and confusion.

In December 1965, the festival's board of directors (which by now consisted of Theo Bikel, Ronnie Gilbert, Alan Lomax, Ralph Rinzler, Peter Yarrow and Mike and Pete Seeger) sent a letter to "performers, volunteers, staff, press and audience" that spent as much time detailing "the problems that arise with a festival the size of Newport" as it did celebrating the festival's successes. And it asked some pretty fundamental questions: "Should there be more workshops? Fewer? Can they be made smaller and more intimate? Should there be more traditional music? More contemporary? How can we improve the relationship of the police to the festival-goers? How many performers? Which ones? Or as one board member laments, 'I wish that an invitation to Newport wasn't looked upon like the Good Housekeeping Seal of Approval.' Another was heard to mumble, 'I never thought I'd be considered the Establishment.'"[1]

At the height of the festival's cultural importance, outside observers were already finding fault with it. (Indeed, the very fact that Newport had become such a touchstone was a problem, and to some observers the Utopia days were never quite that.) In the minds of its critics, by 1965 or even earlier the Newport Folk Festival had gotten too big for its britches. Even many of the organizers felt the same way.

Paul Nelson forecast the problems to come at the beginning of 1965, when he wrote a long essay/review of the 1964 festival in the *Little Sandy Review* (a staunch outlet of folk traditionalism that had previously derided Peter, Paul and Mary as "dazzling in their atrocious artificially canned, commercial enthusiasm"[2] and called *The Freewheelin' Bob Dylan* LP "a great disappointment").[3] "We come to praise Newport, not to bury it," Nelson wrote, "but, alas, it fairly greets us with a shovel in its hands, an embarrassed grin on its face and the Folkways ANTHOLOGY at its feet."[4]

He added that the Thursday-night 1964 concert of elder traditionalists was "a night in which they rose to . . . a sad dignity to a place of eminence in which they would be allowed to remain, virtually unnoticed like the classical paintings in the back room of a museum, in the days and nights that followed, the Days and Nights of the Heroes." Such days and nights, he said, drew "the fraternity folklorists, the Bronx Baezes and Ramblin' Jack Somebodies, the record company presidents, the press agents."[5] Indeed, the assumption of the star-making potential of Newport, fueled by the myth of Joan Baez's 1959 performance as career making, hung over the festival for much of the '60s.

Barbara Dane wrote that "folk-biz-stars need the Festival more than it needs any single one of them, and the notion that 'they draw the people who bring in the money for all the worthwhile projects' should not become an excuse to favor one or slight the other."[6] (That dynamic could cut both ways: In 1968, Ellen Willis wrote that "the electric performers" resented "the Newport game, which decreed that they were mere crowd-pleasers and that Libba Cotton [sic], Henry Crowdog and Buell Kazee were the real VIPS."[7])

That conflict between old-style players and singers of traditional songs and tunes and the new school of singer-songwriters never went away, as Judy Collins recalls. Indeed, behind the scenes, the organizers were having some of the same battles. "It was hard to get the festival to think about young singer-songwriters," she says of her years on the board of directors, "but I think we made a big dent in that over time. . . . That was one of the in-house fights that went on. Pretty loud and raucous for a bunch of liberals." She remembers that Joyce Wein was essential to "damping down the flames of irate reactionary criticism of what was going on. She was good. There was a lot of shouting and a lot of controversy and—it didn't last too long. Nobody came to blows, I don't think."[8]

Bruce Jackson, now the James Agee Professor of American Culture at the University of Buffalo, the author or editor of thirty-three books and maker of five films, remembers occasional "heated arguments" at board meetings: "Alan often had somebody he had discovered. And sometimes the person would be absolutely wonderful, and sometimes the person would be absolutely terrible." Board members would also make decisions on requests for foundation grants—"some of them were for a lot of money, like up to 25 thousand bucks. Some of them were for almost nothing, just a couple hundred bucks for somebody who needed to replace his guitar which had imploded."[9]

Speaking about the history and the influence of Newport, Collins easily conflates the concepts of folk music and singer-songwriters, but at the time they were considered very different musical bags. She calls the distinction "funny," though: "Pete Seeger, the founder of everything, was a singer-songwriter! How could that escape notice? I don't know. There were a lot of people with their noses in the air that if it didn't originate in the Oklahoma hills—Woody Guthrie! The major singer-songwriter of all times!"[10]

While the directors of the Newport festival were arguing over the merits of singers, songwriters and fiddlers, another battle was going on: one faction of directors saw the businessmen in their midst, chiefly Wein, as at best marginally useful, at worst part of the cultural problem that a folk festival was intended to fight against in the first place.

This split had long existed—in January 1964 Lomax, in a letter to Charlie Seeger explaining opposition to Lomax's scouting idea, wrote, "George Wein just wants to keep hold of the money."[11] But in the mid-'60s, suddenly a lot of people with no experience around money were the guardians of lots of cash, and they had questions about where it was going.

At the same time, people inside and outside the festival organization were suspicious of the financial arrangement among the folk festival; the jazz festival; Wein's umbrella corporation, Festival Productions; and the new Festival Field, Inc., the Wein-led corporation that had secured the festival grounds off Connell Highway and that collected rent from the jazz, folk and opera festivals for its use.

Sing Out! managing editor Ed Badeux wrote to the Newport board, demanding to see the foundation's financial records. He claimed that the fame of the festival had grown to the point where such information was essentially public property:

> Certainly all of the performers and others who have contributed their
> services to Newport over the years have the right to feel that Newport is
> their organization.
>
> Frankly, we feel that up to now the Newport Foundation has not been
> as candid with its friends and supporters, as well as with the public at large,
> as it should be. This is only helping to build up an atmosphere of suspicion
> and mistrust which works against the cause of folk music in general. One
> crucial aspect of this has been the air of mystery built up around Newport's
> finances.[12]

Writing in *Sing Out!* a few months later, Barbara Dane, who also had no formal connection with the festival, insinuated the same and added a suggestion that "we" form committees "to produce books and records in the name of Newport and in keeping with its spirit, independent of private business concerns."[13] Meanwhile, Bruce Jackson was dispatched by *Sing Out!* editor Irwin Silber to write "a hatchet job" (Jackson's words) on the festival organization.

Jackson was a graduate student in comparative literature at Indiana University in the early '60s when Pete Seeger came for a gig at the coffeehouse on campus. Jackson says that Seeger's twelve-string acoustic guitar was either lost or broken, and Joe Hickerson, later a longtime archivist at the American Folklife Center at the Library of Congress, asked if Seeger could borrow Jackson's. "[Hickerson] said he would come by and pick it up," Jackson remembers, "and I said 'Fuck you; I'll bring it around—I want to meet Pete Seeger.'" Later, Jackson wrote an article on how to tune a twelve-string —"it's a bitch to tune"—that Seeger included in a booklet that accompanied his instructional album on twelve-string. "And he didn't credit me. So I wrote to Folkways and said 'At least you could send me some albums.'"[14]

That's all it took to become a folk critic at the time, and Jackson says he had written a few reviews when Silber approached him: "He wanted me to show that George was using Newport to underwrite his jazz festivals," Jackson remembers.[15] The organizers gave him full access to the board, as well as meeting minutes and financial records.

While Jackson did his work, Alan Lomax supported the idea of an independent audit of the festival's finances, echoing Badeux's sentiments by telling board secretary Elliot Hoffman in a letter in March 1966 that while he didn't doubt anyone's integrity, "our structure is too large to continue to be informal."[16]

Hoffman was not amused, replying, "My own reaction is simply to invite you to learn more about your own Foundation, and to satisfy yourself that it is not, except in the manner in which the directors are permitted to conduct their own meetings, the least bit informal."[17]

Lomax pressed on. At the festival board meeting in April 1966, he suggested an outside auditor, and the board agreed. At the same meeting, it was suggested that the foundation hire Willis James as a scholar and scout at a salary of $10,000 a year.

James's bona fides aside, the disconnect between the demand for financial scrutiny and the new expense of another hire was too much for George Wein, who had already written to festival accountant Arnold London in December 1965, "I am very concerned about the financial situation of the Folk Festival." He wrote a rare letter to the board after the meeting, saying, "There was such a general desire on the part of the Board to increase Foundation activities that the fact that we had no money in the treasury at the moment did not seem to take hold."[18]

He didn't stop there. In a long diatribe, he unloaded financial and other frustrations he'd evidently had with the board for a while. He proposed splitting the foundation from the festival, arguing that "I think we are only headed for chaos if this is not done." Referring to Dane's *Sing Out!* piece, Wein wrote, "If this type of criticism and concern is what causes worry to the Board concerning the books and the running of the Foundation, then my feeling is that we are only headed for complete destruction."

He added that the board "should have come right out and said, 'George, why don't we have money? Has the Newport Jazz Festival been using our funds? Have you been unfair in splitting up the expenses that accrued to the festivals? Are the budgets valid?' Any of these direct questions asked of the chair would have been much more honest than the insinuations and the actions of several members of the Board." He allowed that folk festival money had at times "temporarily helped Festival Productions Inc. on a short-term basis," but added that "at this point funds of Festival Productions Inc. and Festival Field Inc. are making it possible for the Newport Folk Foundation to stagger through to festival time or such time as ticket money comes in."

It may seem as though the Newport Folk Festival shouldn't have had to stagger through at that point, but Wein wrote that any audit should happen after the 1966 festival, not before, because "at that point, we will have money in the bank, and we will be able to release a public statement that will show that we are a solvent corporation and not an insolvent corporation as we are at this moment."

But the financial quarrel was only one of Wein's dissatisfactions. "I personally feel that our Festival this year is very weak," he wrote, and added that the recent disagreements were taking away from the sprit in which the folk festival was supposed to operate.

> Four years ago we had a beautiful ideal, and we realized it. Now that we
> have achieved and realized something very great, somewhere or other,
> that ideal appears to be lost. When we had no money at all, there were
> no problems. Now that we have been able to do so many wonderful
> projects with the money earned by the Festival and through the generous
> contributions of the artists who have contributed their services, the ideal
> is no longer with us.
>
> We are now concerned with nonprofit, status, expenses, what benefits
> who, and myriad other things that literally disgust me.[19]

In lieu of an audit, the board decided to appoint a Financial Committee to look into the festival's money woes. (An audit, Wein had argued, would explain what money was spent; it wouldn't have, or be able to have, an opinion on whether it was spent wisely.)

The foundation agreed, and the committee comprised Jac Holzman of Elektra Records; Jim Rooney, a board member and a fixture at Club 47; and artist manager Harold Leventhal. They looked at the financial records and interviewed most of the board and officers of Festival Productions. Meanwhile, Jackson's would-be hit piece came out. He remembers finding that "there weren't any bad deeds going on. Some stupid things were funded, but every funding agency does that—you can't predict in advance whether something's going to work. But nobody was putting money in his pocket."[20] Indeed, Jackson wrote at the time, "The word that comes up most characteristically when one discusses Newport with the directors, particularly the originators, is love. At first I felt as if I were in Hollywood and love had become the new equivalent of a defunct darling . . . but it's true, they're serious, they're for real."[21]

In April 1967, the committee of Holtzman, Rooney and Leventhal concluded that the records "appeared to be, without an exhaustive audit, correct," and that "there is no basis for any mistrust or questioning of integrity on either the part of the Wein organization or the board itself." The trio instead had head-scratchingly simple suggestions, such as "No single board member should be permitted to requisition money to initiate any projects" and that "the board should provide oversight to make sure Foundation-backed projects are completed."[22] (This echoed London's letter to the heads of each festival in January 1967, with its nongroundbreaking suggestions such as the use of purchase orders and predetermined budgets, as well as the requirement that each prospective employee of the festivals fill out an application.)

Rooney remembers, "We didn't find anything. And I don't think there was anything to find. . . . We were spending more money than we had in the past; that's just the way it was."[23] He does recall, however, that Wein brought up the incident bitterly in a conversation more than forty years later.

This discord was months away from resolution, however, while the 1966 festival was being planned.

Jackson's piece, published after the 1966 festival but written before, also included six detailed suggestions for improving the festival. The most publicly relevant of them included having many fewer acts—Jackson called the 1964 festival, which featured a total of 228 players, "a beautiful nightmare" and the '65 festival not much better—and more planning on the bill, especially the workshops. "Saturday afternoon," he wrote of 1965, "found six workshops going on at once. It seemed then, and it still does, an awful waste." Some performers, he wrote, "are beautiful in a workshop setting but simply should not be forced out on that stage in front of that sea of faces." Perhaps most embarrassingly, he revealed that "as I'm writing this (June 1) the program is still not complete, and the workshop topics are still in the suggestion stage."[24] (For his troubles on the research and composition of both these pieces, Jackson was invited to join the festival's board, where he served for three years.)

The directors of the festival evidently already felt that more control was needed. In January 1966 they had decided to adopt a suggestion from Alan Lomax that "rather than select talent and then put together a variety show, that the program be planned and talent selected to fill it."

In one sense, there probably wasn't much else to do. Bob Dylan was a pop star now, and he wouldn't return. And while Newport hardly turned its back on artists with records on the charts, inviting the Lovin' Spoonful and Chuck Berry (the latter of whom never showed up) that very year, the musical world around the festival had changed. Folk music had taken over as the music of young people for a time in the early '60s—it's why fans and detractors could even afford to have the argument over whether hosting the Kingston Trio was a sellout move. But the still-growing popularity of the Beatles and of rock in general had taken a chunk out of the crowd. There were still holdouts, Wein says now, but when Dylan went electric, his fans "could follow their friends and join their friends who were also Beatles fans. And that changed the whole world."[25] In Elijah Wald's excellent summation of Bob Dylan's 1965 Newport appearance and its aftermath, he diagnoses, "It was not Dylan who was transformed that weekend; it was Newport. . . . It was not news that Dylan was the future; the news was that Seeger was the past."[26]

Peter Yarrow remembers that "there was another language that was emerging that spoke to the aspirations of the country."[27] Joe Boyd says,

> In '63, '64, '65 there was this dichotomy. If you were a straight youth, you listened to Top-40 radio. And if you were rebellious, and nonconformist, and you thought for yourself and you wanted to be a bit different, you might be a jazz fan; you might be a folk music fan; you might be a blues fanatic; you might be a lot of different things.

But after '65, and once the Fillmore had opened up in San Francisco and all this, the rebellious, antimainstream stance became mainstream. There was nothing unusual about going to a festival in the summer, or going to hear weird music that bore no resemblance to moon-June-spoon. It was still a rebellious statement, but millions and millions of kids were making it. It just wasn't as important anymore.[28]

So for 1966, some of the trademarks of Newport—the Gospel concert on Sunday morning, the New Folks show on Sunday afternoon—remained in place. But, as Lomax suggested, that year's festival was more thematic and theatrical, and it was seemingly an act of atonement for the previous year.

Electricity and pop music were hardly banned, but where there had been star power, now there would be community. The program announced that the opening-night concert would resemble a "kaleidoscope," in which "the entire cast will work together to create the spirit of Newport. . . . Each will appear any number of times for varying periods throughout the first evening, as he will during the following days."

The Children's Day idea was born this year, featuring performers such as Judy Collins, Mike and Pete Seeger, Buffy Sainte-Marie and Skip James. Also new was a display of folk crafts, including a display called "The Wool Process—From Sheep to Loom." And the program—an eighty-page monster—included field reports on various forms of music and crafts, as well as updates from Ralph Rinzler and others on projects that had received grants from the Newport Folk Foundation. Ironically, the inside front cover of that program was taken up by a full-page advertisement for Shure microphones.

The festival began with a concert by Brand, Collins, Phil Ochs, Bukka White and more on Thursday, July 21, but the next two nights saw themed, scripted presentations, in keeping with the directors' decision in January.

So Friday night featured a "Fiddle Contest" hosted by Jimmie Driftwood and including Balfa's Cajun band, Flatt and Scruggs and more; "Blues Cutting" (Son House, Skip James, and Bukka White); "Ballad Topping" (Driftwood, Mike Seeger and others); and a "Gospel Battle" with the Dixie Hummingbirds, the Swan Silvertones and Dorothy Love and the Gospel Harmonettes. Saturday featured a twenty-six-act "Patchwork of American Music" pageant. Both nights featured scripts by Lomax, who hosted the Friday-night show, while Tom Clancy handled Saturday's.

Lomax greeted Friday-night concertgoers with this announcement: "Welcome to the Friday-night Battle of Music. All of us here at Newport, and I'm sure that this applies to everyone in the audience, wishes that all battles consisted of notes and chords and ballads, rather than bullets and bombs. So we're gonna give you a model tonight of the way that the human race could settle its problems in a nice, friendly kind of contest that wouldn't hurt anybody."[29]

Lomax then exhorted the bluesmen—Son House, Skip James and Bukka White—to "get those axes and carve each other to the heart—to the musical heart." In each contest, everyone got a prize for—well, whatever it was they did. Lily Mae Pennington was cringe-worthily rewarded for having "the most beautiful bowing arm I've seen at the festival," one judge said. At the conclusion of the fiddlers' program, Lomax said, "We had to settle the fiddle contest that way, because you know, when fiddlers get crossed up with each other, they're liable to pull out their six-guns and settle it that way instead of with their fiddles."

Robert Cantwell writes that for Lomax, "folk revivalism was a poetic project closely allied to the nineteenth-century literary quest for an American epic."[30] Less delicately, Bruce Jackson says, while acknowledging Lomax's achievements as a collector and curator of American folklore, "he had a real corny aspect to him."[31]

Throughout both nights, the hosts explained the performers and their significance to the crowd, evidently presuming the performers themselves were unable to do this (a presumption demolished by White's story of playing a real cutting contest with a pig for first prize and other moments when the performers got a word in edgewise).

Even Wein, in one of several speeches to the crowd, offered the not-so-ringing endorsement that "I think we've tried a lot of experiments—some have been good, some haven't been so good, but we keep trying up here and we'll see what happens as we proceed through the rest of the festival."

Jackson, reviewing the festival in *Sing Out!* a month after his piece on how the festival could improve, agreed. Of the blues concert, for which he was dragooned into being a judge, he wrote that one of the performers got himself drunk as perhaps the only act of civil disobedience he could manage against the undignified structure. Jackson himself tried unsuccessfully "to sneak away and make everyone forget he had been a party to that mess." He also noted, using thin pseudonyms, that it was patronizing to the less-known and traditional performers only: "One astute observer said afterwards, 'You notice they didn't get Judy Collie, Boffo St. Shawnee or Carolyn Western up there to be judged.' They would have said go to hell Stage Manager, and would have had their way."[32]

He wrote of the rest of the Friday- and Saturday-night shows, "All requisite attention was paid to staging and mixing and positioning and everything anybody could think up or of except music makers and music making."[33]

Jackson wasn't alone. The *Providence Journal*'s Ted Holmberg wrote that if the festival was to be a scripted piece of semitheatre, so be it, but as such, professionalism in the staging was "sadly lacking." He bemoaned "the apparently lost opportunity for each performer to work at some length and develop a mood."[34] And Robert Shelton wrote in the *Times* that "Pedantic attitudes nearly robbed all but the last concert of the fun a festival promises. . . . A committee-run festival is a nobly democratic and representative idea, but it is beginning to bog down."[35] Ellen Willis wrote in the *New Yorker*, "the Folk Festival needs more than a new home. It needs a whole new rationale."[36]

After the festival, Mike Seeger wrote to the board that "at least a half dozen performers were offended by being told not to talk and do only one song or play with others, etc. Some just wished to leave. I found myself explaining and apologizing to Skip James, Dock Boggs, Son House, and other outstanding people. Performers in such productions must be worked with not at."[37] Pete Seeger, on the other hand, actually spoke with, not just about, the artists during his MC stint on the Sunday night, Mike Seeger said. And while he said the Lovin' Spoonful were "good musicians and know folk music," they weren't in keeping with the folk aesthetic. "We must never let ourselves be in the desperate state of mind as we were this year when we were trying to get the spoonful or the byrds [sic] in order primarily to save us financially." He added that the strife between Wein and the board that spring had leaked into the atmosphere of the festival itself: "I missed the warm human atmosphere that was so evident (and so important) in the previous three festivals. . . . Too many people, the uptight staff . . ."[38]

In *Broadside*, Jane Friesen waxed poetic: "Hundreds of disregarded leaflets lay among the heaps of accumulated trash, hardly distinguishable from the lonesome, anonymous guitar pluckers huddled about in scattered clusters dodging the trampling feet of crowds scuffling back and forth."[39]

The total attendance was about 65,000, but many more hung around outside the fences—so many that Wein wrote in a long letter to the board in fall 1966 that the organizers needed "in a sense, to undo what we have done":

> The Saturday night crowd was much too big. The entire Festival structure in Newport nearly blew up Saturday when the kids outside the park tried to storm the fences. . . .
>
> This year, for the first time, I could sense the same tension in town for the Folk Festival that used to be for the Jazz Festival in the late 1950's. There were thousands of kids in town on Friday night who did not come to the performance. They had no business being in town, but were just there because Newport was the place to be.[40]

Wein added that the festival needed to step back from the presentation of star performers not only because the size of the crowds was getting out of control but for aesthetic and business reasons. Show business, he warned, was fickle, and they needed to prepare for the day that the popularity of folk music, already waning, reached niche status: "The Newport Folk Festival cannot hope to exist with any degree of permanency if its primary concern is being part of the 'This is what's happenin', baby" syndrome. . . . We are trying to establish here a series of festivals that will withstand year-to-year changes in the tastes of young people in America." He argued that even though jazz's popularity as an alternative to pop had faded, "I would say the future of the Jazz Festival is more secure than the future of the Folk Festival," thanks to the critical acclaim that comes from presenting the real thing.[41]

The 1967 festival reflected this. In his program note (across from a full-page ad for Fender electric guitars), Wein argued that

> many of the fans of folk-rock are not fans of much of the folk music we have presented at Newport in the past six years.
>
> Therefore, we are taking a great gamble this year. The dedication of the Newport Folk Festival is to foster folk music at its grass roots. This is the direction we have chosen more than ever to emphasize this year. . . .

Can folk music ever die? Can the singing of a song by people who believe and love the music they sing ever disappear?

The bill included folk-rock from the Buffalo Springfield and the electric gospel of the Chambers Brothers, along with blues from Muddy Waters and Otis Spann and gospel from Katie Bell Nubin and Sister Rosetta Tharpe. The grass roots were represented by North Carolina's Dillard Chandler, the Ukrainian-Jewish singer and storyteller Moishe Bressler, Galician piper Antonio Mosquera and his group Los Gallegos D'España and the Glinka Russian Dancers.

The big noise was made by Arlo Guthrie, though, who took the opportunity to trot out what would become his signature song, the twenty-minute shaggy-dog monologue "Alice's Restaurant," for the first time in public at a Saturday-afternoon topical songs workshop. His appearance on the Sunday-afternoon New Folks concert went down so well that he was given a slot on the Sunday-night closing show, for which he was joined by around thirty performers to shout out the opening and closing choruses.

Singer-songwriter Gordon Lightfoot, who went on to have hits such as "Carefree Highway," "Sundown" and "The Wreck of the Edmund Fitzgerald," returned, as well as the Kweskin Jug Band. The crafts shows included dulcimer-maker Edd Presnell and two demonstrations of basket making by Sea Islander Louise Jones and North Carolina's Wilma and Geraldine Ward.

That year saw the revival of the hootenanny tradition, with an audience-participation segment that allowed up to forty festivalgoers to do a song apiece.[42] It was hosted by Oscar Brand, who said it was important to make sure that audience members not only got to play a song but that they "feel they had been heard and they had been judged by someone of importance."

But accountant London told the Newport City Council that ticket sales were such that Joan Baez had to be hastily added to the schedule. The *Boston Globe* reported at the time that "downtown Newport has been unusually tame for a festival week,"[43] and that bad weather kept attendance down.

"The singing of a song by people who believe and love the music they sing,"[44] as Wein called it, can never disappear, Bob Jones said in 2013, but it won't bring in 18,000 people a day. Jones may have been one of the people who rode all over the country with Alan Lomax scouting out unadulterated traditional folk music, but he knew you couldn't fill a festival with it.

The late 1960s, in his view, were an attempt to make the festival work with traditional performers. Bruce Jackson agrees, writing that the mix of "urban" singer-songwriters to traditional artists was 2 to 1 in 1963 but precisely flipped by 1967. He goes on to point out that in 1964, no more than three workshops went on at once; in 1967 there were twenty-two, with microphones disallowed so as to keep the whole afternoon from devolving into a sonic war.[45]

Such traditional artists could only draw so many people, Jones says, adding that the $50-a-day ideal had a downside: it cost just as much to bring Henry Crowdog as it did to bring Bob Dylan, but which one was going to sell more tickets? "We needed people who could draw young adults. And once that started to fade away, I think it became pretty evident."[46]

While the Newport police had always been wary of the presence of the festival and its fans, for 1967 a Newport policeman told the *Providence Journal* that "By now, most people know what the rules are here, and there shouldn't be any doubt about what they are." If there was, it was removed July 12, when the police went beyond their usual dispersal of outdoor sleepers by telling a group of "bearded, barefoot youths singing in Eisenhower Park" to move along. Excessive congregating would no longer fly.[47]

This kind of bummer seemed to run through the whole festival. Silber, in *Sing Out!*, wrote that "the Festival grounds abounded with Cajun bands, old-time dulcimer players, revived blues singers, British ballad-singers and lightning-fingered fiddlers. But the miniskirted teenyboppers who flooded the lobby of the Viking Hotel swapping scraps of information on the sleeping accommodations and arrangements of the Festival's quartet of magic princesses (Joanie, Judy, Mimi and Buffy) knew where it was at."[48]

Silber turned a radical eye toward the festival, and he found Newport lacking in relevance. He declared that while "there was a time when the Newport Festival was able to serve as a synthesis and a platform for much that was new and changing and significant in America," he now called the festival "the annual puberty rites" and decried the playing of the *National Anthem* before the final Sunday show, saying it made the festival "as relevant as a prize fight or a baseball game."[49]

The week of the festival had seen riots in Newark, New Jersey, and to

Silber, four years after "We Shall Overcome," the contrast was striking: "19 people lay dead in the streets of Newark at the moment that most of the singers in the workshop on contemporary songs were expounding on the meaning of love. But point of fact, there was no one at Newport really capable of either acting or reacting to Newark."[50]

He praised a few performers, including the Bread and Puppet Theater and El Teatro Campesino, the farm-workers' theatre from Delano, California. As for the frankly political British folksinger Bob Davenport, Silber wrote that "America in the Vietnam summer was more prepared to snigger at a few raw words than to look into the mirror offered to it." As for the festival's guiding light, "Pete Seeger, of course, is always relevant, although one felt at times that he was playing some latter-day King Lear, blind to the insane self-centered world of his daughter who had taken over the stage."

Silber's solution was to blow the festival up and start over again, perhaps in Boston or New York, in an urban area where ghetto dwellers would be able to afford a ticket: "So long as the folk festival is wedded to the geographical accident of this wealthy and relatively inaccessible Rhode Island resort city, nothing that happens there will really seem important."[51] (The question of whether the citizens of the ghetto would turn out to hear Buell Kazee was left unanswered.)[52]

Barbara Dane was similarly cavalier in her desire to bring the festival to an end:

> If no one offers us a fight, then our actions have been too gentle. . . . Isn't it more fitting that the Festival should die fighting for the needs of its folks, rather than see the best hopes and dreams, traditions and humanity of us folks programmed out to keep the Festival alive? . . .
>
> If we merely collect and admire the cultural product of a human being while he stands before us suffering, we have become tourists taking snapshots of the quaint ragged beggars.[53]

There is no record of whether Dane asked musicians from Appalachia, who were performing in front of the biggest crowds of their lives, or from Louisiana, where the local Cajun culture had been revived, whether they felt like quaint, ragged beggars.

At the same time, the increasing bitterness of the antiwar movement tore at the festival through the late '60s. Whereas the civil rights movement lent the festival some of its most iconic moments, the antiwar movement—and the question of how passionately and openly to embrace it—was a mode of conflict itself. "Politics in the late '6os and early '7os were bitter and violent," Bruce Jackson remembers. "There were riots on campuses; kids were killed at Kent State. My campus (the University of Buffalo) was occupied by 400 policemen; the whole campus was tear-gassed one night. It was a contentious time, and flowers and love didn't have too much of a part in it."[54]

The music reflected this. As acoustic guitars gave way to electrics, the dance-oriented chords and grooves of garage bands gave way to harsher, feedback-laced rock that effectively served as the sonic equivalent of what Joe Boyd, in a different context, called the Boston school of songwriting —privileging individual expression over something that people could get together and participate in, even if only by dancing. And folk was left even further behind. "Musical tastes change," Jackson continues, "and the simplicity of the folk-music scene, to a lot of people, seemed no longer quite appropriate."[55]

Judy Collins remembers that "all of us were doing things, protesting and marching. Anybody who could was out clomping around with a sign. I never felt that was any contradiction to what Newport was about. I mean, maybe formally embracing the idea and therefore marketing it as such wasn't happening, but everybody's heart was in the anti-war movement. . . . It was just a default position—anybody who was out doing this kind of work, music and so on, would have been appearing at anti-war rallies and singing for the right stuff."[56]

On the other hand, there were those who felt that there was no need for more political content than the festival already had. Mike Seeger, in his wrap-up of the '66 festival, remarked that "we cannot rent (a booth) to one action group without renting to all. I think that we should keep such expressions in the musical area, with only the exception of booths selling folk crafts. There is plenty of social comment from the stage, as well as some anti-social."[57]

It may not have risen to the level of a pushback, but some with less-liberal political voices echoed Seeger's sentiments: "I don't want anything to do with tearing down America. . . . If I'd known it was goin' to be like this I'd of stayed in Kentucky," Buell Kazee told the *National Review* in 1968, whose Anthony R. Dolan observed of the audience, "You had to see this bedraggled army to feel the proper sorrow and the proper pity."[58]

Meanwhile, the regional chapter of the Young Americans for Freedom demanded to know how "George Weim" could "let this type of activity go on in view of the serious riots and disregard for law of late?"[59]

By 1970, these tensions had gotten to the point where Bruce Jackson was writing to the board that "I think we could have a nice festival if we were willing to go simple once again and forget fuckhead words like relevant (that word once was usually followed by a preposition; now it's a terminal condition)."

With the war raging, riots in the inner cities, and the recent death of Janis Joplin, Jackson wrote, "I think oh shit how can we sit around and plan folk festivals?" He answered himself:

> Carefully. Because even though these things go on, are out there, continue, get worse, whatall, it is still good to do things like Newport. And if there isn't room for it in our program, then the ratfinks really are winning after all. I still remind myself now and then about Britain starting its Arts Council during the days of the Blitz. I think Theo is right—if we just get together the artists the content will come out however it will and it can't help but express some of the concerns that trouble us all. . . . It is particularly important that we keep Newport alive. Important not for any historical or academic or artsy reasons, but just because it is a pretty good thing. . . .
>
> Early in the year we are always very idealistic and thoughtful; around the break of spring we start to panic and plunge into fads to make sure we make enough money. We did all kinds of clever things two years ago and went broke anyway, so I hope that won't enter into the deliberations this time. I hope there won't be worry and concern over what good Newport is in times like these, because that would miss the point and cause us to do things we really shouldn't. A flower makes it in this world just because it is a flower; it suffers no ontological insecurity about that, it knows being a flower is a perfectly reasonable thing for a flower to be.[60]

By the time Jackson had written those words, the foundation had already called off the festival for that year, due to a combination of forces within and without its control.

While the popularity and influence of rock had obviously loomed over the folk festival for years, including a performance by Big Brother and the Holding Company, led by Janis Joplin, in 1968 ("She wanted to sing with the folk crowd, and she fit right in," Wein says),[61] it was at the Newport

Jazz Festival that the genre made its presence most felt. In 1969, Wein's desire to be a part of the rock-festival craze that he himself had indirectly helped create led him to book the Mothers of Invention, John Mayall's Bluesbreakers and Sly and the Family Stone, among other rock acts, for the jazz festival.

The Newporters feared the rock crowd, and on July 5 a group of fans without tickets to the festival invaded the grounds. They "broke down a 10-foot wooden fence surrounding Festival Field and engaged in a rock-throwing battle with security guards," according to the *New York Times*. "When the main gates were opened, to prevent further assaults on the fence, they swarmed down through the 21,000 spectators, leaping over chairs and railings. As they rushed toward the stage where Sly and the Family Stone, a rock group, was playing, they drove paying customers from their seats, occupied the boxes at the front of the field and filled a pit in front of the bandstand, intended for photographers."[62]

An influx of security guards, a sudden rainstorm and performances by nonrockers the World's Greatest Jazz Band, singer Maxine Sullivan and violinist Stephane Grappelli restored order without any serious injuries. And there were no such incidents at the folk festival two weeks later. Indeed, Judy Collins says no hint of the festival's troubles permeated the atmosphere at Festival Field—above and beyond the usual, anyway. "I think there was always a question of whether we would get that permission to be back in that spot again—would Newport put up with us again? I don't think that was ever off the table; that was always a struggle."[63]

Peter Davis, the Academy Award–winning director of the pioneering Vietnam War documentary *Hearts and Minds*, was filming at the Newport Folk Festival on the penultimate day—July 20, 1969, the day on which Neil Armstrong became the first man to set foot on the moon. Davis and his crew were part of a sprawling project by CBS News to document what people all over America were doing on the historic day, and he remembers his day at Newport as "a loving, tender experience," albeit with a minority of fans demurring when news of the moon landing was announced from the stage (during James Taylor's set, costing him a half hour that he recouped in a surprise appearance at Newport in 2015): under the applause, "there were hoots—I wouldn't call it boos, but kind of hoots—that this isn't what we should be doing now. We should be making sure that everybody in the United States has food and shelter and that kind of thing."[64] (Jim Rooney, who says he announced the landing from the stage, writes that "the audi-ence response was basically, 'Get on with the music!'")[65]

Even with a performance reuniting the Everly Brothers with their father Ike, as well as a young-performers show and impromptu Sunday-night set by a then-unknown Kris Kristofferson, the air had gone out of the sails. "There was an awful lot of money kicking around in 1965," Dave Van Ronk later wrote. "My God, it was the Big Rock Candy Mountain. . . . By 1969 the cold snap had set in."[66] *Rolling Stone* observed, "In an attempt to stay away from the star system, the festival lacked excitement and direction."[67]

The troubles from the jazz festival's violence had already taken a toll —the city required a chain-link fence around Festival Field and an even larger police presence at a festival that some critics were already referring to as "an armed camp."[68] The total cost was $24,000. Rooney remembers that "they also insisted that every off-duty policeman in the state of Rhode Island was going to be on duty that weekend, and we would be paying the overtime."[69] For a festival that had already allowed such indulgences as spending $2,000 to bring in the pioneering Congolese guitarist Jean-Bosco Mwende, it was a crippling blow.

The money was running out, and so was the goodwill. "In the last two or three years, you could feel everything slipping," Wein remembers.[70]

In March 1970, Wein and the board told the *New York Times* that they were looking to move both festivals out of Newport, looking for a perma-nent location where attendees could camp, as was becoming the fashion at big multiday rock shows. Most city officials, United Press International reported, "expressed regret, but agreed that Newport did not have the room to handle the crowds."[71]

But when no new site was forthcoming, they announced in May 1970 that there would be no festival that year. Bob Jones remembers an even simpler reason for canceling: "They thought the festival wasn't strong enough to hold its own and pay its expenses."[72]

Wein said at the time that the next festival would be held "in Newport or not at all." He also said that the 1971 festival would demonstrate that "folk music could communicate to youth in the same way rock music has."[73]

It seemed a forlorn hope—in fact folk music had communicated to young people before rock music had even begun in earnest, and it had been overtaken. But as it worked out, suddenly, in similar circumstances to the previous decade, they were denied the chance.

A 1971 Newport Folk Festival was set for July 16–18, with artists including Baez, Collins, Arlo Guthrie, Mimi Fariña, Tom Rush, Tom Paxton and more. But at the jazz festival held two weeks before, the violence that had bubbled up at previous festivals boiled over.

The more anarchic fans—Wein still refers to them today as "the 'music should be free' crowd,"[74] with a contempt that bespeaks his history in the world of jazz, where performers do not believe music should be free and have no compunction about saying so—were going to rock festivals rather than jazz festivals. But there were no major rock festivals in the United States in the summer of 1971, so the Newport Jazz Festival would have to do. On July 3, swarms of young people without tickets sat on a hill overlooking Festival Field, menacing the musical goings-on for the entire day. As Dionne Warwick sang "What the World Needs Now" at around 10 p.m., they broke through the security fencing surrounding the field and rushed the stage, destroying equipment and chanting and playing drums on and in front of the stage.

Wein told the *New York Times* the next day, "These are the same kids who invaded the festival in 1969. . . . Only they're two years deader, two more years into [being] walking zombies," he said. "They were freaked out on acid. There were hundreds involved in the violence, supported by thousands. . . . They had no concern for jazz, no concern for the festival. They are America's disgrace."[75]

Forty years later, not only can George Wein still remember the details, but he gets impassioned about them. Calling it "a double cross," Wein says, "that never should have happened. I paid the City Council and the police to keep the kids who were coming into town off the hill." Employees came to his office, he remembers, and told him, "They're sending people right to the hill. But that's old news," he says, after bringing it up again. "I don't need to bring that up again."[76]

That ended performances for the night, and the rest of the festival was canceled by Mayor B. Cowles Mallory. Wein broke it to the crowd of 18,000 and added that he agreed with the decision, "even though I was sick about it."[77]

Going back to 1960, all the trouble at Newport festivals had happened in conjunction with the jazz festival, and the papers dutifully noted that the fate of the folk festival, coming up in two weeks, was up in the air. The

City Council scheduled a vote on whether to revoke the permit for the Newport Folk Festival.

Though Councilman William F. Benish asked rhetorically whether the city would "sit back and let a minority group of nuts destroy our festival and our heritage,"[78] Wein's remarks to the council a few days before the vote seemed to indicate an air of resignation and revenge:

> I want to thank the people of Newport for the tremendous expressions of sympathy that have been extended to me and my wife about the misfortune of last weekend. . . .
>
> All of this is wonderful, but unfortunately it means very little. Because I wonder if anybody really meant it. You see, an attitude has continually permeated the relationship between the city and the festivals—the attitude that the festivals are a business that belongs to George Wein and George Wein must pay for everything in relationship to the festivals. . . .
>
> Cities help build stadiums for football and baseball teams. Industry is continually given tax advantages as inducement for moving into communities. Newport has never even authorized a few hundred dollars to put a banner across Broadway to say "Welcome Newport Jazz Festival." . . .
>
> If the city has a direct involvement, the police wouldn't have the excuse that what happened last weekend was because I didn't want to pay for enough police. . . . If the city had a financial and moral interest in the festival the city manager and the chief of police wouldn't have been so quick to cancel the Sunday and Monday concerts. . . .
>
> Several alternative steps could have been taken. But nobody consulted me. Nobody called the councilmen for an emergency meeting. No one thought of the thousands of dollars the hotels and restaurants would lose. Least of all none of the powers that were in control cared about the festival. The only consideration was get the trouble over, let the jerks tear the park apart, and then kick them out and end it all.[79]

Wein went on to say that the board still wanted to have a festival even though, by his calculations, they would lose less money with a cancellation, and he concluded by appealing to the council's sense of fair play.

> At this writing, the city council of Newport has a glorious opportunity—an opportunity to prove that a violence-prone minority in this country cannot

tell an American city that it must give up something that means so much to so many people in the community.

Now is the time to prove that all these years Newport has not just been paying lip service to the festivals.

It is my feeling that if you as a council revoke the license for the Folk Festival, then you are bowing to the elements in our society that all of us abhor.[80]

The council voted to revoke the festival's license. The vote was 5 to 2.

We respect the mistakes we made back then. We weren't even conscious we were making them.

GEORGE WEIN, 1998[1]

IT WAS A SWEET TOWN
WHEN I FIRST CAME HERE

On August 7, 2010, the music at Newport was interrupted when four Newport police officers and the mayor took to the stage at Fort Adams. It wasn't the first time the authorities had visited the folk and jazz festivals, but this time was very different: Mayor Jeanne Napolitano took the stage at the CareFusion Newport Jazz Festival to present a proclamation to George Wein and to declare the day George Wein Day in the City of Newport. She was accompanied by police officers Bob Murphy, Jack Taylor, William "Cub" Costello and Charlie Oxx, long since retired, who were on stage as part of a half-centennial commemoration of the riots that shut down both Newport festivals after their 1960 incarnations.

During the presentation, Napolitano said that Wein "has brought more joy and sunshine to the citizens and visitors of Newport than anyone else."

"I can't say how much it means to me," Wein said, accepting the proclamation, but true to form he insisted on referring to the events of 1960 as "incidents referred to as riots. From where I was, I saw no riots; we were playing music in the park." Nevertheless, Police Chief Michael McKenna joined in the general water-under-the-bridge sentiment, saying, "We hope the festival stays another 50 years."[2]

The feelings between the city and the festival organizers were not always so warm.

The very act of creating the Newport Folk Festival's older brother, the jazz festival, was intended as something of a stick in the eye to Newport as it then stood.

Newport is often referred to as the City by the Sea, and along with the folk and jazz festivals its main claims to world fame include the presence of the U.S. Navy and the mansions that line Bellevue Avenue and Ocean Drive. Beginning in the late 1800s, the barons of the Gilded Age began building such summer "cottages" with vistas of the sea. Coal tycoons, China traders and others commissioned grand buildings such as Rosecliff, the Elms and Kingscote. Perhaps most notable of all was the Breakers, owned by the railroad magnate Cornelius Vanderbilt.

That age didn't last long: taxes and, most importantly, the Great Depression forced the original families out of their grand houses. Starting in 1945, the Preservation Society of Newport County bought many of them and began restoring them. They're tourist attractions now, but the influence of that kind of opulence, as well as Newport's status as a center of society, continue to drive much of the city's self-image and priorities.

Elaine and Louis Lorillard, who originally approached Wein with the idea of a jazz festival in Newport, were a bit different from the typical society couple. Patrick O'Higgins, the publicity man in the early days of the Newport Jazz Festival, has said that Elaine Lorillard "wasn't liked by most of the ladies because they feared her, or they feared that she was cleverer or more amusing or whatever." Of the jazz festival, he said, "In a way I think that it was Elaine's revenge on Newport. . . . I've been on Bailey's Beach and seen ladies suddenly disappear into a cabana so they wouldn't have to say hello to her."[3]

The Lorillards were also having their problems—as Wein has said, Elaine sued Louis for divorce three times before they made it official in 1962—which made an impact on both festivals over the years. "I never knew whether Louis or Elaine were remotely interested in it," said John Maxon, the former director of the Rhode Island School of Design who first proposed the jazz festival, "or whether it was a permutation of their relationship. Elaine had her motivations, and I'm sure that Louis had his."[4]

Elaine Lorillard said in 2004 that "Cleveland Amory wrote, 'The grass is growing on Bellevue Avenue.' That's how dark and dull it was here in the summer."[5]

Even she, however, felt by 1960 that the jazz festival had become too big for its own good. Sacked by the board the previous year, she organized her own festival that year along with the critic Nat Hentoff and the bassist Charles Mingus across town from the Newport Jazz Festival. Known as the Rebel Festival, it completed its full program, even after the riots in town brought down Wein's production.

Elaine Lorillard envisioned the jazz festivals as diversions for the Newport townspeople and nothing more: "My husband and I had a different vision. . . . We wanted it to be local, and Rhode Island, and small and very tasteful."[6]

Newport (city) was home to 47,049 people as of the 1960 Census, but its population fell to 34,562 by 1970. It's home to the nation's oldest tavern —the White Horse Tavern, established in 1673—and the oldest men's club, the Newport Reading Room, established in 1852. An influx of 20,000 or so young people crazy to hear jazz and folk music was a lot for the city to handle in the early days.

And by their own admission, the organizers didn't spend a lot of time pondering what a strain the festivals put on the city at that time. Looking back in 1998, Wein told the *Providence Journal*'s Andy Smith, "We respect the mistakes we made back then." Later, he singled out Mayor Denny Sullivan as someone who "represented a lot of people who hated the festivals. But they were right. . . . You can't take a town like Newport and inundate them with 20,000 people like we used to do."[7] Making matters worse, he adds, after the shows let out around midnight in the center of town, the city's nightclubs would stay open late to make money from the crush of people looking for more music, more to drink, or both.

The 1964 festival had been the biggest yet, with 74,000 people attending the festival and 15,000 at the closing concert in Freebody Park. As it turned out, that was too big for Newport. The businessmen of the city, particularly the hotel, restaurant and bar operators, loved the estimated $1 million of business the jazz and folk festivals brought in, and the festivals had been peaceful. But young people were sleeping on beaches, on lawns and in parks; they rang residents' doorbells to ask for a spot on the porch to sleep or to use their bathrooms. Traffic was beginning to clog the streets. Residents' complaints began to rain on City Hall almost as soon as the festival ended.

Scarcely two weeks later, the Newport City Council voted unanimously to prohibit the use of Freebody Park for future festivals. In December, an agreement was reached: Wein would lease the thirty-five-acre site in the north end of the city off Connell Highway, a half mile from the dump and across from the city's U.S. Navy base. Wein's plan for a permanent performing arts center in Middletown was voted down by that town's council after a lobbying effort by certain elements of the town's Catholic clergy, but the Connell Highway site, named Festival Field, proved suitable. After throwing together a makeshift facility for the 1965 shows, Festival Productions built a permanent venue, with a shell and other structures, the next year.

The process was a learning experience for Wein: "I began to realize that when you go into the city with the intention of attracting thousands of people, you need to know what sort of accommodations are available. You must examine traffic and parking issues and the general effect this influx will have on the city. . . . [Back then] we felt that, whatever happened, we were right. How could we be wrong, when we were presenting marvelous music?"[8]

Many people thought the festival producers were, in fact, wrong. "There are people [in Newport] who don't even speak to me now," Lorillard said in 2004 about the explosion in the size of both festivals. "They hated it. I don't blame them, because it was a sweet town when I first came here after the war."[9]

One history of the city basically agrees with Lorillard, at least about the festivals of the 1960s:

> To the annoyance and concern of city officials the Jazz Festival added rock music to its repertoire, while Folk Festival attendees wore the questionable attire of the young at such gatherings everywhere in those hippie days and slept outside in parks and on the beaches. Observers were completely delighted, however, with the newly-founded Newport Music Festival under director Glen Sauls, a rich offering of classical chamber works by notable artists who performed in Bellevue Avenue mansions and the properties of the Preservation Society.[10]

Not everyone in town felt that way. Lifelong Newporter Tom Perrotti remembers the festivals as "like the circus came to town. . . . I really had no idea about any of this stuff; it just came to us, and we discovered it."[11] In a separate conversation, his childhood friend and erstwhile bandmate Peter Lance says that "every summer was an amazing time for me. . . . It was like being at the Cavern in Liverpool and hearing the Beatles."[12]

While many in the city had problems with the presence of the two festivals, in the 1960s the younger set tended to greet the annual visits with great excitement. Outside of major urban centers, the kind of changes generally thought of as "the '60s" happened in little moments here and there, and for Perrotti and Lance, the annual visits of the festivals to their hometown provided their taste of the decade's currents.

Perrotti's father, Gene, is a longtime member of the local Kiwanis Club, which ran the concession stands at the folk and jazz festivals throughout the 1960s. Gene Perrotti told radio journalist Rhonda Miller that "they didn't have the money like the people at the jazz festival. But it was a nice festival; I think we had less problems with the folk festival."[13]

Thanks to his father's avocation, Tom Perrotti sometimes got an up-close look at some of the performers. His greatest memory involves the combination of the folk festival and his father's food. "My father handed me a plate to bring over to this guy, who turned out to be Mississippi John Hurt. I had no clue who he was, but I'll never forget the huge smile on this guy's face. Because I left there and I said, 'Wow, he's an unusual-looking guy.' I didn't take to the blues early on when I was at the festivals, but I just remember his huge, grateful smile when I handed him the food."[14]

While the town may have had a problem with rough sleepers, Tom Perrotti didn't: "If you were at the top of Memorial Boulevard, looking down on First Beach, you saw a quilt. You didn't see any sand—just a quilt of blankets. It was a beautiful image."

The younger Perrotti calls the folk festival "the best education I ever had," and the music was only part of it: reading the literature from the Congress of Racial Equality and the Student Nonviolent Coordinating Committee gave him an inkling of some of the conflicts going on outside the city. Later in the decade, the representation of the antiwar movement in music and at the tables changed his mind as well: in seventh grade, he had written in an autobiography school assignment that he wanted to be a Navy chaplain. "Listening to Phil Ochs," he says now, "kind of cured me of that." Lance agrees, saying "I was just riveted" by Ochs, beginning at a workshop in 1965. "He was pure to the form of topical songwriting," especially after Dylan had moved on to electric music with kaleidoscopic lyrics. Both friends took the example of Ochs and of the glimpse into another world that the festivals provided, in different directions through life.

Perrotti "picked up a guitar in high school, probably because of the folk festival," and he has been in the world of music ever since—and not only on the stage. He remembers sitting at Festival Field, waiting what he considered an intolerably long time for the next act to start, "thinking, 'I could do this better.' I'm being cocky here, because George Wein is one of my heroes." But it left a mark: Perrotti cofounded and since 1993 has run Common Fence Music, a folk music coffeehouse and arts program in Portsmouth, Rhode Island, whose mission statement says it "draws its inspiration from the early days of the Newport Folk & Jazz Festivals where the public encountered musicians both in concerts and in workshops; and human expression, not financial profit, was the bottom line." Perrotti books the kind of music that fits his definition of folk—which sounds a lot like the Newport definition: "The music's been morphing for a while, but it's still connected through roots, and it's connected through sensitive, thoughtful singer-songwriting."

Lance went into journalism, where he won an award for exposing the slums that existed in the supposedly gleaming city, and he continues to this day with books such as *Deal with the Devil: The FBI's Secret Thirty-Year Relationship with a Mafia Killer*, all the while, he says, "still with that ethos from the '60s."

He says that the festivals had a similar effect on the city: "There was clearly racism in Newport. There was de facto segregation . . . there was slum housing. So Newport, even though it was this jewel of a resort town, the City by the Sea, also reflected many of the same social problems that America was affected by." Both festivals "had a really important role in helping Newport get though the '60s and become a more tolerant, modern city."

Perrotti isn't so sure. He says that the international reputation of Newport as a mecca for music doesn't carry much weight with the powers that be. "People come to Newport thinking that we support the arts . . . that's not ever been the case. . . . There's a certain gallery presence in town, because the wealthy folk can afford paintings and that kind of thing, but . . . the mansions on Bellevue Avenue still kind of dominate and kind of repress any other kind of true artistic expression in this town."

If Newporters had a variety of attitudes toward the festivals, the organizers and fans responded in kind. In the *Broadside* of September 1966, Mary Walling wrote an ode to the city residents who charged attendees to sleep in their spare rooms and on their porches, entitled "Just Call Me 'Ma'" and sung to the tune of "Only a Hobo." The chorus went in part,

> The Folk Music Festival's
> Come round again
> So hustle those folkniks
> Yes, hustle them in.

And at around the time the city was deciding that the festivals were more trouble than they were worth, the board of directors had just about had their fill of the city in return.

While the minutes of a festival board meeting in August 1964 note that "the Portsmouth, Middletown and Newport Town Councils are all for the Festivals" and count Nuala Pell, wife of long-standing Rhode Island U.S. Senator Claiborne Pell, as a "friend of the Festival," some of the organizers felt that there wasn't enough support in the city and state. In October 1964, during negotiations for the new site of the folk and jazz festivals, Eliot Hoffman, the lawyer for the Newport Folk Foundation, told Nuala Pell in a letter that the festivals of that summer had generated $28,000 and added,

> I am distressed that not one single citizen of Newport, whether in high or humble position, has defended aloud either the Festivals or George Wein. Not one person has publicly admitted that the Festivals are anything more than a nuisance. . . .
>
> You hope for smaller audiences, for better-behaved visitors, for shorter programs, indeed, for changes in the Festivals themselves—all designed to accommodate Newport's comfort and convenience. Not one of you has announced to Newport that the fault lies not in the Festivals, but in Newport itself, for failing . . . at the very least, to find a way to absorb the Festivals without changing them.
>
> I am sorry if what I say sounds presumptuous, arrogant or severe; but the words of this letter must be said. Make no mistake, Newport needs the Festivals more than the Festivals need Newport.[15]

A week later, the board discussed the possibility of moving the folk festival out of Newport, "with no real conclusion. It was felt that the same possible objections would exist anywhere, though the political climate could be more favorable."[16]

By the end of 1969, when the festival's survival was in doubt, not least because the violence at that summer's jazz festival led the City Council to require the $24,000 fence around Festival Field as well as increased police overtime, Oscar Brand, one of the MCs for the first-ever folk festival, wrote to the board, "Let's get the hell out of Newport. It's a center of snobbery, and one of the obscene capitols of the establishment. It is a monument to the U.S. Navy and the beautiful people, and they are the enemy. They hate us. They surround us with police and they despise our friends. At their best they are condescending. At their worst they are a police state and they suffocate us."[17]

A week later, Wein responded, "as to the matter of moving the Folk Festival from Newport: In theory, I am in agreement. The costs at Newport with police, rent to Mr. Bucolo, etc. have become too high. For example, the taxes alone on the buildings have tripled in four years."[18] The board discussed possibilities including Brown Stadium, in Providence; the Yale Bowl, in New Haven, Connecticut; and the Powder Hill ski area, between New Haven and Hartford, but found problems with each.

By December of that year, it was generally agreed that the festival was done with Newport, although to announce it immediately would put Wein in a fix, as he still had to run the jazz festival there. The minutes read that Wein had to "live with Newport for his jazz festival this year and [such a caustic announcement] could just as well be made after George is finished with them in July." These were not unanimously held opinions —Ralph Rinzler held productive meetings with city officials in the fall of 1970. But it was academic: the jazz festival violence of 1971 ended both festivals' relationship with Newport.

Right around that time, however, Newport was changing. One of the city's most distinguishing features was born, while another disappeared.

An ambitious program of urban renewal (Elaine Lorillard would call it destruction) began in the mid-1960s, tearing down and rebuilding the city's downtown, building new businesses and especially hotels, with an eye toward making Newport, formerly a navy bastion, fishing port and rich person's playground, into a tourist destination.

The Newport Bay Bridge (now known as the Pell Bridge) began construction in 1965 and was completed in 1969. When finished, it cut the driving time from points south of the city by about an hour, making access to Newport from New York and other major cities much easier. That made a Newport focus on tourism more possible. Not long after, such a focus became necessary, as the navy's presence in Newport, which reached 162,000 people at its height in 1944, was suddenly decimated.

In July 1973, after a *Shore Establishment Realignment* study, the Supply Center and the entire Cruiser Destroyer Force, Atlantic, was moved from the Newport base. Other operations were consolidated. The Quonset Point Naval Air Station, across Narragansett Bay in North Kingstown, was shut down as well.

There still was a large navy presence in Newport—there still is. But 17,000 military personnel, plus their families, and about 6,000 civilian workers left the city. In total, an estimated 38,000 jobs were lost—navy civilian jobs or services dependent on the navy. Unemployment rose to 10 percent. The state lost between $14 million and $16 million in income taxes. State cash flow was down an estimated $300 million; retail sales lost more than $200 million. For the first time, Rhode Island's population dropped. The population of Middletown, which borders on Newport, plunged 41 percent.[19] Meanwhile, the new hotels that had sprung up along the waterfront as part of the urban renewal of the mid- and late 1960s hadn't drawn enough tourists to fulfill predictions; some had already gone bankrupt. (While some maintain that the removal of the fleet was motivated by President Nixon's desire for revenge against New England—Rhode Island had only narrowly gone for him in the 1972 election, and Massachusetts, which also lost a navy base, was the only state to give its Electoral College votes to George McGovern—the closure had been in the making for some time. Years previously, John Chafee, a former U.S. senator and secretary of the navy and future governor of Rhode Island, had urged the region to look to tourism as its economic future.)

Richard Sardella, a former mayor and city councilor of Newport who first bought a house in the city in the early '70s, says that the city "had to come up with some idea to really focus on what a lot of people knew about Newport but kind of kept to themselves—that it was a great place to visit and live in the summertime. . . . There wasn't anything to fill that gap left by the festivals not being in town."[20]

New ideas were floated. In 1973, Newporters were pitched a jai alai fronton (an arena for the game jai alai, which is played with a ball and a long, curved wicker basket attached to the wrist) as the solution to their problems. It opened in 1975 and survived for some years but never delivered on its promise. That same year, developers proposed opening casinos in some of the city's grand mansions. After several years of debate, including strong opposition from the Catholic Church, the idea was voted down in 1979. Some ideas took hold, however: the America's Cup races drew well—as long as the Americans were winning—and the Tall Ships festival, pegged to the U.S. bicentennial in July 1976, brought 400,000 visitors to Newport.

And in 1979, a jazz festival was held in Cardines Field. While Wein's organization wasn't involved and the event was "plagued by poor weather, electrical failure and long waits," the most influential factor evidently was "the peaceful behavior of the crowds."[21]

So by the early 1980s, Newport was more than ready to host big annual events. And Wein and the rest of Festival Productions were ready to return.

This music is timeless.
We're here; they're there.
What's different about it?
BILL MORRISSEY[1]

HE WAS AMAZED AND I WAS AMAZED

By 1985, the definition of folk music had broadened and its place in cultural life had changed. The singers and songwriters who took their cue from Bob Dylan, Joan Baez and the rest of what Joe Boyd had termed the Cambridge school were firmly and uncontroversially included under the umbrella of folk. And the music itself was no longer a world-changing mass communication among American youth—if they sought an alternative to the musical tedium and implicit conservatism of the mass airwaves, they found it in indie rock (then known as college rock), punk rock and hip-hop. Instead, folk had become a durable niche entertainment, intended for the same generation that had always listened—who still carried the discontent with mainstream society that Pete Seeger and Ralph Rinzler had spoken about and that Murray Lerner had seen through his lens, whose concerns had changed as they had aged and who wanted music that kept up with them. The Newport Folk Festival returned to a different atmosphere, and it's not surprising that the programming changed, George Wein's native guide changed, and the festival's reason for being changed.

Other changes were in store, some brought about by the necessities of the new landscape and some by the simple passage of time. The nonprofit ideal went by the wayside; the once-feared businessmen were welcomed as indispensable collaborators, and even as the artistic criteria that defined Newport became more fluid than ever, the perception of the fabled history of the festival slowly changed from albatross to selling point. This all made it possible for the festival to continue for two decades, but collisions were inevitable.

After the violence of 1971, it didn't take long for the Newport Jazz Festival to find a new home. New York is one of the meccas of jazz, and George Wein had based his Festival Productions operations there for years, so it wasn't a huge surprise that the Newport Jazz Festival–New York went off virtually on schedule in 1972.

The folk festival was another matter. Other folk festivals, such as the Philadelphia and Mariposa Folk Festivals, continued, but in terms of the centrality and importance that was part of the definition of Newport, Wein says, "We were dead. . . . Rock smothered the contemporary folk scene."[2]

The debts had reached about $30,000 (about $168,000 in today's dollars), and an attempt at producing a tour of what the organizers hoped would constitute miniature Newport Folk Festivals was unsuccessful—it took about two years just to pay off the fees owed to the tour's advance-publicity man.[3] In July 1972, a pair of benefit concerts at Carnegie Hall featuring Arlo Guthrie, James Taylor, Pete Seeger, Mimi Fariña, Richie Havens and others paid off some of the foundation's debts.

Oscar Brand told the *New York Times* at the time, "We're a proud people. We could have declared bankruptcy after the festival was canceled . . . but that would have meant paying back a penny on a dollar, and that isn't the way we do things."[4] And while the Newport Folk Foundation had given out thousands of dollars over the years, it had never seriously pursued any support from foundations itself, despite a recommendation to that effect from the Holtzman-Rooney-Leventhal ad-hoc committee in 1967. Wein explains now that times were very different, with the big money concentrated in fewer hands: "You see all these computer whizzes—if they come up with an idea, they have no problem getting the money for it. Back then it wasn't like that." It also just wasn't in his nature at the time, he says. "If I couldn't make money, why ask people to give me money? And if I could make money, why did I need people to give me money?"[5]

By this point, the festival's image didn't help. Brand told the *Times* that the association of the Newport name with violence contributed mightily to the failure of the college tour, even though the folk festival itself had never seen any such trouble.

In 1979, the legendary New England concert promoter Frank J. Russo tried to schedule a festival for Labor Day weekend in Newport with performers including Tom Rush, Buffy Sainte-Marie, Ramblin' Jack Elliott, Bob Gibson, John Hammond, and Mary Travers and Peter Yarrow. But Russo pulled the plug in mid-August after only 780 of the 25,000 tickets had been sold. He later told the *Washington Post*, "There has been more interest in the cancellation than in the event itself." He saw a permanent shift in musical tastes: "The kids who were in their early 20s 10 years ago now have families—responsibilities, mortgages, car payments. The adult entertainment [*sic*] dollar is really tight now, and they just can't afford it. The 18-year-olds today were under 10 then. They never heard of Muddy Waters."[6] But the groundwork for a new Newport Folk Festival began to be laid not long after.

In 1981, after a series of moves that reflected a mix of sentiment and business sense, George Wein revived the Newport Jazz Festival. A quirk of nomenclature made it possible—Wein's jazz festival in New York had picked up a corporate sponsor in KOOL cigarettes (which had been sponsoring jazz festivals run by Wein's Festival Productions since 1975), resulting in two years of the KOOL Newport Jazz Festival–New York. After that, though, Brown and Williamson, KOOL's parent corporation, decided they didn't want the name of a competitor (Newport cigarettes) in the name of their festival.

They offered Wein $1.3 million to give up the Newport name. Wein debated for a while before taking it, and once he did, he writes, the move "left an uneasy feeling in the pit of my stomach. . . . What could I do to preserve the memory of the old Newport Jazz Festival? The obvious answer: go back to Newport."[7] Wein said in 2004 that he was partly motivated by a desire to keep someone else from "grabbing the name," but added that "Newport is a destination. It's an important name in American folklore, and American history. . . . They say you can't go home again, but I decided that I was going to go home again anyway."[8]

The changes that had happened in Newport since 1971 were evident: "When I left Newport, nobody wanted me back there," Wein remembers. "And when I came back, everyone wanted me back there."[9]

There were changes in the relationship between the festival and the city, though. The two most obvious ones were the location and the hours. No longer would the festival take over the center of Newport until the wee hours of the morning; the festivals would be held at Fort Adams, a massive

Revolutionary War–era fort (Fort Ticonderoga, Fort McHenry and Fort Sumter can all fit inside it) on a peninsula overlooking Narragansett Bay. And the shows had to end by 7 p.m.—well before sundown in a New England summer.

But music was back in Newport, and it wasn't long before thoughts of a revived folk festival began to kindle.

"Ye gods, we're having another folk music scare!" Dave Van Ronk exclaimed to the *Boston Globe*'s Jeff McLaughlin in early 1985. "Serves us right."[10]

Folk music—of any stripe—was no longer the biggest-selling music in the world, but despite Russo's protestations, the generation that had grown up with Bob Dylan and his singer-songwriter descendents was still not only alive but had more money to spend on concert tickets than they used to. Artists such as James Taylor, Judy Collins and Joan Baez were past their record-selling primes but far from finished as artists or concert draws. And in a 1980s pop-musical landscape that got louder and more electronic, their fans were looking for an alternative more in line with the tastes they'd been developing for years.

And they found it. Not only were the now old guard still in force, but a new generation of singer-songwriters had come up in their place. Artists such as Suzanne Vega, Greg Brown, Michelle Shocked and more began to make an artistic impression—and sell tickets. Warner Communications re-released the Elektra Records folk and blues archives of the '60s. And in Boston, a folk veteran was showing that the concert audience was still there.

Tom Rush had been a member of Cambridge's Club 47 scene, an influential performer with classics such as "No Regrets" and "The Circle Game," the latter coming from a 1965 album of the same name that Rolling Stone said kicked off the singer-songwriter era. His covers of songs by Joni Mitchell, Jackson Browne and James Taylor gave them invaluable exposure in their early years.[11]

But he didn't release a studio album between 1974's *Ladies Love Outlaws* and 1984's *Late Night Radio*. And while some of his hiatus was on purpose, Rush says he and his fellow singer-songwriters couldn't get any traction in the record industry. "They'd gone off pursuing an age group instead of a group of people," he remembers. "They decided their market was fourteen- to twenty-two-year-olds."[12]

One of Rush's solutions had been to continue playing live, and he'd made an annual tradition of taking over a Boston club at some point between Christmas and New Year's and putting on a show featuring himself and a rotating cast of friends. The series began at the Jazz Workshop, moved to Paul's Mall, and eventually was held at the Paradise, in Boston's theatre district.

As the decade turned, Rush says, he had to face some facts: his first year at the Paradise, he put on four shows in two nights at the 400-capacity club and sold them all out; in 1980, he played two shows in two nights, and neither sold out. But thanks to an unlikely source, Rush got an idea. Earlier that year, he says, a University of New Hampshire business major contacted him, wanting to work with Rush as part of the student's thesis. Part of the plan, the student said, required doing some market research. Rush says, "I didn't even know what he was talking about, but I said, 'Sure; go ahead.' And we passed out a questionnaire to the folks at the Paradise, and they were all out there at [intermission]—it looked like an exam room, bless their hearts."

One of the things he learned about his audience from the surveys was that "these were all professional people—they were all doctors, lawyers, dentists, accountants. . . . It occurred to me that these are not folks who would like to stand in line and get their hands stamped. They were also people who had cars; there's no parking near the Paradise," which he says was his venue of choice more out of habit than anything else: "It's the kind of place you played because that's the kind of place you played five years before and ten years before."

So in the face of declining audiences, Rush didn't go smaller; he went bigger, booking his Christmas 1981 shows at Boston's Symphony Hall, with a capacity of 2,365 and the panache of a high-toned venue. He'd been trying to book it for several years, saying "everybody except me knows that nobody goes out between Christmas and New Year's," but finally the management relented.

The bill followed the same formula as previous years—Rush and a few friends, this time celebrating Rush's twenty-five years of performing. "I don't think there were any big names," he remembers, yet even at a ticket price that was double the previous year's, "we sold it out, way in advance. And everybody was stunned by this, including myself. I had a hunch it would do well—I didn't think it would do that well. . . . Everybody in the business said, 'Wait a minute; there is an audience.'"

While chasing the youth-oriented market, Rush says, the music industry let the Baby Boom walk away from them. Instead of saying, "These guys are our best customers; they've got more money than anyone in the world has ever had; let's figure out how to keep them buying records," they just decided that they weren't buying records because they'd gotten older. The mantra was, "They just don't have the disposable income," which is just ludicrous, because these are the people who are spending twenty bucks on a bottle of wine twice a week, and money on books and movies, on televisions and cars—they're disposing of a ton of income. . . . They hadn't all died at the same time; it would've been in the papers.

The Symphony Hall shows only got more successful from there. For 1982, Rush contacted WGBH-TV to see whether the public television giant would be interested in broadcasting the show locally; they countered with an offer to take it nationwide. The bill included Rush, David Bromberg and Buskin & Batteau and was televised in 1983. "It was a big deal, career-wise," Rush says, "because it put me in front of an audience that was so hard to reach through the conventional ways."

It didn't stop there—the two 1983 Christmas shows were broadcast live on NPR. And at the end of 1984, a Club 47 reunion show sold out three shows at Symphony Hall. "Richie Havens and Joan Baez signed on," Rush remembers, "but they signed on after most of the tickets were gone. So it was just the event itself, and I guess the name Club 47—we had a lot of the old guard. . . . And [Bob] Jones, and a lot of people, took note of this."

Indeed, Jones told Carolyn Wyman of the *Christian Science Monitor* that Rush's Symphony Hall shows, the revival of *Sing Out!* from near-bankrupt, occasional newsletter status to regular publication, the popularity of the folk music–laden *Prairie Home Companion*, and the release of Vega's first album all told him and Wein that it might be possible to put on a festival that would survive commercially.[13]

In September 1984, Wein wrote the following in a letter to Ralph Rinzler:

> Before you read about it in the morning papers, I want all of the concerned Trustees and Directors of the old Newport Folk Foundation to know that I am thinking of holding a Newport Folk Festival, probably on the site that I have been using for the Newport Jazz Festival at Newport, Rhode Island.

I have some general plans and dates in mind, but before I do it, I wanted to (a) tell you about it; (b) ask you for your help and approval. I don't know whether a folk festival can make any money at this time, but I am thinking about some kind of formula which would make a contribution out of profits to the Newport Folk Foundation or some other deserving organization that could do some good deeds for the folk world. Please let me know how you feel about this and whether you would encourage me to proceed.[14]

Jones says that the State of Rhode Island was interested in doing more events at Fort Adams to help make money for the trust that took care of the buildings and land. The fort was falling down, Jones says, "and there were goats inside the place—although they kept the grass down, I might add. So they asked, 'Can you put something together?'"[15]

In 1985, Wein made Jones his third native guide to the folk world, giving him the go-ahead to begin booking a Newport Folk Festival for Fort Adams, to be held over the first weekend of August. Jones was living and working in Cincinnati, producing KOOL Jazz Festivals for Festival Productions. He didn't have a lot of time to put a bill together, but it turned out he didn't need much. Word of the possibility of a Newport revival had spread through the folk world, Jones says, and people were already excited. "The festival had not lost any of its cachet among folk people. If you played the Newport Folk Festival, even fifteen years ago, you had a check mark."[16]

Jones assembled a bill heavy on people who were booked to play the 1971 festival but hadn't gotten a chance: Tom Rush, Tom Paxton, Bonnie Raitt, Taj Mahal and more. He also put on old favorites including Joan Baez, Judy Collins and Ramblin' Jack Elliott.

Even with the addition of newer singer-songwriters such as Greg Brown, Bill Morrissey and David Massengill, Jones recalls the 1985 festival as "a very, very safe event."[17] And with good reason, he says—the festival was legendary, but there was no commitment from Wein or anyone else to make it happen for more than one year.

And so it happened that Ramblin' Jack Elliott, after driving across the country for five days to get there (and turning fifty-four en route), stood on an eight-foot-high stage on August 3, 1985, and reinstituted the Newport Folk Festival, playing for twenty minutes to a sun-baking crowd.

After playing, an evidently exhausted Elliott said, "I'm going on the energy of my memories of the past."[18] He wasn't the only one who felt that way. Indeed, much of the weekend was considered a reunion.

Baez's "Please Come to Boston" included the reworked lines, "Please come to Newport in the summer . . . take our old wooden guitars out of their cases and smile and laugh with so many old faces." Bonnie Raitt, who was booked to play in 1971, told the sold-out Sunday crowd, "I am sooo glad to be here. I missed this the first time around. So let's do it every year."[19] Each day ended with a benedictory sing-along of "Amazing Grace," led by Baez on Saturday and Collins on Sunday.

Arlo Guthrie returned to perform "Alice's Restaurant," which he had debuted at Newport in 1967. In the audience, Andy Nelsen, from Troy, New York, said, "All I had to hear was that first strum, and I got goosebumps. I felt like I was 18 again."[20]

He had gone through a lot of changes over the years, and so had a lot of people there. Nelsen, the devotee of Guthrie's shaggy-dog hippie essential, had become a pharmacist. Baez said at the time that the audience was different "in just about every way possible" from the kids who packed into Festival Field in the 1960s; "I just think that the adrenaline is someplace else in the 1980s."[21]

Laura Rifkin came to Newport in 1985 with her husband and two children from Green, Maine, and told the *Detroit Free Press*, "The music's great. It just seems a lot less politically tied in. It's just different; it has evolved."[22] And Michael Bates, of Brockton, Massachusetts, added, "In the old days, a lot of performers would come who were not scheduled. That's not happening as often this weekend. Also, the main concerts were at night, and people got a lot more geared up for them. Sometimes too much. This is a lot quieter, a lot more mellow."[23]

Thomas Quin, of Sharon, Massachusetts, was a vice president of finance for Healthfirst Inc. and said he attended the 1969 festival as a navy officer candidate at the Naval Education and Training Center, in Newport. At the time, he felt that "I was a subject of a lot of the protest songs, yet I was part of the spirit; I felt the same way." In 1985, he said, "They're singing about family and small towns and everyday lives. That's what folk music is about today."[24]

And Louis Ricci III, of the Rhode Island State Marshal's office, standing guard at Fort Adams, said at the time that there was "no trouble whatsoever," adding that "it's been great for me—I really love this kind of music, and I've been able to enjoy it."[25]

Many critics felt that the festival was a succession of musical successes but without a unifying theme or ethos. Wein had acknowledged in June of that year, when the festival was announced, that that might not be possible anymore: "To recapture the concept of four or five days of a festival that takes over a town—that's not going to happen," he said. "We are going to recapture the essence of what happened in the old festival."[26]

As to whether they accomplished that, reaction was mixed. Mike Boehm of the *Providence Journal* expressed his view:

> Musically, the folk festival was clearly a crowd-pleaser, but there was little of the tension and surprise that can make an event tingle.
>
> Known performers did what they are known for, and almost all of what they did came off well. Generally missing was the expectancy that surrounded Newport festivals of the past, when audiences knew they might witness the making of an undiscovered talent's career.
>
> Jones admitted it was "troublesome" that he had to stack the bill with known draws, sacrificing some artistic excitement to improve the festival's economic prospects.[27]

Jon Herman wrote in the *Boston Phoenix*, "With three-quarters of the first day gone, Newport seemed less a festive pilgrimage than a parade of outdoor performances, with short, disconnected (though often outstanding) sets, and promoters nervously rushing from one act to the next. And as the sun crept off to the west, 6000 half-baked sunbathers still lay desperately seeking an anthem, a cause, or a new clutch of icons to sanctify the festival." And while Taj Mahal and Bonnie Raitt gave standout performances, Herman wrote that in the end, "Newport 1985 provided folkie memory with no new milestones, no symbolic enactments that promise the world can be saved with a folksong. Baez tried to bring Bob Gibson along for a guest set, but her former mentor was attending a bar mitzvah. . . . Music may not be in the throes of another folk revival, but there is an unarguably aroused interest in acoustic songwriting and picking. It's too bad that Newport didn't know what to do with it."[28]

Tom Rush essentially agreed at the time, though he was more optimistic: "It will be interesting to see who emerges as the new star—that was what it was all about in the '60s. This year, without a financial cushion, they went for name power. Next year, 1 think you'll see more up-and-coming talent."[29]

Not that such talents were absent: David Massengill, for example, played for the sold-out Sunday crowd of 6,500, and afterward he told the *Boston Globe* that previously the biggest crowd he'd ever played for was 700 to 800 people at the Philadelphia Folk Festival. "This was incredible. 1 thought I'd be nervous, but 1 was just all pumped up. Everyone was so supportive 1 just had to give it everything I've got."[30] After Sunday's "Amazing Grace" finale, according to Boehm, Massengill bounded off the stage and implored Jones, "That's the nicest thing 1 ever saw in my life. Please, do this again." All Jones could offer was, "We'll try," but underneath he was optimistic.[31]

The *Globe* wrote that Jones "would not come out and say there would be another Newport festival next year, but he smiled broadly when he said, 'We'll be making that decision in the next few weeks.'"[32]

Jones remembers that Wein was with a tour in Japan at the time and missed the folk festival. When he told Wein about the success, especially the Sunday sellout, Jones recalls, "he was amazed and 1 was amazed." Jones says that performers were paid their usual market fees, yet the organizers cleared $80,000.[33]

But what of the Newport Folk Foundation? While Wein's Festival Productions had brought off the reincarnation of the festival, the old nonprofit organization still existed. (It still does, Bob Jones says, and acts mostly as a repository for its share of royalties from Murray Lerner's *Festival!* film, usually donating them to Pete Seeger's Clearwater foundation.)

On January 23, 1986, Wein wrote to Ralph Rinzler, "It is time to face the question of whether my organization or the Newport Folk Foundation (or neither of us) presents a Folk Festival at Newport in the summer of 1986. . . . It really does not matter to me which of us puts up the budget, signs the contracts and promotes the Festival. If the Board would rather do it, 1 would give it every encouragement. Otherwise, 1 tentatively plan to promote it through my own organization." A meeting of the board of directors was set for March 3.

No one seems to have kept a record of the meeting—"There wouldn't be," Wein says[34]—but in the end, the foundation decided not to get involved with the reborn festival.

Wein recalls the meeting as involving Pete and Toshi Seeger, Theo Bikel,

Peter Yarrow and others. Jones says that Bernice Reagon (of the Freedom Singers and Sweet Honey in the Rock), Jean Ritchie, the Reverend James Kirkpatrick and possibly Rinzler were also there.

"You could see it wasn't gonna happen," Wein recalls now. "Could not recapture what we had in the '60s. . . . We just decided it couldn't work. Times were different. And that was a conscious decision."[35] He says it wasn't a rancorous meeting—"There just wasn't the same spirit. The old folk world . . . they were a different breed of person. . . . They just couldn't feel it."[36]

Jones remembers it slightly differently. "I won't say it was a stormy meeting," he says now, "but a very tense one."[37] He describes some members of the board as having "strident, politically strong ideas" about how the festival should be run. "It was a very political scene, including Bernice [Reagon] and others . . . who wanted to go in a totally different direction."

Jones remembers that Pete Seeger, in many ways the father of the festival, didn't say much. "Which would lead me to believe he probably [didn't] think it was the best idea to come back in the same way, which maybe the others read into it." At the end of the meeting, Jones says, "They were getting ready to leave, and Toshi Seeger came up to George and myself and said, 'You need to put this festival together. You don't need to get involved in this scene. This is too complicated to bring back under the old system.' And we sort of took her advice, and we never called another meeting. We just kind of went ahead and did it."[38]

So Utopia was over. But there was still a festival to put on. And while some of the people who had put on the old folk festival were dropping away, people from that generation were still coming out to the shows.

The fact that the Newport Folk Festival had become a musical institution was cause for some hand-wringing in the 1960s, but as the 1980s turned into the 1990s, some began to treasure that institutional quality. Catie Curtis was a Brown University student from Maine when she went to her first festival in the late '80s, and she says "that was really how I discovered what I wanted to do with my life—going to the Newport Folk Festival and seeing a whole day of this music."[39] She went on to play the festival several times between 1994 and 2001.

Dar Williams was a regular at the festival from 1994 to 2002 and says now that when she started, "I think we were still lucky enough to be haunted by scenes from the great folk revival. . . . Maybe it's just because of where I was in my career, but there was a sense that there was folk royalty and lineage and history."[40]

But in the first couple of years of the revived folk festival, George Wein and Bob Jones each had a major decision to make—and each got it wrong. The way they recovered from them, however, tells a lot about the history of the festival, the changing definitions of folk music and the changing nature of social action in the late 1980s and 1990s.

Buoyed by the success of the 1985 return to Newport, Jones booked for the 1986 festival a slew of artists that, he says now, reflected the same pattern of mistakes he saw others make in the late 1960s. "I decided, 'Well, this is doing OK.' I came out of that group that was more interested in keeping the traditional things alive, and I went with a much more traditional festival."[41] Shortly before the festival began, he told the *Providence Journal*, "Maybe we made too much of nostalgia last year, but we wanted to reestablish the festival in Newport and now we will find out if we have or not."[42]

The biggest names for 1986 were John Sebastian and Richie Havens, along with Odetta and Tom Rush. The Cajun classicism of the Savoy-Doucet Band, the fierce gospel of Sweet Honey in the Rock and the prodigal fiddle of Alison Krauss were musical highlights as well. When it was over, the *Journal*'s Mike Boehm wrote, "Nostalgic thrills aside, the weekend's best performances were more exciting than anything Baez, Collins and Guthrie were able to achieve when they held the stage a year ago." But the festival drew a total of only about 6,000 people over its two-day span.[43]

The *Journal*'s Barbara Polichetti wrote that it had become an open question "whether folk music '80s-style can still sell in festivals '60s-style."[44] And Wein and Bob Jones told Boehm that "they'd have to rethink the festival's economics and drawing potential before deciding whether to try again next year."[45]

"There has to be a basic public that goes beyond the coffeehouse folk culture," Wein said at the time. "We have no young folk people who are reaching out to a larger audience." He also said that they faced the choice of finding a corporate sponsor, or lowering overhead to "where 3,000 people could allow us to break even. If we can do that, I'd stay with it two or three years until we build our own public."[46]

For the next year, a little of each happened—the State of Rhode Island lowered Newport's operating costs, and the festival found a corporate sponsor. This allowed them in turn to bring back Guthrie, Baez and Collins, as well as the Roches and Richard Thompson, and to spread out artistically with such acts as blues guitarist Johnny Copeland and swamp-pop star Katie Webster.

It was in the late 1980s that the festival began to stretch the definition of folk again. By 1988, Robert Cray and Los Lobos were on the Newport bill; in 1990, Michelle Shocked began her set by herself with an acoustic guitar and by the end was backed by the Bay Area funkateers, Tower of Power. Jones remembers that 1998's "Texas Day" included "people from Texas, and maybe people who had flown over Texas. We were certainly moving, not toward the edge, but to a larger definition of folk," he says. "I felt that if people came out of the folk scene, possibly never actually playing folk music, but they were influenced by it and had a great respect for it . . . I felt they could be presented."[47]

Jones didn't make up these criteria by himself. Obviously, Bob Dylan had transformed before the Newport audience's eyes from the work-shirted singer of coal-mining songs to the spinner of stories about Napoleon in rags with electric hair and "Clarabelle the Clown shirts" (the phrase of Doug Hindley, of Lincoln, Rhode Island, a 1965 audience member).[48] Perhaps even more importantly, it was Mike Seeger in 1965 who wrote to the board of directors that performers should be invited only if they had some "connection in form and content to what we in general call the traditions of folk music."

This sounds like a restriction, and maybe at the time it was, but in fact it blows a loophole into the definition of folk music that the Newport Folk Festival strides through to this day, to the enjoyment of thousands and the consternation of a few (with some overlap between the two groups).

While a corporate sponsor for the folk festival was a helpful development, the choice of Nestlé Foods Corporation was the second misstep of the late '80s.

In 1977, activists including religious, labor and health groups launched an international boycott against the Nestlé Corporation's aggressive marketing of infant formula in developing countries. The arguments were that Nestlé was creating demand for formula among women who could least afford it, and that the nutritional deficiencies of formula were exacerbated in such countries (where families had less access to the clean water required to make formula and faced the temptation to dilute the formula in order to stretch it out).

The 1987 festival was known as the Nestlé Folk Festival–Newport, the city that had given the festival its name and its cache being sent to the back seat. That didn't last long, as George Gritzbach, whose blues band opened the Saturday show, immediately opened the curtain on the omission, saying from the stage, "It's still the Newport Folk Festival, no matter how they sugarcoat it." Cormac McCarthy later called it the "Farfel Folk Festival," after the droopy-eared dog who then served as the company's advertising mascot.

Other artists had varied reactions. The normally politically charged Joan Baez was agnostic on the topic, saying nothing from the stage during a set that included such pop classics as "Let It Be," "The Rose," the synth-laden apartheid protest "Asimbonanga," and songs by Peter Gabriel and Bob Marley, but before her show hoping Nestlé would "follow through on its promises," referring to the agreements the company made in negotiations to end the boycott. Her set wasn't the only one with a pop emphasis. Boehm wrote, "The pop songbook was quoted at least as often as the folk tradition in the first day of the Nestlé Folk Festival. . . . Nobody sang Woody Guthrie songs, but the audience of about 5,000 heard a sampling of Beatles tunes, a helping of doo wop and even a song by the Talking Heads. Pete Seeger's name was invoked twice, but only as a joke by performers who wanted to lead sing-alongs but felt sheepish about such a blatantly folk-purist move."[49]

Maria Muldaur said, "The God I follow says to forgive people, especially if they repent. . . . If they spend some of the money they made off those poor women, I think it's great."

Bluesman Moses Rascoe, a seventy-one-year-old former truck driver, had even less to say: "(Nestlé) must be a good man; I don't even know him." Told it was the sponsor, he replied, "They got me here, makin' me a little money, so it's all right with me."

Still, not everyone was so quick to forgive. Vendor Michael Marsh told Johnson, "In this crowd, Nestlé has a very bad image, so this is their attempt to regain their good name with the folk music crowd."[50] After a tendentious Sunday, however, in which Billy Bragg and Judy Collins each launched into speeches about the problems of Nestlé as a sponsor, the sponsorship ended after the one festival. For 1988, the festival was sponsored by the ice cream giant Ben & Jerry's, and the city name was restored, making it the Ben & Jerry's Newport Folk Festival. This went over much better: Ben Cohen and Jerry Greenfield spoke on the second day of the 1988 festival about their One Percent for Peace program—Wein remarked that it was the first time he'd ever seen a corporate sponsor get a standing ovation.

While Ben & Jerry's was a huge company, it was started by childhood friends Cohen and Greenfield in 1978 after they took a correspondence course in ice cream making and started a shop in a rehabilitated gas station in Burlington, Vermont. By 1985, the Ben & Jerry's Foundation was funding "community-oriented projects," and a few years later they set their sights on Newport.

It was a perfect fit, says Greenfield. "I think Ben & Jerry's coming to the Newport Folk Festival was a breath of fresh air. And for Ben & Jerry's it wasn't just for sponsorship. . . . We were more partners in it, rather than simply writing a check."[51]

By 1992, Rick Carr, senior editor of the International Events Group Sponsorship Report, told the *Providence Journal* that event marketing had grown tenfold, from $300 million to $3 billion, in the previous decade. The number included sponsorship of sporting events and other ventures, but Carr said that musical events were continuing to grow and called the Newport festivals a leader of the trend.

From the company's standpoint, an official said, the sponsorship had unique value: "On a TV commercial, you don't get to meet Ben and Jerry; you don't get a chance to try the ice cream; you don't get a feel for what we're all about. . . . It's hard to say if it affects sales. Certainly if we thought it was hurting sales, we wouldn't do it."[52]

Greenfield and Cohen regularly addressed the audience during the Newport festivals they sponsored (through 1999, when they sold the company to Unilever, starting the festival on a series of sponsors) on subjects such as a proposed reduction in military spending; booths on the grounds sold twenty-five-cent postcards that audience members could use to express an opinion to their elected representatives. And the company helped groups such as Clean Water Action set up shop at Newport to spread the word about their own campaigns.

While the Newport Folk Festival of the 1980s and 1990s lacked the kind of direct action of the civil rights movement of the '60s, those who were there say that's because the political sense of the festival simply changed with the times. Amy Ray, of the Indigo Girls, says,

> I feel like the thing that made it activist to me was that it was Ben and Jerry's festival. To me, that company was an activist company. And [that] made it automatically a community event and put it in that mindset for me. . . . The spirit of the people who went to the festival, and if you walk around out into the audience where the booths are, there was definitely an activist spirit. But it wasn't politicized in the way that it probably was in the '60s. That was the '60s, you know? But whenever we were there, we were talking to people in that way—what recent benefits we'd done, or what organizations we thought were cool. It was like networking—the good side of networking.[53]

Greenfield and others point out that the animating factors of 1960s radicalism (at least among white people)—the Vietnam War and particularly the draft—were no longer, and while many worthwhile causes were important to the lives of the people at the folk festival, nothing really coalesced in the same way. Catie Curtis says, "I didn't think of it as community, as a politically like-minded group. I saw it as entertainment, as music that touched my life. But I didn't think of it as music of a movement of anything like that. . . . You can't have a group sing-along if the energy's not there—if it's not a time in our country when everyone's feeling the same about something, for or against. I just don't think there's consensus about what the message would be."[54]

Dar Williams, who performed at the festival regularly in the 1990s, says that the activism of the '80s and '90s was less dramatic but no less effective: "The '90s was about sort of buddying up with people. It was about the little decisions you were making in your heart every day about confronting authority and personal power, and how you share the power. . . . This was about the drops of water that broke down the wall; this wasn't about the stick of dynamite." The political battles of the '90s, she says, were not only tactically different; they were fought on different ground. "I call the '90s the Gender Decade," Williams says. Referencing her breakthrough hit, "When I Was a Boy," she adds, "It's not about being a lesbian; I never thought I was. I was singing about gender . . . it was saying 'Some women are men, some men are women, some women sleep with men and they're still men themselves inside.'"[55]

Amy Ray, who along with fellow Indigo Girl Emily Saliers has been an out lesbian for most of her career, says on the other hand that she found "less emphasis on gender and sexuality at that festival, because I think there was an assumed acceptance. And we had a very diverse cross-section of people at that show. That's one show where I felt our audience was incredibly diverse. . . . It wasn't a place where I felt like there was an emphasis on that—bad or good. It really felt like it was around music, and the assumption was that you were seen as a musician, and not as specifically gay or African-American or Hispanic or whatever."[56]

Williams, in a separate conversation, thinks Ray is underselling the Indigo Girls' effect, saying that

> preaching to the converted at that time was [the way of] the feminist/ LGBT community. And then these people went off into the world, where the Indigo Girls weren't such a normalized force. They had hits, but that doesn't mean that their lifestyle was normalized. . . .
>
> And I think breaking the back of the gender thing, of fascistic gender roles, especially in men, it's like—wars won't be fought because of that! Letting guys have some shit going on besides just being rigid.[57]

Williams's characterization of the politics of folk music in the 1990s, and her metaphor of drops of water, could apply to the changes in the music itself. The old struggle between what Boyd's New York school (with an emphasis on collective activism typified by crowds of people singing along to a well-known tune) and the Boston school (typified by singer-songwriters expressing their singular viewpoints and poetics and hoping that a satisfying percentage of the crowd could empathize) had, at least at Newport, been decisively won by the latter. Of the communal, everybody-sing-it-now spirit of the 1950s and '60s, Williams says, "I didn't need that by the '90s. I was used to the paradox that you played music with all these people, you really appreciated them; you really loved them, and what you really talked about were airports. And you played your songs for each other."[58]

For Williams that was an artistic and professional blessing, but she says the backlash from older performers and observers was real.

> It must have been a real letdown to these folks to see all these little college-educated songwriters going off and whittling these fancy little ornate

songs, and coming in to say "I'm going to perform this all by myself." They must have experienced that as a real blow. And that's absolutely what I was. . . .

They were all reminiscing, and all talking about Dave Van Ronk. They all had these stories about each other, and they had this collective force of memory and community. And I really respected that. And I totally understand what the perception of the '90s must have been. And I'm in the crosshairs.[59]

Just as the only truly new music is made when new instruments are invented, the changing focus of the Newport Folk Festival—from a nonprofit's mission to present an accurate representation of the far-flung regional American music to a popular if diverse group of singer-songwriters with traditional musicians sprinkled in to taste—required new people, who had been in the field from the beginning, to take charge. And if Bob Jones had become George Wein's native guide to the folk world, Jones himself found someone who knew the territory—who was able to identify what Wein had called "young folk people who are reaching out to a larger audience" —and he didn't have to look far.

Bob and Marguerite Jones's daughter Nalini went to the 1981 Newport Jazz Festival as a ten-year-old with her brother and sister and remembers, "I guess what was most compelling to us was the fort, because . . . it looked incredibly dangerous in ways that appealed to us."[60] As for the music, she found the jazz of Newport and other Festival Productions efforts sometimes abstruse, even if compelling. She recalls watching Count Basie at a Saratoga festival, "and all I could think was that I didn't sound like that at my piano lessons, and [that] I wanted to stop taking piano lessons. It seemed incredibly unreachable and unattainable, like I couldn't even follow with my mind what he was doing." The music at the folk festival, when it came back, was different: it was "much more immediately . . . recognizable."

Jones and his wife, Marguerite, continued to play music around the house that came from and was influenced by Bob Jones's Club 47 days, and over the course of her childhood Nalini Jones quickly advanced from strolling through the Newport crowd selling programs to spending summers in downtown Newport answering phones at twelve to being in charge of ground transportation for artists at age sixteen ("I could probably barely drive myself without smashing around").

As is the case at many small businesses, she began to pick up more and more responsibilities simply by starting to do them. "My dad is a great big-picture guy. I love some kinds of details; he loves, like, banners. He really likes making sure that the trailers are plumbed correctly. Things like guest lists cannot capture his attention for long. . . . Slowly I grew into those roles too, because I was detail-oriented in that way, and it worked out."

She began working full-time as an assistant to her father in 1994, but already by the time she was in college in the late '80s, the generational influence was working in the other direction as well. Bob Jones was taking the musical tastes and recommendations of his daughter and her friends seriously. She says now that they were "just a convenient group of young people," but that singer-songwriters would come to her college and coffeehouses in the area.

> I think that [the organizers] realized: "Here's a group of young people; let's notice what they're listening to and see where that takes us in terms of an audience." . . .
>
> And sometimes our taste was bad—there was really no getting around that. But through me and some of these friends, [Bob Jones] had a kind of road into what young people might be interested in for a little while here and there.

And as she grew into the job of booking the festival, Nalini says, the philosophy was variety.

> We had some really popular programs, for example, that would have had, say, the Indigo Girls and Mary Chapin Carpenter, Joan Baez all on it. And that was a nice thing to do for the audience, because they were so thrilled, and it was a nice thing maybe to do for the musicians, because it was fun for them to play with their friends. But those aren't, to me, the most interesting lineups; those are sort of fairly obvious lineups.
>
> To me what was interesting was when you put people into a kind of resonance possible. I think there was one year where Ani DiFranco played and then right after her Joan Armatrading played. And that was very interesting because a lot of the audience who had come to hear

Ani DiFranco had never heard Joan Armatrading before, or had never listened seriously to her. And so for them, she was a new artist, and it was astonishing to see their response to her; they loved her. That was the kind of thrilling, interesting booking to me.

And that was just amongst songwriters. You open that up to "What kind of bluegrass can you put here that's going to make everybody more interesting by contrast?" So I think that was what we were slowly, slowly working toward.

There was nothing slow, however, about the rise of the Indigo Girls during the 1990s, particularly at Newport.

The Indigo Girls blended Emily Saliers's singer-songwriter moodiness and Amy Ray's love of punk rock, and even when they played as a duo, eschewing the rhythm sections that drove many of their recordings, the energy behind their poetry remained. They first played at Newport in 1990, shortly after their self-titled major-label record came out, including their signature hits, "Closer to Fine" and "Kid Fears."

Bob Jones says the duo was one of the acts his daughter and her friends turned him on to. "I'm looking at the age of these kids and I'm thinking, 'Hmm; something must be here.' So I gave them a listen and put them on. I had no idea what would happen, but they were fabulous as far as audience was concerned. And they had great respect for the festival." He drove them to the airport after their first Newport appearance and remembers that "we talked about the festival and what it meant. They knew about it; they were cognizant of the fact that Joni had played and Joan Baez had played. They loved coming to the festival, and we loved having them."[61]

They proved an instant success at Newport. From 1991 to 1999, they headlined a festival day (by themselves or with Joan Baez and Mary Chapin Carpenter in the ad-hoc quartet Four Voices in Harmony) eight times, virtually every one a sellout. Their 1995 and 1996 performances bookended an entire year off—they wanted to play Newport even when they didn't want to play anywhere else.

Amy Ray says Newport "was so formative for us, because we started doing it so early in our career, and we met so many people." But despite their popularity, Ray, like Judy Collins and Jim Kweskin before her, says that partaking in the atmosphere and traditions of Newport formed her best memory:

The most important part of that festival to me was not actually when we played, but going around to all the other stages. . . . And I would put aside the whole weekend and make sure I could go to every show, and all that. . . .

You'd meet other musicians and see people you didn't know were going to be there—it was remarkable to have that kind of camaraderie. I felt like the Joneses were just crucial to running that festival, and I saw Nalini grow up, and kind of take over for a while and—it just felt like family. . . .

I knew the history, Dylan and everything. And I knew, just knowing what Bob Jones's history was, I felt like I was a part of a folk tradition that had branched out.[62]

Ray says that "the audience there kind of loved everybody; it was very embracing," but others had a different opinion, describing the Indigo Girls fans as a pushy lot who were there to hear their favorites only, showing indifference or worse to the rest of the bill. "The fans of the Indigos were a little bit assertive, shall we say," says Johnette Rodriguez, of Wakefield, Rhode Island, who along with her husband, Bill, has come to the Newport festival early enough to pitch a blanket in the front row every year since 1969, "and we had to really prepare ourselves to be stepped all over when the Indigos came on, even though we'd been sitting there all day."[63] Betsy Siggins also remembers bills topped by the Indigos and including other lesbian artists that produced "some harsh lesbian moments that were not communal. They had an axe to grind and a point to make."[64]

But the success of the Indigo Girls, both on the charts and at Newport, helped pave the way for female singer-songwriters, who found an inviting stage and an appreciative audience. Catie Curtis says, "The Indigos were great about bringing everybody out at the end for 'Closer to Fine.' So for three years I got to go out and sing 'Closer to Fine' with a big group of great performers. So that was a great folky moment, with lots of voices on stage."[65] The ratio of women songwriters at Newport rose to the point where by 1996 the Boston Phoenix's Seth Rogovoy dubbed the festival "the Weekend of the Women," with the Indigo Girls, Joan Armatrading, Suzanne Vega, Michelle Shocked and Ani DiFranco only some of the women playing.

Nalini Jones makes no apologies in regard to gender—"Sometimes you throw a lot of offers out there, and some people say yes, and there were years when mostly women said yes, and years when only men said yes. And then you'd sort of piece it together as best you could"—but adds that "some things were intentional and some things just weren't, but we skewed a lot toward women. And then I remember wanting to scramble back from that, starting to feel tired of that, so then there were years where we really explicitly wanted people like Guy Clark, Lyle Lovett. I don't know that you get more manlier than Guy Clark." In regard to style, though, she concedes that "we probably did give over a little too much of the festival to songwriters for a while."

Starting in 1998, more stages sprang up around Fort Adams, mainly to give the quieter singer-songwriters a place to get close to the audience while full groups got people dancing in front of the main stage. Song circles, where a group of songwriters who were linked in some thematic or geographical way, were another method of getting more acts in front of audiences. "If he could have had a thirty-day festival with sixteen stages, that would have been fine with him," Nalini Jones says of her father, "because there was enough good music out there."

And while the acts tended to hold to Mike Seeger's stipulated "connection in form and content to what we in general call the traditions of folk music," Nalini Jones says, "I was always articulating to myself, 'How does this person fit into a folk lineage?' And sometimes, admittedly, it was thin."

Siggins, the doyenne of Cambridge's Club 47 scene, which had fed the festival so many star performers in the 1960s, had faithfully headed to Newport every year since they'd returned and says, "I think in the '90s it wasn't clear what it wanted to be. It knew it needed money, and there were acts I didn't know, and I don't think made much of a difference."[66] Peter Yarrow says that returning to Newport in the 1980s and 1990s with Peter Paul and Mary "was a commercial gig. . . . Wonderful in some ways—a lot of ways. But it was a gig."[67]

The weekend before the 1994 Newport Folk Festival, the Lollapalooza Tour took over the old Quonset Point Naval Air Base. With the Smashing Pumpkins, the Beastie Boys, L7 and the Breeders topping an enormous bill of acts, it was a raucous affair that jammed traffic in southern Rhode Island for more than a day and resulted in several hospitalizations, including one for a stage-diving-induced broken neck. The weekend after Newport, the Woodstock 25th-anniversary festival brought '60s originals such as the Band, Santana, Joe Cocker, Country Joe McDonald and John Sebastian (Dylan also played)—as well as more current acts such as Metallica, Aerosmith, the Red Hot Chili Peppers and Nine Inch Nails—together in Saugerties, New York, where the organizers had intended to hold the original Woodstock festival. Some of the highlights of that sometimes-rainy weekend included a legendary mud fight between Green Day and the audience (as well as a less-celebrated one between the crowd and Primus).

In between, at Newport, John Morton, twenty-five, told the *Providence Journal's* Mark Johnson that he was "on my way to taking a nap," while Long Island schoolteacher Brian McCarroll read *Lonesome Dove* while listening to the Saturday show. And Daniel Nash, who had been to the first Woodstock, preferred coming to Newport to the Woodstock revival: "Everything that they're talking about for another Woodstock—this is more like it. Less commercial."[68]

While the day's bill included hit makers such as Sarah McLachlan and Michelle Shocked, Nash was essentially right. Still, the essential snooziness the concertgoers described (except when the Indigo Girls came on) proved to be a problem in later years. The setting and structure of the festival had changed permanently, and so had the place it occupied in the lives of the people who came out to it. Bob Weiser, who first came to the festival in 1985 (he went to Newport for the 1969 festival but missed the music when he was arrested for sleeping in a car) and has been to nearly all of them since, refers to Newport as an all-day concert rather than a festival:

> I began to define a festival as a place where you camped out for a couple of days. . . . At a festival, the whole environment changes as night falls. This big open space, with all this stuff going on, closes in as night falls. And the audience's attention gets more focused and less scattered. And that's a huge part of the process of the festivals that I consider to be real festivals, as opposed to concerts. That process brings an audience together into a place where they're having an experience with each other. . . . In daylight you're entertained; you're wandering around; there's all kinds of stuff going on. So the attention of the audience to the performer on stage never gets really tight.[69]

While Weiser concedes that that kind of diffuse focus is unique to festivals, and the tight focus is evident at any concert, he argues that the nighttime feeling at a festival is earned in a different way: "It has the contributing factor of people already being in that place. They've gotten that focus after being engaged with each other in different ways all day. And, when the concert breaks up, [campers] go off and play music together."[70]

Observers of the Newport Folk Festival can hold forth on the differences between "the original festival" and "the way it was when they came back," and for all the philosophical and artistic distinctions they draw, the simple structural fact that the festival changed from a nighttime urban affair to an event held under (often baking) sunlight and essentially in a harbor may be the most underrated factor. The new venue also set up a striking visual contrast, as for three decades now the music has blared out to the audience and past them to an array of boats ranging from rowboats to yachts to cruise ships bobbing or lumbering in Narragansett Bay. Asked for their impressions of Newport, performers ranging from Pete Seeger to Oscar Brand to Jeff Tweedy remember the sight of the boats before anything else. And in 1985, Bill Morrissey may have been the first to send a shout-out to "the 'Boat People'" and note sardonically that "they can afford a boat like this, but they're too cheap to pay the cover,"[71] but he was far from the last.

Of course, Newport saw some of the kind of moments that only happen at festivals. In 1992, a downpour cut short Four Voices in Harmony's set and inspired an audience conga line to keep warm as well as a Ben & Jerry's ice cream giveaway; in 1996, Michelle Shocked's band missed their plane, so she played while backed variously by her brother Max Johnston, Clarence "Gatemouth" Brown and the audience (on an a cappella "Quality of Mercy"). In 1998, Nanci Griffith was unstoppable on Texas Day, hopping on stage to sing with Eric Taylor, Rodney Crowell, Jimmie Dale Gilmore and Lyle Lovett, as well as doing her own set, on which she was joined variously by Amy Ray, Taylor, Lovett, Alison Krauss and Tom Rush. In 2003, Nickel Creek pulled off an impromptu serenade for the audience members waiting in line for a shuttle bus to the parking lot.

Some old critical conflicts managed to rear their heads as well, with one unnamed writer calling the inclusion of the Violent Femmes in 1997 "an insult," but the *Providence Journal*'s Vaughn Watson celebrating the forward-looking perspective evidenced by the inclusion of the jam-band String Cheese Incident and the folk-funk of the group Toshi Reagon and Big Lovely. But considering later debates over authenticity in relation to the epic struggles of the festival's early days, the lack of centrality that Joe

Boyd pointed out as starting in the mid-1960s seems to have created an anything-goes atmosphere. The folk historian I. Sheldon Posen strikes a chord, writing in 1993,

> The striving after authenticity is no longer a burning issue in whatever it is nowadays that occupies the folksong slot in popular culture. . . . It is hard to say in a few sentences and general terms just how this relaxation of angst came about. At some point in the 1970s, people seemed to tire of the whole argument about authenticity and just decided to play and listen to what they wanted. Very 1970s. . . .
>
> Now, in these postmodern, postfusion early 1990s, most folk performers offer a personalized collage of material, executed with references to all manner of past styles and sources. . . . Maybe this casual approach to folksong, not to say life, is healthier than searching for a culture to be at home in and agonizing over how to be authentic. I must say I've tried to give that up myself.[72]

Meanwhile, even as 1990s Newport performers such as Joan Armatrading, Randy Newman and Jonatha Brooke of the Story had no problem saying explicitly that there was nothing folk about them, artists such as Steve Earle and Lisa Loeb would continue to call Newport the badge of honor for a singer-songwriter.

But if the Newport Folk Festival as a whole was a parade of artists each doing their thing—what Jon Herman had called "short, disconnected (though often outstanding) sets"—it lacked a coherent reason for being. In his 1966 *Sing Out!* article, Bruce Jackson wrote, "If Newport is no more than JUST a big concert, it is inexcusable." That might be a strong word for the festivals of the 1990s and early 2000s, but if there were a better place for fans to hear their favorite act or acts, they would take the alternative.

That's exactly what happened as the century turned: the festival got squeezed in between two forces—one massive and corporate; the other, small and grassroots.

All through the 1990s, casinos began springing up all over the Northeast, many of which had sometimes-lavish performing venues attached: the Foxwoods Casino, with two music venues, opened in 1992; the Mohegan Sun Casino, which now has four, in 1996. Both are in Connecticut, a mere half-hour's drive from Newport. And in states where casinos weren't legalized, concert giants such as Clear Channel, which spun off its live-entertainment division into Live Nation in 2005, had begun moving in on the concert game, taking a lot of bigger-name artists who might otherwise have come to Newport. "A lot of booking ideas that would have been really kinetic and exciting basically didn't happen," Nalini Jones says.

The effect was a kind of echo of the revelation Tom Rush had had in the late 1970s. Fort Adams is on a peninsula that is itself on an island—there are only a couple of small roads leading to and from the venue. And Newport is simultaneously too small to have massive hotels blocks from the venue and not isolated enough to allow for organized camping. And the rough-sleeping opportunities of the early 1960s were long gone (not that many of the more mature fans were likely still interested in sleeping outside anymore).

Suddenly, fans who wanted to see the Indigo Girls or Suzanne Vega, Robert Cray or B. B. King had more options, many of which were more comfortable than an afternoon in the sun and crowds of Newport. And for fans of artists who weren't such blockbuster draws—singer-songwriters such as Cheryl Wheeler, David Massengill, or Greg Brown—a whole new network of venues had sprung up around the country, particularly in New England, allowing a chance to see them up close and without spending hours in traffic.

Festivals had sprung up across the country and across the region during the Newport Folk Festival's history, in places such as Cambridge and Lowell, Massachusetts; Philadelphia; Berkeley; Chicago; and dozens of spots in between—some independent of Newport and some directly inspired by it. Bruce Jackson wrote in 1984, "The large festivals gave way to many more smaller festivals. . . . More folk festivals go on now than ever went on during the 1950s and 1960s, and many of them reflect real sensitivity and sophistication in programming."[73]

And coffeehouses had always existed, but while spots such as Club 47 had been hip, late-night spots, these new venues, such as Rhode Island's Mediator Fellowship (which opened in 1979), the Stone Soup Coffeehouse (1980) and Common Fence Music (1992), were community-oriented nonprofits run by musicians and fans. Pete Seeger, the man who did so much to make the Newport Folk Festival possible, helped make some of these venues possible as well. Bill Harley, one of the founders of Stone Soup, says that the idea for the venue came directly from Seeger during a People's Music Network/Songs of Freedom and Struggle workshop in Liberty,

New York, in 1980, at the height of the antinuclear movement and opposition to interventionism in Central America.

"We need places to play, where these kinds of songs should be heard. Everyone should go home and start a coffeehouse," Harley remembers Seeger saying.[74] And while no individual venue could put the Newport festival out of business, the new small venues provided a credible alternative for the older, '60s-era fans Newport was trying to attract.

Indeed, even as the mid-1980s folk revival began to gear up, folksinger Dave Van Ronk told the *New York Times* that he had reservations about the staying power: "I sense an upsurge, but I'm not convinced there's a mass base," he said in 1985. "The majority of the audiences are in their late twenties and thirties. Where are the students?"[75]

So the festival went from 9,500 the first day and 10,000 the second in 1996 (with headliners including Joan Armatrading, John Hiatt, Suzanne Vega and Ani DiFranco the first day and Indigo Girls, Bruce Cockburn and Michelle Shocked the second) to 4,200 and 6,200 respectively for the two days of the 2001 festival (even with Indigo Girls headlining the second day).

In 2002, as the festival was looking at its second year in a row without the corporate sponsorship that organizers had earlier deemed crucial, a resident at a Newport City Council meeting said, "The festival is losing its legs." A council member expanded on the metaphor, saying, "The folk festival has to stand on its own legs, if it's going to stand." In response, the best Wein could tell the *Providence Journal* was, "I will not let it die as long as it's possible to keep it operating. It will not die this year."[76]

The low point might have come in 2006, when an announced crowd of 4,000 came on Saturday, August 5, to what was now the Dunkin' Donuts Newport Folk Festival to hear a bill headlined by the pop meanderings of a past-his-prime David Gray (who showed his appreciation by signing autographs "make music, not donuts"), and only 4,600 made it out to hear the once-mighty Indigo Girls. While George Wein calls them "the only singer-songwriters that came through [the revived folk festival] that had any meaning," he also simply says, "They don't do business for us anymore." Of Gray, Jim Gillis of the *Newport Daily News* remembers, "He wasn't very good, and he didn't draw a lot of people, and he complained a lot. That's a bad three-way combination."[77]

The culturally important moments weren't happening, and the tickets weren't selling. Around this time, George Wein said, "We have some new ideas about what to do with the folk festival. We have to do something or we won't be able to do it anymore."[78]

In 2002, the prodigal son returned. Thirty-seven years after he set the worlds of folk and pop music on their respective ears, Bob Dylan came back to Fort Adams to play at the festival he had unwittingly done so much to make and unmake.

The run-up to the occasion gave everyone a chance to relitigate Dylan's 1965 performance, with eyewitnesses variously reminding each other in the pages of the *New York Times* that he had been booed and that he hadn't; that "nobody there that night had ever heard anything like it, not live at least," and that the Butterfield band had played with electric guitars earlier that day.

Peter Stone Brown went to the festival that day, and his impressions, written later on for Dylan's Web site, captured some of the ways in which the festival had changed:

> The festival along the sides of an old fort is packed. Walking in, the tiny "Roots Stage" is jammed in with the vendors, almost a souvenir stand, a bunch of singers with guitars sitting while one of them performs. There is barely room to stand and watch. Thirty-nine years ago this would have been called "The Broadside Workshop" and I wonder if Bob Dylan, Phil Ochs and Tom Paxton who were all making their Newport debuts had to perform under such circumstances, if we'd ever have known who they were. We make our way past all the vendors to wherever the main stage is. The lawn is a sea of people and blankets. . . . Someone's on stage, I don't know who. It's too hot to really care. . . . Checking out any other part of the festival means navigating a human traffic jam.[79]

George Wein wrote in that day's *New York Times* that Dylan had been invited back to Newport every year since the revival of the festival and concluded by saying, "The question is what will he do at Newport? We have never asked. Whatever it is, it will be all right with me."[80]

That was the prevailing attitude in the crowd. And it seemed to be an attitude that Dylan was anticipating and playing with. While almost everyone at Fort Adams was looking to Dylan for what he was, he treated the Newport Folk Festival like what it had become.

Backstage, numerous observers say they were informed that "Mr. Dylan" could not be addressed, or even looked at directly. The audience was informed that "the next artist" would not perform if anyone was taking pictures. The banners for the sponsor—at this point, the juice company Apple and Eve—came down. And then, on came Dylan, wearing a white cowboy hat, a fake beard and a long, stringy-haired wig. If the audience was waiting for a grand speech from Dylan acknowledging the significance of this performance and all that had happened since his show in 1965, they weren't getting one.

Sage Francis, a rapper from Providence who fought the crowds to see one of his idols, wrote later that Dylan didn't speak to the audience except for brief introductions of the members of his band. "He held his guitar like an old gun. . . . He didn't say hi. He didn't check the mic. He didn't fiddle with his guitar. The music started right away and two bars into it, he steps to the mic and sang."[81]

By then, Dylan was on what came to be known as the Never-Ending Tour, and he had been peppering the beginnings of his sets with acoustic renditions of traditional songs, which he'd been exploring on his records *Good As I Been to You* and *World Gone Wrong*. The effect was to bring long-forgotten artists such as Elizabeth Cotten, the Stanley Brothers and more to a new audience. Peter Stone Brown wrote at the time, "The irony is that this is what quite a few members of the original board of directors of the Newport Folk Festival had been attempting to do all along, and here was the all-time bad boy of Newport, the guy who dared to say, this rock and roll just might be folk music too turning more people onto Jimmie Rodgers, Leadbelly and the Carter Family than they ever could have imagined."[82]

So under the hot sun of Newport, Dylan and his band started with an acoustic version of the traditional "Roving Gambler." Behind the stage, the luminaries included Richard Gere and Al Gore. In front of the stage, John Lucas, a mailman from Scituate, Rhode Island, told the *Providence Journal's* Karen Ziner, "Think about it! There's no one else." Ziner wrote the next day,

> If you were young then, if you tie-dyed your own shirts in the sink instead of buying them off the rack, or if you slid around in the mud at Max Yasgur's farm, then you would understand.
> Or if you watched thousands of hippies streaming into Boston in the

1960s and sleeping out on the Common, or you got busted for your politics, or you watched your high school friends return home in that continuum of caskets from Vietnam, you would know how this feels.[83]

Dylan, who had done none of those things, played on.

After four acoustic songs (including the classics "The Times They Are A-Changin'" and "Desolation Row"), Dylan and this band put on electric guitars, prompting a wiseacre in the crowd to shout, "Judas!" in the style of the anonymous London fan immortalized in the film *Don't Look Back*.

The joker in the audience may have drawn some knowing chuckles from the crowd, but it didn't seem to do anything for Dylan. He proceeded to play a set heavy on hits but in the style he'd been putting on for the previous few years, in which even his best-known songs are twisted, rearranged and re-melodicized to the point where a solid verse goes by before fans can recognize the song—"most likely because he didn't want the show to turn into a sing-along," Francis hypothesized. "I can't help but think this show meant something to him. It's like 'I win. You know it. I know it. I am the winner. Talk about me all you want and say what you will . . . but you're here to celebrate what I do. I win.'" Brown concluded, "The guy underneath the hat may have looked a little strange, but in the end it was the music that mattered and just maybe that's what he's been trying to say all along."[84]

Laurie Lewis, who had heard Dylan's performance, wrote a song about it the next morning and played it on the Newport stage that afternoon. The *Providence Journal*'s Vaughn Watson wrote approvingly, "This was very folk."[85] Dar Williams rolled in to play and remembers that "it was like all of these twelve-year-old, fourteen-year-old boys had grown up loving Bob Dylan and here he was coming back to their festival. . . . And it was heartbreaking that he continued, as he always had, to give them so little. And that it was still enough. That they were high as a kite when I got there the next day. They were all saying, 'He was fantastic.' And he was purposefully not fantastic. And you know what? Great."[86]

By then, Dylan was off to Augusta, Maine, to play the next night. And that was it.

Jim Gillis of the *Newport Daily News* says, "It was a much bigger deal to a lot of people than it was to Bob Dylan, I guess. Maybe he felt something; we'll never know."[87]

*Perhaps they looked at us
as some sort of an ideal that
could possibly help to make
this world a better place.*
GEORGE WEIN

SHE WAS MY GIRL

On August 15, 2005, a week after that year's Newport Folk Festival, Joyce Wein died in New York of complications from cancer. She was seventy-six.

Joyce Alexander Wein was the granddaughter and niece of slaves. After graduating from Simmons College she worked as a technician at Massachusetts General Hospital and, after moving to New York with her husband, in enzyme research at Columbia Presbyterian Hospital. But her duties for Festival Productions, which at first could be handled over a couple weeks' vacation time, expanded with the company, and quickly she became an irreplaceable behind-the-scenes component of Festival Productions as an executive vice president of the company until the late 1990s. She continued to contribute until her death.

Joyce Alexander and George Wein met in 1947 at a Sidney Bechet concert. She was a biochemistry student at Simmons and wrote a jazz column for the college paper; he was a piano player and ran Storyville in Boston.

Wein writes in his memoirs that the girls he met in his own neighborhood "observed their mothers' materialistic agendas," whereas Joyce Alexander's love of music and poetry "added a new dimension to my life."[1] Still, while they were an almost instant match, it took a while before they were married.

Wein's parents liked Joyce and had her in their home many times, he writes, but they objected to the two getting married—"It would be a shanda [embarrassment] for the neighbors." One of the funniest passages in Wein's book recounts his hapless attempt to break up with Joyce, going so far as to spend what was intended to be a romantic weekend in Rockport, Massachusetts, with another girl who knew Joyce and knew full well that Wein was in love with her. On Sunday of that "total drag" of a weekend, Wein drove back to Boston and called Alexander's house, where he was informed that Joyce was at Fenway Park watching a Red Sox game.

Off he went, scouring the bleachers for her. "Then, amazingly, there she was," he writes. "She saw me as I approached. 'Oh shit' was all she could say. We were off to the races again."

It took an ultimatum from Joyce—"I'll give you until I'm 30 years old," she said at age 27—for Wein to propose, and still his parents objected. When they got married without the Weins' knowledge, Wein's father said he would never speak to his son again. That lasted seven months.

Wein describes in his memoirs an experience of walking through New York with trumpeter Frankie Newton. The two men looked for a place to get a drink and eventually came across a bar that seemed to Wein's liking, but not Newton's. "'What's the matter, Frankie?' I asked innocently," Wein writes. "'Why don't you relax? This place looks OK.' He said, 'George, you've never been black one day in your life.'

"I've been trying to compose a proper response to that statement ever since."[2]

It wouldn't be accurate to say that the Weins' interracial marriage—illegal in nineteen states when they were wed in 1959—was the event that opened George Wein's eyes to the persistent racism in the society around him. But the realities they faced and hopes they shared influenced their work and gave it extra meaning.

Late one afternoon in 2009, near the end of an hour-plus conversation with George Wein about the folk festival, I asked him about an incident—detailed in his autobiography, *Myself among Others*—from 1964, in which an all-white Sacred Harp singing group from Alabama was riding a shuttle bus to the festival grounds when the bus stopped to let on the all-black Georgia Sea Island Singers, who were also headed there.[3]

The bus was full. There was nowhere for the Sea Islanders to sit. According to the book, there was an awkward pause while everyone weighed their options. And then, only a few years after the idea of a black woman sitting with white people on a bus provoked many white Southerners to riot in the streets, the men of the Sacred Harp group rose and offered their seats to the women.

Wein confirmed that it had happened, though he added that he hadn't seen it personally. Then he said, "Very moving things happened like that. There were a lot of incidents."

Some of those incidents were grim. Wein told the story of folklorist and musicologist Willis James, whose reservation the Hotel Viking wouldn't honor when he showed up in person in 1954 for the Jazz Festival and they realized he was black; and of the musician Robert Pete Williams, a guest in the Weins' Middletown, Rhode Island, home, asking George and Joyce where the toilet for black people was.

In 1967, the Student Nonviolent Coordinating Committee and the Congress of Racial Equality distributed literature at the Newport Folk Festival, and tension between the activists and the all-white Newport police reached the point where the SNCC members were pushed out of Festival Field. A promised lineup, in which the activists would be able to identify their tormentors, was canceled at the last minute, and that spelled the end of the SNCC's involvement with Newport.

Some stories were more hopeful. Wein recalled times when Joyce would be directing traffic backstage and would often give white Southern men detailed instructions on where to go and what to do. "And they would say to her, 'You're the finest woman we've ever met!' It was a big thing to them. Here she was feeding them, taking care of them, telling them what to do—they never had that happen. . . .

"Very beautiful things happened."

His use of the passive voice couldn't go unremarked.

Wein changed the subject, expounding on how wild parts of Newport had been in the early days of the festival, with "bucket of blood" bars along the shore featuring bands playing "shitkicker music" all night.[4] I waited for him to pause, and he finally did.

"You knew what you were doing," I said, without referring back to our previous subject, or having to.

He paused. "Oh yeah; that was intentional."

For the next half hour, Wein related examples of the ways his business intersected with the world as it was and how he wanted it to be; what he thought he had helped to change; and his frustrations over what he perceived as an assumption on the part of folk music observers that he was at most a passive observer to all of it.

The integrated life the Weins shared, and the integrated world of music they built around themselves—by the early 2000s, Festival Productions was staging thirty-five festivals worldwide—influenced both Newport festivals in different ways. "The jazz festival was an instruction on how things could be if people worked together," Wein says. "Jazz was ahead of its time. But it wasn't political in its integration; it was personalized integration. . . . The folk festival was very political. The jazz festival was more demonstrative, in the mixing of musicians. But the political stance that the folk festival took . . . created some people against it, and more people for it. It was an exciting situation."

Wein said of the process that put black and white performers not only on the same bills but the same buses, "I can't say we were color-blind; we knew that we had to do these things if we were gonna be a representation of what we were supposed to do."[5] Wein could still recall with pride not only the "We Shall Overcome" moment of the 1963 folk festival but how much of an anthem the song became after that. In his book, he calls the performance "a moment never to be forgotten" and says, "I still get emotional when I think of it." He also got emotional talking about its aftermath.

On March 15, 1965, President Johnson spoke to Congress a week after a white civil rights activist was killed in Selma, Alabama, part of an effort by the state government to prevent a march on Montgomery demanding an end to voting discrimination. It was only the latest in a string of casualties brought on by the racism that Johnson himself had grown up in. Indeed, Johnson had spent two decades in the U.S. House and Senate voting against every civil rights bill before him.

On the afternoon of the speech, a group of activists had sung "We Shall Overcome" on the steps of the Capitol. And that night, Johnson introduced the Voting Rights Act of 1965, which eliminated barriers to voting such as poll taxes and literacy and knowledge tests (which weren't given to all prospective voters, and whose difficulty varied widely depending on who was taking them). After outlining the parameters and goals of the bill, he spoke of the importance of passing it:

> What happened in Selma is part of a far larger movement which reaches
> into every section and state of America. It is the effort of American Negroes

to secure for themselves the full blessings of American life. Their cause must be our cause too. Because it's not just Negroes, but really it's all of us, who must overcome the crippling legacy of bigotry and injustice.

And we shall overcome.[6]

Today, the phrase is iconic, unobjectionable; at the time, Johnson's use of the civil rights movement's words were a blessing to some, a bombshell to others, and a signal to everyone that enough was enough. Nearly fifty years later, George Wein was still capable of getting worked up over that moment.

"Lyndon Johnson is reading from 'We Shall Overcome' on television!" he exclaimed in 2009. "And that was because of the folk movement! Maybe not the Newport Folk Festival, but the folk movement." It was, for Wein, an acknowledgment of the work done on the front lines of American society by, if not himself, then compatriots such as Seeger, Ochs, Dylan, Baez and other spokespeople for whom Wein had endeavored to give a platform.

Among the other festivals Wein started or ran, the New Orleans Jazz and Heritage Festival is perhaps the most prominent, and the dealings Wein had with the city and the state comprise perhaps the most eloquent statement of his principles. Wein was first contacted by officials in New Orleans about establishing a festival in 1963, before the Civil Rights Act or Voting Rights Act were passed. When they outlined their vision of a segregated festival that would celebrate jazz in general and New Orleans's contributions to the genre specifically, Wein couldn't oblige.

"I'd love to do it," he remembers saying, "but you have laws on your books that are a problem. You don't allow integrated audiences, and I have people who have clauses in their contracts that they won't play for segregated audiences." The city also wouldn't allow integrated bands, which most of the biggest names in jazz had by that time, and had separate hotels for black people—treatment that legends such as Duke Ellington had long since outgrown. Wein says, "They sat there, trying to figure out a way around their own laws! . . . [They couldn't] but I never confronted them."

Two years later, after the passage of the Civil Rights Act and with the Voting Rights Act imminent, Wein was called back to New Orleans, and negotiations resumed. But when the city wouldn't allow black and white players in that summer's American Football League All-Star Game to stay in the same hotels, protests ensued, players boycotted the game, and the city's officials decided, Wein says, that another integrated event would be pushing it.

In 1968, they called him again, saying that they were going to put on a festival, but that they had chosen Willis Conover to run it; they couldn't give Wein the contract because he was married to a black woman. Again, he says, his response was "'Fine; if you ever change, call me.' I never got mad." Finally, in 1969, Wein was in New Orleans again, this time because his own finances had gotten rough enough that he'd taken a piano gig at the Hotel Sonesta. This time, he was told the contract with Conover would be broken, and Wein could run the festival.

"I never fought them or tried to get them to change their way of life," Wein says. "That's how I did my fighting; by just being there. And when Joyce came down there, they treated her like a queen."

Despite this, Wein continued to feel that the folk music world hadn't given him his due in this area. "A lot of the folk people thought I was just a businessman—that I didn't know and I didn't care. Pete [Seeger] understood me differently. He knew me for what I feel about myself." He recalled with some bitterness the International Folk Alliance conference, held in Montreal in 2005, which gave an award to the Newport Folk Festival—the entire festival, not Wein personally. "I wouldn't go. Nalini went up there; I said, 'You take it.'" Theodore Bikel, who lived in Montreal, also accepted the award. Wein remembered sarcastically the acclaim Bikel had received for his political stances while on the Newport board—"Theo was on the board because I put him on the board! . . . The folk world never acknowledged me. They just thought I was a businessman. The fact that maybe I was doing something I loved never entered their head."

But Wein is a businessman, particularly since the Brown and Williamson deal of the early '80s made him wealthy. As such, his primary influence on society lies in what he allows to happen and sets up to happen, rather than what he makes happen.

> That's been my life. I lived an integrated life. And everywhere I went, I think, I left my mark with people. . . . I never wanted to be a rebel. I never thought I was doing anything different by marrying Joyce. I wanted the same kind of respect my father had as a doctor. I wasn't going to live an outsider's life; I was part of society. And to this day I still am. And that's why I've lasted all these years, I think. I don't compromise, but at the same

time I don't tell anyone else they're wrong. They have to find out that they're wrong.

And they'll find out.

When Joyce Wein died in 2005, George Wein could only say, "She was my girl since 1950."[7] But soon after, her death was another factor that put into motion more of the changes that would transform the festival yet again in the middle of the decade.

IN THE WOODS THEY
GOT ELECTRONIC INSTRUMENTS

The changes that George Wein intimated were on the horizon in 2005, when the Newport Folk Festival was in difficult shape, beset by declining attendance and a lack of a sense of purpose, turned out to be some of the biggest to hit Newport since Dylan plugged in. Within five years of Wein's baleful assessment, the festival had changed in more ways than he could have imagined, thanks in large part to Wein's next native guide—one who, like the others before him, set a new definition of folk music and envisioned a new generation of people flocking to see it.

Wein set these changes in motion himself. "Joyce's last words to me were that I had to keep living," he says; "I had to keep doing my thing." But as 2007 began he was 81, and after her death he had begun operating "on the basis of 'stop worrying about going out there and trying to make a living.' [So it was] the concept of cashing in—'Let's see if I can live my last years and not worry about making money.'" Toward that end, "I sold everything in one year."[1]

He sold most of the properties of various kinds that he accumulated thanks to his decades of producing music and the money he got from the 1980 Brown and Williamson deal—his share of the New Orleans Jazz and Heritage Festival; his house in France; his brownstone in New York, which he had bought for a song in New York's dark mid-'70s; and much of his and his wife's collection of art, which included pieces by African American masters such as Romare Bearden, Norman Lewis and Edward Mitchell Bannister, as well as a Chagall and a Renoir.

And on January 24, 2007, he sold the Newport Folk Festival—along with the rest of Festival Productions, which produced thirteen festivals a year—to a new company called Festival Network, run by Chris Shields.

It wasn't the first time Wein had considered selling; he and Black Entertainment Television had reached an agreement in principle for a sale in 1998, a deal that fell apart late in the negotiation process over "the legacy of Newport," as Wein explained in the *New York Times* at the time.[2]

The *Times* said that Shields had been founder and president of the festival-production company Shoreline Media. He'd also worked for Festival Productions for two years in the 1990s and produced several other musical events, including components of the Olympics in Athens in 2004 and Turin in 2006. Shields told the *Times* when the sale was announced that he was interested in creating and maintaining "destination" music festivals. "It doesn't mean that large cities can't be destinations as well; we're not talking about small, affluent destinations alone. But when you think about Monte Carlo, Jackson Hole, Nantucket, Newport, there's brand in the names already." While the term "brand" was twenty-first-century buzzworthy, the idea behind it wasn't new and had been debated since the second day of the first festival in 1959 — a debate that was about to reopen, if it ever closed.

The aim of Festival Network was to buy up small music festivals across the country and run them as a unit, with artistic decisions being made individually but benefiting from economies of scale. The staff for one company running ten festivals could be slimmer than that of ten companies running ten festivals; artists and agents could be convinced to give package-deal rates for playing more than one festival if they were dealing with the same producers for each.

The deal between Wein and Festival Network included a provision keeping the Festival Productions staff in place for three years (including Wein: he was now an employee of Festival Network, even though he said his job title was "Boss"). But new people came on board immediately as well, and one of them would eventually become George Wein's new native guide to a new folk music world.

Jay Sweet grew up in Essex, Massachusetts, and went to high school in Newport, at St. George's, from 1984 to 1988. He spent the postgraduation summer of 1988 hanging around Newport and sneaked into that year's folk festival. "I was blown away," Sweet remembers: he'd seen concerts by James Taylor, the Grateful Dead and REM, but Newport was his first festival experience.[3] He went on to the University of Colorado, during which time his friend Don Strasburg opened the Fox Theatre in Boulder in 1990.[4]

"That's kind of where it all came together for me," Sweet says. The first night at the Fox was headlined by the reconstituted classic lineup of the Meters, and he remembers thinking, "'Oh Lord, this is amazing.' That kind of set my life."

At least, it set the rest of his life as he envisioned it unfolding. But after he graduated from Colorado, he says, "My mom said I had to get a real job." That led to a master's degree in education and a job teaching creative writing at a private day school in New Jersey. He left after a year (he says he didn't have a good answer to a writing student who protested his grade by saying, "What have you ever done?"), then flew to Ecuador and went as native as he could: "I climbed these mountains and kayaked the headwaters of the Amazon and saw the Galapagos and drank *ayah uasca* —I was that way; I finally broke." He also wrote two screenplays "about a young teacher who gets called out because he hasn't done anything," one of which was made into the "lackluster" (Sweet's word) film *West of Here*.

On a trip to the Nantucket Film Festival to hawk his scripts, he met the directing duo the Farrelly Brothers. He eventually worked on the crew of their movies *Dumb and Dumber* and *Me, Myself and Irene*, then as a music supervisor on six movies between 2000 and 2003. Along the way, he began to write for the new music magazine *Paste*, eventually becoming an editor at large. An assignment for *Paste* brought him back to the Newport Folk Festival in 2005.

That was the year that the Monsters of Folk were already pushing the boundaries of what could be presented at the folk festival. The three front men were Jim James, of My Morning Jacket; Conor Oberst, performing under the name Bright Eyes; and the indie-rock singer-songwriter M. Ward, with the remainder of My Morning Jacket serving as a loud and proud backing band to the very different and idiosyncratic song structures and lyrical twists of the front three. Sweet talked with them and My Morning Jacket drummer Patrick Hallahan after the show. It was Sweet's second time at the festival, his first trip backstage—and he says, "I just, again, started to fall in love with this thing."

The Monsters were "by far the youngest artists on the bill," Sweet remembers; in a festival that included Emmylou Harris, Elvis Costello, Odetta, Buddy Miller, Jim Lauderdale, Arlo Guthrie, Nanci Griffith and Chris Smither, "they obviously stuck out." They came from ostensibly different musical worlds, but in their minds they were the heirs of the old singer-songwriters who had become Newport's backbone. "I remember talking to them about what an honor it was for them to be part of the bill," Sweet says. "We were talking about what they should do to bring this back to what they had envisioned when they thought about the words 'Newport Folk Festival.'"

Shortly thereafter, Sweet says, Chris Shields approached him for advice on whether to buy Festival Productions. Sweet's response ran eighteen single-spaced pages. Festival Network acquired festivals from all over the world: Mali's Festival in the Desert, the Pemberton Music Festival in British Columbia, and more. But Sweet called Newport "the granddaddy of all music festivals" and urged Shields in the strongest terms to buy. He remembers Shields asking, "Do you want to put your money where your mouth is?"

Sweet did. He gave up Sweet & Doggett, the self-described company of "music pimps" Sweet began with adman Scott Doggett that worked in music consulting and licensing, "putting together brands and bands" for films and commercials, as well as *Paste*.

The first time Wein and Sweet met was not an auspicious beginning, Wein says. "We had a meeting and he was talking, like he can talk—he can talk like crazy. And I said, 'Who is this guy? What the hell is he talking about?' I didn't like him at all. . . . His personality really rubbed me the wrong way. . . . And when I started to work with him, I could see that he had something a little different. And so we built up a relationship."[5]

When Bob Jones first met with Sweet, Jones says, he called Wein "and told him, 'This is the guy.'"[6]

Sweet's title was director, as well as associate producer for the Whistler and Jackson Hole festivals and the Newport Folk Festival. Festival Network's ownership of the Newport Folk Festival lasted only two years, but its influence on the musical aesthetic of Newport continues to this day.

It was nothing new for rock bands to play at Newport of course, stretching back to the Los Lobos/Robert Cray shows of the late 1980s, even to Big Brother and the Holding Company in 1968 and of course Dylan before that. Indeed, the Monsters of Folk show that led to the rekindling of Jay Sweet's love affair with Newport was booked by Nalini Jones, and the last pre-Festival Network festival, in 2006, included the Meters, Bettye LaVette and Grace Potter and the Nocturnals. In 2007, during which Nalini Jones remembers that the old Festival Productions crew was "still allowed to run things the way we wanted," the Allman Brothers Band finished off the festival with a two-and-a-half-hour show.[7]

But when Festival Network took over, such acts weren't just the icing on the cake. It was easy for an old-style singer-songwriter fan to believe that the rock bands on the main stage were there to draw the crowds, sell the tickets and pay the bills while the "real" stuff was happening on the side stages. But when Sweet and Festival Network took over, the message was clear: the young people with electric guitars were, in fact, the real stuff. Sweet's aesthetic was simple to understand: if you wrote songs and sang them, you were a singer-songwriter. The fact that you played an electric guitar for people drinking beer rather than an acoustic for people drinking coffee and tea was of little importance. To this day, Sweet doesn't use the word "rock" very much in conversation, preferring to say "expanding the definition of folk."

> Joan Baez played on a guitar in a coffeehouse and people went and saw her. Chan Marshall[8] played in Brooklyn and people drank beer and saw her. But it was just her and a guitar. It was an electric guitar, but . . . two women sitting on stools in these dungy fucking places in the boroughs of New York, lyrically talking about the struggles of being a young woman in their times, in these places—I just see it as a natural progression. Because I think anyone who's singing in a coffeehouse in Chan Marshall's time—to me, they might be trying to copy the past.[9]

Wein puts it more simply: "You go to Africa, you go to India, everybody's got electric instruments. In the woods they got electronic instruments."[10]

At the 2008 festival, Sweet and Festival Network put this philosophy into action in sometimes jarring fashion. On the undercards, names such as Chris Smither, Cheryl Wheeler and Martha Wainwright gave way to Damian and Stephen Marley, Jakob Dylan and Cat Power. But the most visible changes came at the top of each bill: for the Friday-night concert at the Newport Casino, it was Brian Wilson; for Saturday at Fort Adams, the Black Crowes; for Sunday, Jimmy Buffett.

The combination of new leadership and an untraditional lineup inspired criticism from some venerable quarters. Joan Baez told the *Boston Globe*'s Joan Anderman, "I don't like the idea that it's just dissipating into another festival like so many others. It seems that it's all about money and not much about holding onto something that's been pretty precious for a lot of years."[11]

Betsy Siggins of Club 47 and at the time the executive director of its successor, Passim, called the lineup "the death knell for traditionalists," though she considered it a sign of hope for the future. Saying that recently featured artists at Passim had also stretched the definition of folk, she called Newport "a strong concert" and added, "Do I hope they bring in more traditional music down the line? Yes. But it's a tough time for folk; they're looking for a home run the first time out of the gate, and I wouldn't miss it for anything."[12]

The Black Crowes' Southern roots and their opening acoustic songs —the traditionals "Girl of the North Country" and "He Was a Friend of Mine"—allowed an observer to squint at the right angle and see a folk connection, at least until they whanged into "Jealous Again." But Brian Wilson's opening Friday-night show at the Newport Casino was just puzzling, as many of the Beach Boy's solo shows are. And Buffett's performance pushed virtually the entire idea of the festival to one side.

When he was announced as a performer earlier in the year, Buffett had told Anderman that he would play a muted set, either solo or with one other player, that would hearken to the Cambridge singer-songwriter he once was. (Indeed, one can easily imagine a resetting of "Margaritaville," "Come Monday," "A Pirate Looks at Forty," and others of his early songs that would work well in such a context.) "I threatened to do Newport before I was gone, and I seriously want to honor the heritage of the festival," Buffett said. "I came up as a folk singer. I've always loved the idea of being a balladeer. You know, I might do Gordon Lightfoot's 'Canadian Railroad Trilogy.' I am not going to do a Parrothead show," he said, referring to his notoriously rowdy, impressively dedicated fans.[13]

As the August 3 show came to a close, though, Buffett had left his horn section at home but otherwise was in full roar, and so was the crowd. An acoustic encore of "Blowin' in the Wind," a mostly acoustic "Come Monday," and a version of Gillian Welch's "Elvis Blues," performed with Welch and David Rawlings, were the only tips of the hat to his unique surroundings; otherwise, "Cheeseburger in Paradise," "Fins," "It's Five O'Clock Somewhere," and the rest of his usual set blared away. Meanwhile, Sweet was scrambling backstage for answers to give journalists who wanted an explanation. The best he could come up with was, "Was it a folk show? No. Was it a stripped-down version of a Jimmy Buffett show? Yes." He also called the content of the show "a surprise" to the organizers.[14]

While Buffett's show was going on, though, Sweet recalls a moment that would prove a symbol of things to come. "Half the audience was there strictly for him," he recalls. "The other half, the minute he walked onstage—mass exodus." At the time, the festival's smallest stage was right between the waters of Narragansett Bay and the access road out of Fort Adams. Anyone who was leaving would have to walk right by it. And while the Avett Brothers' loud, fast, roots-oriented performance was supposed to be finished by then, they were running overtime, which meant that anyone who was fleeing Buffett was forced to give them a listen. "And that tent was five times capacity, and [the Avetts] were sweating, wearing tweed suits, and they were killing it. And people started freaking out."[15]

It wasn't the only classic-folk moment of that year. During a downpour on the same stage the previous day, the Felice Brothers played through a power outage, clambering down to the wet ground and leading a series of raucous, all-acoustic sing-alongs; at the same time, the American Babies were rewarded with a main-stage set when the Marleys balked at playing during the brunt of the rainfall. The historical references were clear, and Sweet was anxious to capitalize on the momentum.

But the 2008 festival was the only Newport Folk Festival that Festival Network fully produced. While the startup company was running the Newport festivals as well as festivals all over the country, the bills had piled up and the attendance numbers hadn't supported the overhead. By January 2009, Festival Network still owed the state $150,000 of the proceeds from the previous year's festival. "We got promissory messages," said Larry Mouradjian, at the time chief of parks and recreation for the Rhode Island Department of Environmental Management (DEM), which runs Fort Adams, "and then that date would go by."[16]

Festival Network's debts to private contractors and vendors were reportedly much bigger than those owed to the state. Bob Jones says, "I started getting these phone calls from vendors in Newport saying, 'We haven't been paid; can you give us a helping hand?' I did the best I could."[17] In January 2009, the DEM canceled Festival Network's contract with three years still to run. The company eventually paid the state, but "we communicated to them that we still held them in default," Mouradjian says, "because we had no confidence." Newport evidently wasn't alone: Festival Network quickly shut down operations completely. Sweet recalls trying unsuccessfully to contact anyone from the organization before finally heading to their New York offices from Essex and finding the doors chained shut.

Several observers say Festival Network's demise was no surprise. Nalini Jones recalls that she "left when the Festival Network people came in. . . . [So] I don't know exactly where they went wrong, but I saw them throwing money around in ways that were just delusional, when you think about what a risk any entertainment industry is. . . . You have to really look at the fact that some people might not come to the field that year, and that it might rain, and there's a lot of things that could go wrong. And I think they spent like nothing could go wrong."[18]

Sweet says that Shields's Festival Network concept was "in theory, a great idea," and that his model is being followed today by companies such as the Bowery Presents and Huka Entertainment. "But he went out at a sprint, not a jog." He also fell victim to the general economic malaise of 2008: "The funding dried up, and everyone thought the funding would be unlimited." Still, Sweet says, "Everyone gets worried when you see money flying out that doesn't need to."[19]

Jill Davidson, director of the festival since 1996, says that Festival Network's "perspective on everything was just unlike anything I had ever seen. They had crazy ideas . . . just spending money on crazy things like tents and white linen tablecloths on everything. They were all about wanting everything to look luxurious and stuff, and we were just watching all this money be spent, knowing that it's very expensive to do these festivals, even on the cheap side. So we knew they were going to get into trouble eventually."[20] Wein simply says, "I was working for them, [and] they never listened to me."[21]

So as the fiftieth anniversary of the Newport Folk Festival neared, it had no producer, no sponsor, not even a permit. Sweet says he had "a lot of doubt" as to whether the festival could be resurrected.[22] Wein, however, says that he couldn't let his life's work end so ignominiously. "Newport was my legacy," he says now; "I said, 'Hey; I still like these festivals; I wanna keep them going.'"[23]

"Once we knew that," Mouradjian says, "then we began to work with him."

By March, Wein had approval from the state, and the necessary permits from the city weren't far behind. He told the *Boston Globe*'s James Reed in March 2009, "I just reacted to a negative situation that involved my legacy. I'm not trying to go back in business. I'm just trying to keep Newport going. . . . That's my life, those two festivals."[24] (While Wein was, and is, sincere about that, the quick turnaround between Festival Network's demise and Wein's reentry probably wasn't an accident. He says now that there's "no question" that the DEM knew that he would resume producing the festivals if they canceled Festival Network's contract, and he surmises, "Maybe they would've treated them differently if I wasn't there; that's another story."[25])

Reed also quoted a statement from Shields thanking Wein for "assisting with the groundwork to ensure the legacies of the Newport Folk and Newport Jazz festivals"—a statement that provoked laughter from Wein years later: "He keeps saying he's looking forward to working with me; I'm not working with him."[26] Reed also wrote in 2009 that Festival Network's Web site "still includes the Newport Folk Festival and JVC Newport Jazz Festival on its homepage, noting 'new site coming soon!' in the upper corner."[27] As of June 2016, that's still true.

When Wein took the reins back, he cleaned house. Almost all of the employees of Festival Network were let go, with two major exceptions: Jason Olaine, whose knowledge of the contemporary jazz scene still informs the programming of the Newport Jazz Festival; and Jay Sweet. "He represents a world that I don't know," Wein would say later that year.[28]

The 2009 fiftieth-anniversary edition of the festival was called George Wein's Folk Festival 50. While Wein had reserved the rights to put on a festival in case of the default of Festival Network, he had leased the name "Newport Folk Festival" to the new company, and that property was tied up as an asset in bankruptcy court.[29] Wein pressed Sweet, Bob Jones and Nalini Jones into service to book and arrange the festival in a hurry. These days, the process of booking and scheduling the folk festival begins in October, two months after the previous festival ends, and some feelers are put out before that. In 2009, they began in April, three months in advance. Artists were secured for the festival at unusual speed—Sweet acknowledges that they "were doing George a favor."[30]

Colin Meloy, of the Decemberists, recalls the group's manager telling him, "They may not be able to pay you," but they took the gig anyway.

"This festival is clearly very important. They [were] trying to rehab it and relaunch it, and as long as you're willing to take that leap of faith—well, you can see very clearly that it's an American institution and an American folk music institution."[31]

For his part, Wein was energized; getting back into the game had proven a tonic. At an event that summer to announce a new sponsor for the jazz festival, the guitarist Howard Alden—who had known and played with Wein for twenty years at that point—said, "It's amazing how he's more full of life than ever," and called their recent gigs together with the Newport All-Stars "very inspiring and very exciting." Michael Dorf, owner of New York's Knitting Factory and City Winery, agreed, saying, "I think he's rejuvenated."[32]

And another old hand was called on deck to celebrate the milestone: Pete Seeger, making his first Newport appearance in years and one of only two outside his county in upstate New York that year. He was the touchstone of the Newport Folk Festival, and his national profile was higher than ever, his having turned ninety that spring, a milestone that was celebrated with an all-star bash at Madison Square Garden including Dave Matthews, Bruce Springsteen, Joan Baez, Richie Havens, Billy Bragg and more. (Seeger played the concert because it benefited his Clearwater Foundation, but he said, "I wasn't enthusiastic about it actually. The best music I've ever made was to a few hundred people, although there was one concert to about a thousand people that wasn't bad.")[33]

The Newport formula had always consisted of young, popular acts and the older ones who had inspired them, and in 2009 the older generation was represented by Seeger; Ramblin' Jack Elliott, playing on his seventy-eighth birthday; Joan Baez, fifty years after one of the crucial gigs of her youth; Mavis Staples; Judy Collins; Guy Clark; and Del McCoury. Youth was evidenced by the Decemberists, Elvis Perkins in Dearland, Fleet Foxes, the Avett Brothers, Joe Pug and Rhode Island's own Deer Tick and Low Anthem[34]—all of whom bounce off the folk and/or singer-songwriter traditions in various ways, while incorporating drums, distorted electric guitars and head-rush harmony vocals to varying degrees.

And each day ended with a Pete Seeger trademark: a sing-along, which saw the hip and the historic get-together for chestnuts such as "Guantanamera," "This Little Light of Mine" and, naturally, "This Land Is Your Land." The sing-alongs were the emotional centerpieces of each day's show, with performers of various eras joining in a celebration that was part music lesson and part passing of the torch. "It wasn't the equivalent of the [baseball] All-Stars crowding around Ted Williams at Fenway Park," the *Providence Journal* noted—"actually, yes it was."[35]

Meloy of the Decemberists recalls that singing along with Seeger was not only a chance to rub elbows with a hero but a solidifying moment for performers of his generation: "That experience, especially around those people who had taken the same leap of faith with us, who wanted to step in and be a part of this thing and give it new life—that was really exciting."[36]

Tao Rodriguez Seeger, Pete Seeger's grandson, performed with Seeger that weekend, as well as playing with his own electric band; he organized the sing-alongs, to the extent that they were organized. In 2011, he recalled teaching some of the younger musicians the chords to "This Land Is Your Land"—not a complicated song—and explaining how organized the performance should and shouldn't be.

> People asked, "What do we do?" And I said, "Just have fun, man." Because that's what my grandfather's all about—just find a microphone. I remember people wanted direction, and I said, "The direction is, it's a gas. It's a hootenanny." . . .
>
> At one point [during "When the Saints Go Marching In"] I stopped singing and I just leaned out to see if I could hear the audience. And I could, and I could see that they were really doing it, and that just filled me up. Because that's all my grandpa cares about. And when I'm [performing with him], all I really care about is whether my grandpa's happy.[37]

Tao remembered his most striking memory from the sing-along:

> My grandmother was sitting with George [Wein] on stage, and they were holding hands. It was just real sweet to see real powerhouses, people who sacrificed so many things in their lives, for better or for worse. George never had kids, so the festival's his child. And to a certain degree, my mother is an adopted daughter of George, so to a certain degree George is one of my grandparents. So I just want to help 'em; I want them all to feel like they didn't fail.
>
> My grandpa often feels like a failure. He tells me pretty much every opportunity he gets, how much he failed. And I can't take it. I can get it, because I know how you can put yourself in that place, but every chance I

get I try and show him how he didn't fail . . . to exemplify how what he and others did changed our lives.

It made our lives better, whether it's a directly musical thing or something as simple as recycling. . . . It's not just music—it's life; it's the earth; it's all of us; it's humanity, together. And I don't want them to feel like they failed.

I want them to feel like the journey continues.[38]

On Saturday, while the Decemberists played, another drama was unfolding backstage.

"Pete was lost," Jay Sweet says. "By which I mean no one could find him on the grounds. And everyone started freaking out—they thought he had fallen into the ocean, or he'd gotten into somebody else's car, or he hitchhiked, or he'd gotten on a boat. Not because he was daft, but just because he would think, 'I wanna get out of here.'" After some searching, Sweet got another piece of news: a security guard ran up to him and informed him that "There was a guy thirty feet up on the scaffolding, and he won't come down. And sure enough, it's fucking Pete Seeger. He'd climbed thirty, forty feet in the air, and he was just hanging, in his Wrangler jeans and a purple shirt and the big white hat, looking down at the Decemberists. And I stood there for five or ten minutes, and then he came down. And I was scared shitless . . . I just said, 'Man, what the hell are you doing?'"[39]

At dinner with Wein in Newport the night before, Sweet had told Seeger that he would likely enjoy the Decemberists. As Sweet remembers it, Seeger had been told exactly the opposite. The next day, "he said, 'It was the only place I could go listen to these guys without people wanting a piece of me, wanting my autograph or wanting to take a picture. I just wanted to listen to the music. And if you say I'll want to listen to them, I'll listen to them.'"

Sweet remembers Seeger saying, "I thought they were great. Great lyrics, and they have control of the crowd." Singer and chief songwriter Meloy had gotten the crowd to make like whales during "The Mariner's Revenge Song," which struck a chord with Seeger, the sing-along evangelist.

What neither of them knew was that at the moment, while half the band was playing "Cautionary Song," the other half was strolling through the audience with marching and handheld percussion to perform a low-comedy reenactment of Bob Dylan's 1965 electric performance, complete with a Pete Seeger losing his temper and threatening to cut cords with an axe. "He didn't see that, because he was talking to me," Sweet says. "Which is probably a good thing." Sweet told Seeger that people were upset about the booking, and Seeger replied, "Well, if you're not pissing someone off, you're not doing it right."

Attendance had ticked up for the previous two years, from a total attendance of 8,600 in 2006 and 13,500 in 2007 to 15,000 in 2008 and 17,000 in 2009, including 9,200 on Saturday, the most since Dylan's return to Newport in 2002. How much of the 2009 attendance surge was due to the milestone factor of the fiftieth anniversary is unknowable; Sweet conjectures that "everyone thought it was going to be the last one."[40]

Sweet told Wein that he wanted the job of producing the festival. He says he told Wein that if the festival didn't sell out within three years, Wein could fire him. Wein took Sweet up on it. So in planning the 2010 Newport Folk Festival, Sweet had all the responsibility, as well as all the power, and he put his philosophy into effect.

*It changed the course of so
many things. . . . Why are we
not using that?*
JAY SWEET[1]

LET THEM KNOW THAT
YOU KNOW WHERE YOU ARE

Sometimes the Newport Folk Festival as it is currently constituted doesn't sound or seem much like a classic folk festival: when Band of Horses buzzsaws their way through "Weed Party" at ear-covering volume; when Lake Street Dive purveys sunny swing just six months after Rolling Stone named them one of "10 New Artists You Need to Know for 2014"; when Wilco kicks up a racket that includes whooshing synthesizers; when Hozier runs through the megahit "Take Me to Church"; when *Glide* magazine previews the folkiest and least-folkie acts heading to the festival; or when the *Providence Journal* runs a fashion-photo spread celebrating the put-together looks of some of the festivalgoers (a few of whom clearly didn't plan on dust, dirt or rain).

On the other hand, it feels very much like a folk festival when Mavis Staples joins Lake Street Dive for a cameo; when Deer Tick's John McCauley brings his mother on stage to sing "Margaritaville"; when My Morning Jacket backs Pink Floyd legend Roger Waters; when the rapt onlooker at a small-stage show turns out to be Jack White or Jackson Browne; or when the shouts and applause from one stage reach another.

It has another thing in common with the classic mid-1960s festivals: success. Buoyed by the popularity of young, smart rock groups such as Dawes, Deer Tick and My Morning Jacket; modern singer-songwriters such as Blake Mills, Jason Isbell and Joe Pug; and groups that revive traditional acoustic sounds with young energy, such as Trampled By Turtles, the Avett Brothers, the Felice Brothers, Langhorne Slim, Pokey LaFarge and hit-makers the Decemberists and the Lumineers, the festival has regained a commercial power it hasn't had in decades.

Today's Newport Folk Festival doesn't match Pete Seeger's mid-'60s vision of a dozen or more stages with everyone from the famous singer-songwriters to the backwoods fiddlers, where someone could ask Seeger the chords to "Waist Deep in the Big Muddy" and get an immediate private lesson.[2] But music and musicians occupy nearly every corner of Fort Adams for three days, and while the hipsters, the hardcore and the hippies traipse around the grounds together, the older folks in tie-dyed shirts are steadily and increasingly outnumbered by young men in fedoras and dress shirts and women in retro-'70s gear. All around, artists who have already played, artists whose sets aren't for another day, and artists who aren't even booked stroll the grounds, many as excited to be there as the fans, hanging around in order to soak up the fellowship—a dynamic that Jim Kweskin or Judy Collins would recognize from the 1960s and Amy Ray from the 1990s—and in many cases to continue the process well into the night at various clubs throughout the city.

Newport "has begun to feel more like a state of mind than an annual event," the *Boston Globe*'s James Reed wrote in 2014, describing the festival as "all over the map. That, of course, is exactly how most young people experience music these days."[3]

Yet while at least two of the organizers independently use the phrase "this festival moves forward," the structure and spirit of Newport—as well as a lot of its success—come from a conscious evocation of the past by the organizers, artists and fans that mirrors and profits from the Utopia days, echoed in the celebrated bubbling up of tradition-inspired music that's taken place in the twenty-first century.

Jay Sweet is proud to point out that he beat his own sellout guarantee to Wein: the Saturday show of 2011 was the first sellout since Dylan's return in 2002, which in turn was the first sellout since the Indigo Girls in 1998. Each year after that, the festival broke another barrier: in 2012 the festival sold out both days; in 2013 it sold out both days in advance. And in 2014 and 2015, the festival not only added a third full day of programming but also sold its allotment of 10,000 tickets for each day before the lineups were announced.

The festival added its second stage in 1998, a third in 2003. Since then, the number of stages has climbed at an even faster rate. The Family Tent, added in 2012, has gone from hosting a formally scheduled roster of children's acts to becoming the jam hangout for artists, particularly when the main stage on the north wall of the fort is being changed over between sets. (Indeed, adults vastly outnumber children in the tent, and like a good children's movie, the material generally runs to the kid-friendly rather than the expressly kid-centered.) The small stage on the edge of the harbor was replaced in 2010 with a bigger stage set on the parade ground inside the fort, a mostly enclosed area that has turned into what operations manager Tim Tobin calls "a festival within a festival,"[4] with an audience and universe of vendors, glad-handers and star-studded guest appearances all its own. Performances began in the 100-seat Museum of Yachting in 2013, and the nooks and crannies of Fort Adams buzz with small-stage performances for radio broadcasts and podcast recordings.

And while the artists no longer huddle and jam in communal, dormitory-style rooms or Blues Houses when it's all over, the close of each day of the festival marks the beginning of the after-concerts throughout downtown Newport, with impromptu collaborations and sing-alongs into the night —all of which sell out almost the moment they're announced.

The Rhode Island–based band Deer Tick first played at Newport in 2009 and immediately began to revive the tradition of music at night after the concerts were over—first at a couple of donors-only events inside Fort Adams, later a rowdier and less formal gathering of colleagues and friends at the Newport Blues Café in the downtown. Their shows and others include on-the-spot collaborations on the performers' own material, as well as relatively modern rock classics. Chief singer and songwriter John McCauley says, "The festival ends early every night, and a big portion of the crowd, and the musicians themselves, don't want it to end."[5]

"It's phenomenal, because I really didn't see it coming," says Jim Gillis, who has been covering the festival for the *Newport Daily News* since 1985. "I'm not exactly Kreskin when it comes to these things, but I didn't see it bouncing back to this level, where it's become one of the hottest tickets in the country in the summer."[6]

The experience begins months before the shows do, when tickets are snapped up. Acts are then announced piecemeal over the twenty-first-century word of mouth that is social media. The Newport Folk Festival no longer advertises, and since 2014 they haven't done so much as send out a press release—which only contributes to the paradoxical appeal of a sold-out event that operates under the radar.

Gillis recalls his first brush with the new way of getting the word out—during the 2008 Avett Brothers set that served as a virtual anti-Buffett outpost: "There were a lot of kids near the stage. And I remember talking to them, and they knew all the songs. And I asked them, 'How do you know about these guys?' They weren't on any kind of commercial radio. And they said, 'the Internet.' The whole formula has changed in the music industry. And this festival is definitely part of it."[7] By 2015, the festival had so thoroughly absorbed the immediacy of electronic media that last-minute announcements and changes were more often announced through the festival's Twitter account or smartphone app than by someone heading to the stage to talk on the microphone.

The current success has led Wein to declare Sweet "as perfect as he can be . . . as far as what we're looking for from a contemporary folk festival." Not only are the tickets selling, he says, but "there's a whole new feeling that started growing a couple of years ago. It's very exciting; I'm very happy with it." He adds that Sweet "always showed respect to the old folk festival —and he always respected Pete Seeger. That was very important to me."[8]

Sweet not only showed respect to Seeger's model for the festival; he did his best to emulate it in modern circumstances. Upon taking control, Sweet immediately moved to eliminate titular sponsorship. The festival, he said, would never again be known as the Dunkin' Donuts Newport Folk Festival, or the Ben & Jerry's Newport Folk Festival, or the Apple & Eve Newport Folk Festival.

"Nothing can be greater than the words 'Newport Folk Festival,'" Sweet remembers saying, "because the only way this is going to come out is to rebuild the brand as the one and only Newport Folk Festival. . . . If you look at the first six years of this festival, it rocked the world. And that's not an overstatement. It changed the course of so many things. So I said, Why are we not using that?"[9]

It was a mix of slick branding and a respect for history—it also meant forgoing a sizable check each year—but Sweet argues that it made business sense as well. Sponsorship money, he says, gets eaten up by acts who know that there's extra cash floating around, and other performers hike their fees in response. "And you have this name above your name, and all the money you're spending on marketing is pushing their brand, not your brand. I'd rather say, 'Look, we don't have any sponsors; we're broke. If you want to do it, great; if you don't, I understand.'"[10] Many of the other organizers objected but eventually signed on, in some cases with a touch of fatalism, Sweet says: Given the festival's financial situation in 2009, "Jill [Davidson]'s response was, 'Well, what else are we gonna do?'"[11]

It wasn't the only move Sweet made that echoed the festival's past. While he had a newfangled idea of how the Newport Folk Festival should sound, he had very old-fashioned ideas on how it should operate and what it should mean. Sweet says the eighteen-page paper he wrote to encourage Chris Shields to buy the Newport festivals was taken directly from the original manifesto the Weins and the Seegers wrote up in the winter of 1963 at the Seegers' half-finished house before bringing their nonprofit ideal to life: "I went back and looked at every one of their past books and studied their things, looked at *Broadside*. I became a student."[12]

Since becoming a student, Sweet might be better described as what historian Benjamin Filene years previously called a "memory worker"— someone who institutes and cultivates "a set of goals and cultural strategies—an effort to string lines between past, present and future."[13] And while previous examples of memory work involve individual artists and genres, Sweet's efforts constitute a kind of memory work on behalf of the institution of the festival itself.

In *Romancing the Folk: Public Memory & American Roots Music*, Filene compares in consecutive chapters the discoveries and careers of Lead Belly and Muddy Waters, two roots musicians whose credentials are today thought to be impeccable. But the handling of their careers and legacies differed, and as a result their places in the American public memory differ.

What made the difference between Lead Belly—a figure more respected than popular—and Muddy Waters—a figure who not only had a long, popular career but was instrumental in the popularization of his brand of music with at least two generations of players and fans—came down to what Filene calls the memory workers in charge of each man's career and legacy. And the differences between the methods of those memory workers find parallels with the different models of stewardship of the institution of the Newport Folk Festival and, by extension, folk music itself.

Lead Belly was discovered in the Angola prison farm (the Louisiana State Penitentiary) by John and Alan Lomax, and after his release he became something of an employee of the father-son duo, Filene says; in return, they brought Lead Belly to the concert stage and professionalized his music to an extent he could not have thought possible.

While the Lomaxes "depicted a much more robust folk tradition"[14] than collectors such as Francis Child and Cecil Sharp—in part because of their use of the record rather than the printed page as the primary means of communicating folk music—the way they managed Lead Belly's career reflects the same kind of trapped-in-amber, preservationist impulse that characterized the early collectors. Indeed, the very fact that they were at Angola was driven by John Lomax's belief that prisons, operating at a remove from the mainstream of society, were the place to find something unadulterated, homegrown and untamed.

In the same way, Filene argues, they may have built Lead Belly's career, but they also limited it. For the most outward example, John Lomax made Lead Belly perform in his old prison uniform, something the singer hated. While Lead Belly was described by others as a sharp dresser and having a formal, even haughty personality, the Lomaxes made sure that in his public persona he never strayed far from being the singing murderer, rescued from jail by the force of his musical talent (although the story that Lead Belly's first release from prison was spurred by his writing and singing a song about the governor of Louisiana was more legend than fact).

While John Lomax smoothed out various aspects of Lead Belly's music, lyrics and delivery, he continued to cast the singer as the primitive, untamed savage. "Penitentiary wardens tell me I set no value on my life in using him as a traveling companion," Lomax wrote in a publicity letter, and, as Filene documents, the stories written about Lead Belly early in his career take a similar tack. "The Lomaxes' handling of Lead Belly resonated with a current of primitivism that ran through early twentieth-century modernism," Filene writes.

But while that othering may have brought Lead Belly to a certain level, it kept him from progressing any further, Filene argues. Joe Klein wrote that many folk singers turned into "museum pieces, priceless and rare, but not quite marketable to the mass culture." Lead Belly spent much of his postprison life on public assistance and died in 1949, months before the Weavers recorded their hit version of his "Goodnight Irene." For much of the 1950s and 1960s folk revival, Lead Belly was a source of songs and a touchstone of authenticity—all of which worked out well for those who succeeded him but didn't do much for the man himself. "The 1960s folk revival did more to cement Lead Belly's reputation than had all his own efforts while he was alive," Filene writes. "After his death, then, Lead Belly himself became an authenticating agent, one who could bestow legitimacy on performers and fans searching for a sense of roots in the midst of ephemeral pop culture."[15]

This, Filene argues, is the result of memory workers who place too much value on old-school definitions of authenticity, not only as a clue toward the discovery of a performer but the continuing narrative of his career.

Jay Sweet's handling of the Newport Folk Festival, on the other hand, more closely echoes the handling of Muddy Waters's career by a succession of actors who steered his "move into American public memory."[16] As Filene documents, Waters came up from Mississippi to Chicago—he crossed paths with the Lomaxes and made some recordings for their Library of Congress project, but they went their separate ways afterwards —and he began playing in the old country-blues style. But soon he fell in with producer Lester Melrose, who put him in group situations which, of necessity, smoothed out some of the eccentricities inherent in solo country blues so that others could play along.

From there, Waters began to record for the Chess brothers, who were famously more attuned to their standing in the marketplace than the historical purity of the music they released, and for a largely black audience, which Filene says didn't have academically exacting standards on what was real and what was fake. This worked on more levels than one. By making records that would sell in the Chicago of the 1950s, Waters was identifying and catering to an underrecognized demographic: African-Americans who, like himself, had come up from the South and wanted music that echoed their roots while tapping into their current surroundings. Commercialism, as Filene argues, actually allowed Muddy Waters to be authentic: he represented a culture, albeit not one that had been fetishized yet.

In this process, Waters met and collaborated with Willie Dixon, who gave him some of his best-known songs, such as "Got My Mojo Workin'" and "Hoochie Coochie Man." These are considered hard and heavy, unfiltered blues now, but as Filene points out, the presence of identifiable verses, choruses and bridges made them a pop-blues hybrid in the context of the time. Waters also benefited from Dixon's zeal in assembling the American Folk Blues Festival roadshow, which was instrumental in spreading the Chicago blues to England, influencing a generation of British future rock stars and enshrining Chicago electric blues as the genuine article over there.

Waters recorded the passing-the-torch album *Fathers and Sons* with Michael Bloomfield in the late 1960s, and the blues-rock guitarist Johnny Winter produced four albums for Waters in the late 1970s and early 1980s.

Waters died in 1983, and his estate was a client of Dixon's Blues Heaven Foundation, founded the same year and dedicated to the proposition that "the blues are the roots; the rest are the fruits" (Dixon's words). From its home at 2120 South Michigan Avenue in Chicago, the old Chess studios, the foundation preserves the legacies of the old masters, propagates the tradition among young people and makes sure older players and their estates get their financial due. In the process, Filene writes, the foundation "implicitly canonize[s] blues musicians,"[17] as well as the genre as a whole.

In short, the greater influence and higher place that Muddy Waters has in American cultural memory than Lead Belly, Filene argues, is partly due to what he calls the inextricable connection between memory and popularity (and in turn the musical flexibility required to pursue a durable popularity), but it is also due to the conscious efforts of memory workers who "attempted to sense (and direct) the underlying current" and "advanced visions of America's musical past."[18]

This threading together of the traditional and the new has been a part of the festival's ethos since the beginning, and it has fueled its recent renaissance. Where other memory workers labored on behalf of an artist, a stable of artists, or even a genre, Sweet's efforts since taking over the Newport Folk Festival constitute a body of memory work on behalf of the institution itself. The festival evokes its past in the return of what few artists from the earliest festivals remain, such as Ramblin' Jack Elliott and the Kossoy Sisters, as well as the celebration of milestone anniversaries of landmark events. Such celebrations also reflect conscious integration of the past in framing the present. In 2015, the fiftieth anniversary of Bob Dylan's electric performance was celebrated while the thirtieth anniversary of the return of the festival and its establishment at Fort Adams was ignored, an echo of Filene's observation that "history is something we consciously make." And the emphasis on younger artists, as well as the artistic flexibility required to continue expanding the festival's horizons, keep not only the commercial life but the cultural importance of Newport alive—popularity and American cultural importance so often being intertwined.

Bob Jones reverses the causal relationship between Sweet's methods and his success, arguing that "The weight of the festival and its tradition has been able to carry Jay on to do what he wants."[19] Sweet doesn't disagree but says that he consciously cites that very weight and tradition to be able to make his decisions with confidence. All artists looking for advice from Sweet on how to win over the Newport crowd are told, "Let them know that you know where you are. If you think you're gonna come in with whatever the set is that you bring out on tour, and they know you're just doing your set, you're gonna get crushed." The recent popularity of the festival helps him in this regard: "I always say, 'Remember—they didn't buy a ticket to see you necessarily. They had no idea you were playing. You have to impress them, because they're not there to see you.' The artists who come back realize it immediately."[20]

But is Bob Jones right that the festival is riding a cyclical high, with the implication being that the force of commercial gravity will someday soon take over? It's not preposterous to think so, particularly given a recent resurgence in music festivals nationwide, but Sweet believes the interest in the festival is more broadly based than in a small group of artists. Dom Flemons, formerly of the Newport alums the Carolina Chocolate Drops, says the interest in acoustic and roots-based music that has gotten mainstream attention with breakthroughs such as the *O Brother Where Art Thou?* soundtrack and Johnny Cash's *American Recordings* series may help Newport, but that that interest comes from a deep place:

> We're still in the mindset that we have to keep pushing the envelope
> forward. But in the postdigital revolution, there is no envelope anymore.
> And I feel like we need to be pushing for standardized things. People have
> been referencing Dylan going electric in 1965, and they've been like, "Well,
> he was an artist, and he was interested in progressing forward." But Dylan
> had a cultural memory that everybody shared, that goes back, and then
> he was able to take his idea forward. Now we don't have that. Most people
> don't have a straight knowledge of "Well, this is what traditional music
> means, and now let's move it." Now people just grab what they like and

mold it. Traditional music's not based on that. Traditional music's based on hunkering down and learning it and doing it the same way. . . .

The generation gap of interest in folk music is coming back together. People sigh about the hipsters, but in the early '60s it was the same sort of hipsters and countercultural ideas that were going on. And I think that that movement is regenerating itself. It's access—I think most people who are into folk music in general are interested in this traditional stuff. It's just that it's been so long since it's been overtly presented like, "Here; take this in. Immerse yourself in it."[21]

In Flemons's "postdigital revolution," he adds, there's room for everyone—the kind of side taking that happened between the Kingston Trio wing of folk music and the Lester Scruggs wing, or for that matter the Pete Seeger–Bob Dylan schism of the mid-1960s, he argues, no longer has to happen.

But the rising of a new generation necessarily comes with the ushering aside—sometimes the shoving aside—of an older one, and that can happen on either side of the stage.

Previously, each time George Wein picked up a new native guide to the folk music world—changing from Albert Grossman to Pete Seeger and from Pete Seeger to Bob Jones—it was accompanied by a hiatus in the production of the Newport Folk Festival. This time, however, Jay Sweet acquired more and more power and responsibility while Bob Jones was still in the picture.

Jones was slowed by a bout with the stroke-like nervous-system disorder Guillian-Barre Syndrome in 2004, which first confined him to a wheelchair and still requires his use of a walker. His daughter Nalini and her friend Tracey Meade did much of the booking for the next several years, before Festival Network took over.

Still, Wein says, it was a difficult transition. "All of a sudden, I was saying, 'Bob, work with Jay.' . . . It was very difficult for him—it's still difficult for him. But nothing succeeds like success, and when we sell out the three days, Bob understands that. . . . Bob is very precious to me. But I still had to make a move and tell him to work with Jay Sweet. And then, slowly but surely, it became an autonomous thing with Jay Sweet. . . . But believe me, Jay still calls Bob once in a while about certain things."[22]

Jones now calls himself retired, and as the 2014 festival blared around him, he declared that "I have no responsibilities . . . I've got all the time in the world. . . . As far as I'm concerned, it's his ballgame now."[23] Still, Jones manages to get his opinions in: "I couldn't care less what [Sweet] does on this event," he said at the 2014 festival. "I just want to make sure that he keeps the musical level up," citing the performance of the blues–hard rock group Reignwolf as a failure to do so. He also warns that while Sweet is riding high with annual sellouts, he too had success in his time: "I hope it continues like this, but these events are very cyclical."[24]

Sweet responds that while Jones and Wein have their criticisms of his opinions and decisions, "the biggest thing they did for me" was to never let an agent or an artist go over Sweet's head to them. And he laughs as he recounts that Wein will never miss a chance to say, "'He thought he knew everything; he knew nothing!' He'll tell this while I'm standing there. He'll tell it to my wife."[25]

A generational changeover began in the audience as well. Jill Davidson said in 2014, "We've turned over the audience almost completely in the last five years. People who were coming here five years ago are almost gone, and a whole new group of people are in here now."[26]

Beer sales were expanded, Davidson says, to cater to the younger audience that was turning out to see younger acts. Artists were beginning to make more and more signing appearances at merchandise tents after their performances. And the entire area in the front of the main stage, which used to hold the blankets and lawn chairs of the earliest arrivals, has been given over to an area where only standing and dancing are allowed, giving the venue the feeling of a concert, rather than a stay-all-day festival atmosphere.

That's drawn mixed reactions from some longtime observers. Johnette Rodriguez and her husband, Bill, from Wakefield, Rhode Island, first came to the Newport Folk Festival in 1969, the year the headliners included Johnny Cash and June Carter and the new-artists stage featured Van Morrison, James Taylor, Joni Mitchell and more. She recalls the multistage experience as "hectic" but fun enough that she went to the revived jazz festival starting in 1981. And when the folk festival returned in 1985, she and her husband, along with her sister, were excited enough to see Judy Collins and the rest that they showed up early enough to be first in line when the gates opened, so they could spread a blanket in a prime spot in front of the stage (the only stage at that point). They've done so every year since.

The first year, she remembers, "We were next to these two guys who were surreptitiously recording and one of them was from South Carolina and one of them was from Birmingham, so we kinda introduced ourselves, and the next year they were back." That began a tradition that's lasted nearly thirty years and counting. The Group, as they began to call themselves (with T-shirts to prove it), grew as the years went by, to about twenty by the mid-'90s, Rodriguez says.[27]

Members of the Group came from Connecticut, Washington state, Alabama and plenty of places in between, and they formed a tight bond over the music and through their lives. In 2007 in the literary journal *Balancing the Tides*, Rodriguez wrote,

> We share our water, rain ponchos, sunscreen, hats, the blanket/tarp space and, of course, the music. We also share lifestyles and life situations, such as our friend in a wheelchair and his large black Lab service dog. We enjoy each other's enthusiasms, tolerate overwrought reactions to the on-stage "stars" and try to understand each person's needs and foibles. We continue to befriend neighbors on adjacent blankets and temporary visitors who ask to sit with us for a particular set.[28]

For Rodriguez, the female acts had an extra appeal: seeing Bonnie Raitt, Nanci Griffith, Iris Dement, Mary Chapin Carpenter and others "cemented the sisterhood of my front-row female friends, re-affirming the inner strength we all need to 'perform' in our daily lives."

She can recall getting a bandana from Willie Nelson, take umbrage at having been obliquely referred to as a "grandmother" in an Ani DiFranco–inspired jostle, bristle as she remembers that "we had to really prepare ourselves to be stepped all over when the Indigos came on," and share a dozen other anecdotes from decades of attendance at what she remembers Bruce Cockburn calling "a festival of friends."

At Newport, she wrote, "I encounter a new artist whose talent knocks me over, enjoy a favorite musician whom I am thrilled to finally see in live performance and almost always make a new friend."

Many of those new friends were added to the Group, and it grew in other ways. Rodriguez wrote that "the guy from South Carolina brought his fiancée the next year and the following year she accompanied him as his wife. They brought along the oldest of her three children and the year after that all three of them. This past summer, they arrived with two of those kids (who'd now been coming for almost twenty years) and a grandchild!"

Six years later, in 2013, however, the Group had dwindled to six originals and a few relative newcomers, Rodriguez says. And while Rodriguez, a hardy fan who can be seen at many Rhode Island musical events, continues to attend, she thinks some of the changes at Newport are pushing her away.

The young energy of the revitalized festival, Rodriguez says, has kept the festival alive and interesting, but at a cost. While she could always be found in her front-row spot, occasionally drifting off to another stage during breaks or to see a particular favorite, by 2013 she was a wandering presence, hiding from what she calls "a mosh pit in front of the stage. . . . I think initially Jay had a lot more respect for the people who had come before him than he seems to now. There's the positive aspect that he's keeping the festival going, but there's a balance there. I think he could have done it without alienating so many of the old fans. If we were ever going to be patient with all the changes that have happened, nobody has been patient with what has happened up in front of the stage."[29]

While Rodriguez says she continues to see old favorites and make new musical discoveries at Newport—her 2013 musical crush was on the Milk Carton Kids—she thinks the days of the Group are drawing to a close. "I know people who just aren't coming back. . . . I don't know if we'll come next year. It'll depend."[30] (The Rodriguezes still come to Newport; in 2014, after the recent death of a close friend, they explained that they needed to be somewhere where they could celebrate life.)

Sweet says of the dancing issue, "I made a conscious effort to allow people . . . a section where they can go and commune with the artist. Mostly because artists were coming off the stage totally demoralized because people were . . . doing the crossword puzzle just waiting for the headliner, while people who wanted to engage were left way in the back."[31]

Speaking in 2012 to the *Globe*'s Reed, Sweet said,

> The biggest criticism is that we are popular now. I think a lot of people don't like it when something's successful. . . .
>
> We also get: "This isn't folk music. We've been coming to this festival for 35 years, and what you have booked is not folk music." These are the

first people to claim pride that they were there when Dylan did what he did in 1965. I always tell them, "These young people who are coming to our festival now? This is their folk music."[32]

Some of the problem is about the dancers, Rodriguez says; some of it is the volume. Some of it is about aesthetics ("I have to ask, is some of this folk music?"). But it's also about the feeling. Until recently, she says, Newport carried with it a sense of "everybody being here for the music and each other and sometimes for a political cause. And I don't feel that so much anymore. But maybe those people who are the same age will get it together. I don't know."[33]

While a general live-and-let-live attitude prevails at the Newport Folk Festival these days, the level of explicit political activity is generally limited to making sure people recycle and a general exhortation to treat each other fairly. A paint-by-numbers painting with the words "This Land Is Your Land," which gave audience members the chance to fill in areas themselves, stood as a visual tribute to Pete Seeger at the 2014 festival. The sentiment was lovely, the do-it-yourself aesthetic was pure Seeger, and there were stirring political moments, such as Thao & the Get Down Stay Down's "We the Common" and the incandescent performance by reggae legend Jimmy Cliff. But the festival as a whole didn't claim to be making a point. (The effect of the election of Donald Trump to the presidency in 2016 remains to be seen.)

"The level of politics has diminished," says Jim Gillis. "Tom Morello will always fire that up, but . . . it's probably like that in modern society, too." Gillis recalls that in the 1990s, Michelle Shocked, playing on V-J Day (Victory over Japan Day, which only Rhode Island still celebrates), asked the audience to lie down "because she wanted to see what it looked like when people had been destroyed by bombs. . . . But I just think any kind of protest movement is more factionalized than the civil rights movement was."[34]

Peter Yarrow thinks the nation hasn't recovered from the divisions of the Vietnam War:

> We did things in that war that were extraordinarily reprehensible, and we've never come to terms with that as a country. And . . . when people know that they've done something terrible, or injurious to others, they tend to . . . live in denial of it if they don't come to terms with it, [or] they make up excuses and justify their actions. . . .

We are a divided nation, in such a way that has really killed the spirit of unanimity and hunger for justice.[35]

But Sweet's memory work needed an audience ready to receive it, and as Muddy Waters's work fell on the ears of an audience underrecognized at the time, the reimagined Newport Folk Festival caught the ears of a generation of young fans ready to listen to a new vision of folk. Where Sweet found common ground with the architects of the folk revival–era Newport Folk Festival, so the young people in the twenty-first-century audience and the conditions they've grown up with bear some resemblance to their forebears a half century previous.

A reading of Robert Cantwell's frank assessment of his own generation, which flocked to the folk festival during the early 1960s, reveals such similarities. A generation squeezed by a precipitous economic downturn and an explosion of student-loan debt that the blogger Duncan Black characterizes as having "a mortgage but no home," and growing up in the aftermath of the September 11 terrorist attacks and resulting disastrous Iraq occupation, sounds much like what Cantwell (born in 1946) must have had in mind when, of his own generation, he wrote that "The invention of a folk . . . provides immediate relief from the sense of oppressive change emanating from vast, remote and often inconceivable historical forces, and from an accompanying sense of personal disorientation, diminution, or fragmentation."[36]

Indeed, Cantwell foresaw it himself. Writing in 1996, he pointed out that "with vested interests holding hostage the core agendas of both liberals and conservatives, legislators mired in private obligation . . . the deliberative processes of government effectively grind to a halt."[37] As such, "in successive periods a number of 'progressive,' alternative, or oppositional styles and ideologies . . . continuing today in green, new age, punk, deadhead, grunge and slacker movements, have ridden the waves of generations of youth recoiling from the real world as it confronts them after domestic and scholastic protections have receded, often adopting the more genuinely angry styles and postures of excluded ethnic, working-class, or minority youth."[38]

And while older observers see a generation blunted by material comforts and screen-based gratification, Cantwell reminds us that his own cohort "lacked the disruptive energy of J. K. Huysmans, Lenin, or Tristan Tzara"[39] and was "a generation destined to fall in love with itself."[40]

He adds that "it was . . . the suppression of the earlier political affiliations that enabled the folk revival to flourish as it did,"[41] particularly when the singer-songwriter generation moved the focus from "we" to "I," as Josh Dunson wrote. Indeed, Cantwell reminds us that, going all the way back to progressive social-work pioneer Jane Addams, we can find that a desire to reconnect with whatever is currently defined as folk and folk culture can be ascribed to feeling "smothered and sickened by advantages."[42]

Sweet told Nate Chinen of the *New York Times* in 2012, "The artists understand that playing Newport is an invite; it's not a booking."[43] The rising of a new generation of singers and songwriters means, to borrow a geological term, another layer of history on top of the Newport Folk Festival. A fan such as Sean Maloney, who grew up in North Reading, Massachusetts, sees the Group's era at Newport as a piece of its history. He came to the Newport Folk Festival in 1989 as a punk rock–loving child accompanying his father as part of "divorced-dad weekend" and remembers, "I was miserable . . . you can't listen to DRI and [then] go see Joan Baez when you're ten; there's too much cognitive dissonance there. But now as a thirty-three-year-old, seeing the connections grow and become solid and second nature, it's a beautiful thing."[44]

The sheer weight of history at Newport means that second-generation moments happen. In 2013, Merrill Garbus of tUnE-yArDs began her Newport set with an explanation that Newport was the first festival she'd ever been to and the first festival-gig announcement she was able to impress her parents with. In 2015, Brad Barr of the Barr Brothers explained to the crowd that his and bandmate/brother Andrew's parents' first date consisted of sneaking into the 1967 Newport Folk Festival to hear Arlo Guthrie sing "Alice's Restaurant." Hozier and Dom Flemons both credit Murray Lerner's *Festival!* film with inspiring them to become musicians.

Many of the younger performers speak of Newport and the artists who came before them with reverence. The singer-songwriter Joe Pug says, "When you get on stage, you try not to think about too much stuff and just be in the moment. But it's pretty hard to get on a stage with that much history and not at least . . . be self-conscious a couple of times, just realizing what a lineage you've been allowed to be a small part of."[45]

"There might be some folk purists who might be insulted" by new claims to the mantle of folk music, says Taylor Goldsmith, the chief singer, songwriter and guitarist with Dawes, who have played the festival annually since 2009, and who serves on the festival's seven-member artist advisory board along with McCauley; the Decemberists' Meloy; Jim James; Gillian Welch; and Sara Watkins of Nickel Creek and the Watkins Family Hour. "And maybe they know more about the heritage than me. But I feel that if I'm watching someone sing a song, and it's compelling or illuminating in any possible way, and I feel like I'm getting to know that person through the music—it's hard for me to give more of a definition to the term 'folk.'"[46]

Ketch Secor, of Old Crow Medicine Show, says the first song he learned to play on guitar was Phil Ochs's "I Ain't Marching Anymore," from *Broadside*'s compilation of songs from the first two Newport festivals. The band first played at Newport in 2004, when half of them didn't look old enough to drink. They've been enormously popular since then, working up to mainstage slots and headlining sets. His feelings about Newport are more complicated: "I thought it was gonna be the ultimate venue, and when I got there it was a festival."[47]

He says that when he plays at Fort Adams he thinks about Doc Watson and other hillbillies from the old days—the people who would "ride all the way to the end of the line—southern New England, and be that far away from the mountains of Tennessee." He feels a bit the same way himself. When recalling the group's 2013 festival performance on a rainy Friday evening, he remembers thinking, "This is a crowd that has the most high-tech foul-weather gear. . . . It looked like an L. L. Bean catalog shoot. I mean, there were thousands of dollars of rain gear right at my feet." Introducing Jim Garland's labor song "I Don't Want Your Millions, Mister," "I thought, 'God, who am I talking to? Who is understanding this?'"[48]

Jeff Tweedy, who has played solo sets at Newport as well as performing as the lead singer and chief songwriter of Wilco, says that coming to Fort Adams for the first time, "at least in my mind, it had a mythology similar to Woodstock. It had played a key role in rock history, or something. But getting there and playing a part in it is, delightfully, more manageable. I questioned it when we were originally asked to do it years ago, and I stopped questioning it. If they're asking us to be there, they're obviously asking us to come and do our thing. It's not only a nice ethos; I think it's kind of smart to keep their festival from suffering from Bounder's Disease or whatever they call it. It's gonna die if you don't bring in some other generations."[49]

Others comment on the inviting atmosphere of Newport. "1 was amazed," Jack White said from the stage in 2014, "that there was one place left on Earth that 1 could walk around and listen to bands and it was fine."

"No one stays an extra day at a festival," says Rhode Island–based singer-songwriter Joe Fletcher, who has played Newport several times and hosted a Thursday-night kickoff party in 2014. "[But] a lot of bands took the weekend off and skipped a Saturday night where they could be playing somewhere and making money, just to hang out. People don't do that anywhere else. . . . It's just got a magical feel—the water, the little peninsula of land, the fort—it's aesthetically beautiful. It's 10,000 people; it's not a sea."[50]

And while Deer Tick's McCauley, like Sweet, first experienced the festival by seeing Los Lobos in 1989, he says, "We do our best to preserve the traditions there: an appreciation of early American music, and beyond that . . . to other countries. And an anything-can-happen, communal kind of musical spirit. You never know who might hop onstage with someone, and that doesn't really happen at other festivals. At other festivals, it doesn't happen organically; it's set up by the person who's running the festival. . . . [That's] a disaster for us."[51]

Thao Nguyen of Thao & the Get Down Stay Down made her first Newport appearance in 2014 but says that she learned the traditions of folk music in school. "The Newport Folk Festival was the beacon for me, because the reason that 1 got into guitar-playing . . . was old country, folk, blues, old-time Appalachian—and 1 knew that everybody 1 was a huge fan of had come through here. 1 studied them at school because it was such a pivotal part of American history and politics as well." Even if the festival didn't have decades of history behind it, Nguyen says, "It's still the best festival that we play. . . . And maybe that's out of respect for the history and tradition of this festival, but 1 also think that that's what the creators have promoted and what they stay true to. Everybody relaxes and breathes a sigh of relief."[52]

Sweet's booking ethos of "a curatorial aspect mixed with a familial aspect"[53] may find its prime example in Jim James, who has played Newport with everything from the Monsters of Folk to his own group, My Morning Jacket, to solo acoustic sets and mostly instrumental performances with a semiorchestra. He's also hopped onstage with seemingly anyone who would have him, ranging from singer-songwriter legend John Prine to cellist Ben Sollee to the Preservation Hall Jazz Band. James calls Newport "a magical place":

> For me, [Newport] is the festival that you go to for two or three days, and you get lost in the world of it. The world of Newport is such a unique and strange world, because it's like you're in some bizarre, alternate-universe amusement park. The site of the festival itself, this old fort, and you're playing looking at the water, looking at all the boats. It's like everything's drawn in pastels or something. Finding yourself rehearsing in some crazy mansion the size of a museum that's now just a tourist attraction . . . there's just something about the whole place. I'm a big believer in spirits and ghosts and whatever forces are working that we're not fully aware of, and I just feel like Newport is full of ghosts. It's haunted, in a good way—and in some dark ways; there are some dark ghosts looming there as well. But that kind of makes it all part of the intrigue of the place.
>
> The whole process of Newport Folk is so funny, because so many people consider it a folk festival, and so many people consider folk music to be a person and a guitar. That's so many people's definition of quote-unquote "folk music." But Dylan, most obviously, most famously, kind of proved that folk could be a guy with an electric guitar. So my definition of Newport Folk is whatever I'm personally doing at the moment. . . . And I like playing acoustic guitar by myself, but I also like playing with a full band, and weird electronic stuff, or different types of music. "Folk music" is a limitless term that has come to mean "a guy with an acoustic guitar." . . . but hip-hop is folk music; there are lots of different types of music that is folk music. I think the festival is starting to grow and embrace that a little bit more.[54]

Some of the more outré additions to the Newport bill in recent years have included Beck, the singer-songwriter who made electronics into the backbone of much of his music, particularly on the hit "Loser"; and tUnE-yArDs, the performing name of Merrill Garbus, a virtual one-woman orchestra of drum loops, percussion and ukulele. Sweet says, "I will argue all day long, with anyone, about why Beck is a folk artist,"[55] a modern-day, electro equivalent to a one-man jug band; his acoustic miniset with ageless Ramblin' Jack Elliott in 2013 speaks to Sweet's point. So does the argument Gene Youngblood made in 1967: "This new music may have its roots more in technology than in turf, but because of our affluent and technological society, the Moog Synthesizer, the wah-wah peddle [*sic*] and the Vox amp are as accessible and intrinsic to the new troubadour as the jug and Jew's Harp were to the mountain moaner. And if the message has changed from dirt to dope it is still a message, still personal, still reflective of the attitudes of the 'folk.'"[56]

For years, Wein has been concerned with the ability of both Newport festivals to outlive him. In 2004 he said that he looked forward to the State of Rhode Island and the City of Newport taking the festivals over, but not long after that he began to dream of reviving another tradition from the old days: a nonprofit foundation. And in late 2010, the Newport Festivals Foundation was formed, with the mission of maintaining the two festivals "in perpetuity, to be presented at historic locations, including Fort Adams State Park and other facilities in Newport, R.I." The nonprofit structure reinforces not only the festivals' financial stability but Wein's conception of where they fit in the musical world. The mission statement also includes the declaration "that jazz and folk music as with any art form, is an ever-evolving cultural expression."[57]

The nonprofit status allows the festivals to apply for foundation support and has also resulted in "a huge difference in people's attitude . . . it created a whole family feeling," Wein says.

Presenting a festival at Newport will always be a tricky, expensive proposition—the venue must be built from scratch every year, Davidson explains, and Newport is an expensive city in which to house organizers and artists. Sweet says the festival "basically breaks even" on ticket sales and sponsorships—despite the lack of a title sponsor, Davidson says that the folk festival has only "slightly less sponsorship" money coming in than the jazz festival.

Still, Wein says that "there are no basic problems with us continuing another fifteen or twenty years, with or without me. . . . If I had a dream to keep these festivals going after I'm gone, I think the dream has become a reality."[58] In November 2015, Sweet was promoted to executive producer of the Newport Festivals Foundation, overseeing both the folk and jazz festivals.

Pete Seeger's death in 2014 presented the organizers with an aesthetic challenge: while there would certainly be enough willing, high-powered names to stage a Madison Square Garden–worthy all-star tribute, that was exactly what Seeger wouldn't want—indeed, didn't want.

Seeger himself confirmed this to Jay Sweet, the producer says: "Pete had given me a mandate" in their last conversation saying if he couldn't make it to Newport for the next festival, "I want to make sure there isn't a big fuss about me."[59] Sweet confirmed Seeger's wishes with Tao Rodriguez Seeger and instead helped create a corner of the festival that embodies the ambitions Seeger had for Newport when he cowrote the festival's manifesto in 1962 and over which he even railed against the festival in the late '60s.

In the Museum of Yachting, a small building on the grounds of Fort Adams that holds about 100 people, three days of performances collectively known as For Pete's Sake exhibit the kind of traditional performers and lesser-known singer-songwriters that comprised Pete Seeger's ideal for a folk festival. Curated and hosted by Chris Funk, best known as the guitarist with the Decemberists, the performances ranged in 2014 from a song circle to a bagpipe duo to a hurdy-gurdy band complete with a dog jumping through hoops.

"Pete had said, 'Don't do a tribute to me—bring dancers and bagpipe players: something that encompasses the patchwork of what we deem American folk music, which is vast,'" Funk says. "Specialized instruments and musicians that maybe people don't know as well. Not the Jack Whites, not the My Morning Jackets, not the Decemberists, but bring some younger songwriters or some musicians who are specialists on their instruments." Of keeping Seeger's tradition alive, Funk says, "I think he was one of the greatest Americans. He encompasses American spirit beyond just music. I'm not saying I'm that person, but—shit; it kind of got laid on me, and I said, 'Well, sure.'"[60] He repeated the presentation on the Saturday of the 2015 festival, with Dom Flemons taking over the Sunday and presenting a bill that included a passel of acts presented by the Music Maker Relief Foundation, including the Coma Mamas and seventy-five-year-old Ironing Board Sam.

Seeger's tradition was on exhibit when Jack White, formerly of the White Stripes, announced in 2014 that he didn't have enough time left on stage to play his full set. He omitted the White Stripes hit "Seven Nation Army" and went straight into "Goodnight Irene," Lead Belly's song that had been a hit for the Pete Seeger-led Weavers in 1950—years before almost anyone in the audience was born, and years before many of the audience members' parents had been born—complete with a Seeger-inspired sing-along.

For Wein and Sweet, the moment, capping off a sold-out day, encapsulated what they'd been trying to do for years. "To try to replicate what you did years ago," Wein said later, "you can't do it. But if it just happens, with younger people who can relate to it, it's perfect."[61]

In that spirit, the 2009 sing-along finale inspired a change. While many festivals of the early 2000s ended with whatever song the last act happened to end with, nearly every day of the festival since the fiftieth-anniversary edition has concluded with a group of unrelated artists joining in on a standard of the Seeger or Dylan era, putting an emotional and historical cap on the event. In 2014, Seeger's passing was marked by headliner Mavis Staples and a gaggle of lesser-known acts joining in on "We Shall Overcome," while in other years the elder statespeople have included Jackson Browne (2013) and Levon Helm (several times before his death in 2012). It's effectively an opportunity for young performers to stand toe-to-toe with their heroes and prove their worth.

Of the Newport festival as it was in the 1960s, Robert Cantwell made the following distinction: "If the musically expert and charismatic young revivalists at Newport drew greater audiences and more enthusiastic ovations than the authentic musicians themselves, it is certainly because their performances sanctified the site by demonstrating the successful transmission of the folk character to the young—liberating them, in effect, from their own youth."[62]

James Felice of the Felice Brothers took part in a sing-along finale of "I Shall Be Released" in 2010 with Levon Helm, a member of the Band, which backed Bob Dylan through many raucous and ill-received electric shows after he musically torched Festival Field in 1965; Richie Havens, one of the "new" generation of singer-songwriters who had played at Newport decades previous, before Felice's birth; and many more.

"That's the best part of your life right there," Felice told *Rolling Stone* upon getting off the stage. "It doesn't get quite as good as that."[63]

#DONTLOOKBACK

The 2015 Newport Folk Festival concluded with a parade of performers from the weekend, plus several guest stars, celebrating the fiftieth anniversary of Bob Dylan's electric performance—those fifteen minutes that had so riled observers, ruined Newport in some ways, and continued the process of revolutionizing popular music. Performers shuttled on and off stage, paying tribute to songs that ranged through much of what's considered Dylan's glory days. The duo of Gillian Welch and David Rawlings essentially anchored the acoustic performances, with beautiful takes on "Mr. Tambourine Man," "It's All Over Now, Baby Blue" and more with help from Willie Watson and others. Dawes provided the backing for the electric material, with special appearances including Blake Mills, Deer Tick and most powerfully Robyn Hitchcock, who managed, in the middle of a slam-bang celebration, to make the marathon "Visions of Johanna" mesmerizing.

All the while, many in the crowd of 10,000 were waiting impatiently.

Before the '65 Revisited tribute began, fans buzzed, as they had for much of the day, with speculation that Dylan himself would be part of the tribute. Other names were bandied about—Bono, Paul McCartney—and their tour schedules scrutinized on smartphones for clues as to whether they'd be nearby and free to drop in. But many fans wouldn't give up the dream of Dylan returning to celebrate past glory—never mind that precious few things seemed farther out of character for him, or that the organizers had tweeted, "We can not say this any other way. BOB DYLAN IS NOT PLAYING #NFFI5 #DontLookBack." Jay Sweet says that after a pro forma contact with (and refusal from) Dylan's management, he had no intention of celebrating the fiftieth anniversary of Dylan's feat—"this festival moves forward"—but that he relented after a long-enough succession of artists asked him how the festival would mark the occasion, delegating the job to Welch, Rawlings, Goldsmith and a few other artists. Still, as the show began, one fan even received a text from a friend claiming that he'd seen Dylan, along with Al Kooper, a member of the band that fateful night in 1965, backstage.

The most-anticipated moment of the 2015 finale came when Dawes took the stage to begin the electric segment of the tribute: here, many in the audience thought, was when the man himself, or someone similarly huge, would appear.

Those fans might have been disappointed when Dawes front man Taylor Goldsmith essentially took on the electric-Dylan role, with guest verses on various songs outsourced to Hozier, Deer Tick's McCauley and Ian O'Neil, and others. Goldsmith played "Maggie's Farm" on the same guitar Dylan had played on that night in 1965 — a guitar that had only been rediscovered and authenticated a couple of years before and had been sold for nearly a million dollars to the owner of the Indianapolis Colts football team. (Legend has it that Dylan, who never had much regard for one guitar over another, had absent-mindedly left it on a plane and never bothered to reclaim it.) Meanwhile, Kooper was in fact in the house, returning to the organ for his signature part on "Like a Rolling Stone," and the day wrapped up with an all-hands-on-deck sing-along on "Rainy Day Women #12 and 35," with the Preservation Hall Jazz Band providing the indispensable horn-section wheezes.

"This guitar that I'm holding has been on this stage before," Goldsmith said before "Maggie's Farm." Strictly speaking, of course, that wasn't true. It wouldn't be the first time an artist has erroneously thought that he or she is standing on the very stage at which Dylan went electric, slouching under a stone arch that Mississippi John Hurt passed under or eating at a picnic table that once groaned under the weight of Muddy Waters.

But by "this stage," Goldsmith likely meant the Newport stage, and from his point of view, he was right. At that point, fifty-six years from its beginning, the Newport Folk Festival had not only contributed to the history of folk music, rock music and other musics, but made a history, an ethos and a tradition of its own.

Who decides when a tradition is being upheld? Who decides when a tradition is being betrayed? Opinions can coalesce, but there's never one answer. George Wein still wields authority, but he gave up the day-to-day work of the Newport Folk Festival long ago. Pete Seeger was the touchstone, the North Star of the movement, but he's gone. Bob Dylan never wanted the job. Jay Sweet is the latest in the line of succession. Johnette Rodriguez and Bob Weiser have been attached to the festival longer than Sweet. Where does this credential lie?

A study of the Newport Folk Festival, and the evolution of folk music inside it, reveals that the tradition lies in the tension—the uncertainty. A musical form, or a musical institution, is not a tradition until it's carried on by someone other than the originator; it's also likely not a tradition until someone argues that it's being betrayed. If either the form or the institution have any value, both of these developments will inevitably happen.

And that tension, that uncertainty, that creation of new tradition happens at least as much in the audience as it does on stage. Dar Williams, during her Newport performance in 1994, claimed that the defining factor of folk music was "an audience that listens." The audience provides context and meaning as well as the performers—"We Shall Overcome," as we've seen, wasn't an anthem when Guy Carawan did it at Newport in 1960; it was an anthem when a cast of stars performed it in 1963, during a summer of protest and violence. And while observers can—and do—look at the current incarnation of the Newport Folk Festival and pronounce various versions of John S. Patterson's assessment of the Kingston Trio ("not a record of traditions, but what a mass audience wishes to accept as traditions"), that attitude can presume an objectivity that doesn't really exist.

Robert Cantwell wrote, "Like other noble ideas, the idea of the folk must be an invention, a substance sublimated by an aspiration . . . The performance of a folk song is as much a representation as the pastoral painting or the proletarian novel . . . claiming and attributing but never confirming."[1]

"Maggie's Farm," as John Cohen pointed out years ago, derived from the chestnut "Penny's Farm." At Newport in 1965, though, it wasn't a folk song—it was a blast of jet exhaust, a thumb in the eye to what had gone before. But when Dawes, with the help of Welch and Rawlings, played it at Newport, in honor of the man who brought it there, with the guitar he'd played it on, they revived a well-known and well-loved song and imbued it with a resonance that rewarded anyone in the audience with a knowledge of what had come before.

Together, they made it a folk song.

NOTES

1. PEOPLE THINK THIS STUFF JUST HAPPENS

1. The description of Pete Seeger's 1959 performance comes from the sound recording, "The Newport Folk Festival 1959," released by Not Now Records in 2011.

2. The description of Pete Seeger's 2009 performance comes from the author's observation, July 25, 2009. The quotes from him on that day come from an interview with the author.

3. Devon Maloney, "Newport Folk Festival Wrestles Weather, Evolving Legacy with Beck, Avett Brothers, Feist," www.billboard.com, July 29, 2013, at http://www .billboard.com/articles/columns/music-festivals/5053720/newport-folk-festival -wrestles-weather-evolving-legacy-with.

4. Interview with the author, July 6, 2009.

5. Interview with the author, July 6, 2009.

6. Pete Seeger, interview on *Pete Seeger: The Power of Song*, Genius Products DVD, 2008.

2. THE AMERICAN PUBLIC IS LIKE SLEEPING BEAUTY

1. The recapitulation of George Wein's early life is taken from George Wein and Nate Chinen, *Myself among Others: A Life in Music* (Cambridge, MA: Da Capo Press, 2003). Wein quotes in this chapter are from this memoir unless otherwise noted.

2. Burt Goldblatt, *Newport Jazz Festival: The Illustrated History* (New York: Dial Press, 1977), xi–xiii, xvi.

3. Goldblatt, *Newport Jazz Festival*, xiii.

4. Wein and Chinen, *Myself among Others*, 313–314.

5. Interview with the author, May 19, 2011.

6. Neil V. Rosenberg, ed., *Transforming Tradition: Folk Music Revivals Examined* (Urbana: University of Illinois Press, 1993), 11.

7. Benjamin Filene, *Romancing the Folk: Public Memory & American Roots Music* (Chapel Hill, London: University of North Carolina Press, 2000), 12.

8. Robert Cantwell, *When We Were Good: The Folk Revival* (Cambridge, MA, and London: Harvard University Press, 1996), 307.

9. Ronald D. Cohen, *Rainbow Quest: The Folk Music Revival & American Society, 1940–1970* (Amherst and Boston: University of Massachusetts Press, 2002), 19.

10. Cohen, *Rainbow Quest*, 70.

11. Matusow later wrote the book *False Witness*, in which he said he had been paid to lie in his testimony, and he later served almost three years for perjury.

12. Cohen, *Rainbow Quest*, 76.

13. Cantwell, *When We Were Good*, 280.

14. Cantwell, *When We Were Good*, 162.

15. "Folk Music Today: A Symposium," *Sing Out!* February–March 1961, 27; in Cantwell, *When We Were Good*, 163.

16. Cantwell, *When We Were Good*, 164.

17. An excellent distillation of the political harassment of the folk world can be found in Cohen's *Rainbow Quest*, 80–87.

18. Cantwell, *When We Were Good*, 190.

19. Susan Montgomery, "The Folk Furor," *Mademoiselle*, December 1960, 118. In Cantwell, *When We Were Good*, 327.

20. Cantwell, *When We Were Good*, 89.

21. Eileen Stekert, "Cents and Nonsense in the Urban Folksong Movement: 1930–66," in Rosenberg, *Transforming Tradition*, 95–96.

22. Cohen, *Rainbow Quest*, 136.

23. Cantwell, *When We Were Good*, 8.

24. Robert Cantwell, *When We Were Good*, in Rosenberg, *Transforming Tradition*, 38 and 44.

25. Todd Gitlin, *The Sixties: Years of Hope, Days of Rage* (New York: Bantam, 1987), 75, in Cohen, *Rainbow Quest*, 159.

26. Montgomery, "The Folk Furor," 99, in Cohen, *Rainbow Quest*, 167.

27. Ronald Cohen, *A History of Folk Music Festivals in the United States: Feasts of Musical Celebration* (Scarecrow Press, 2008), 48.

28. Interview with the author, September 11, 2014.

29. Interview with the author, December 14, 2011.

30. "Albert Grossman's Ghost," Rory O'Conner, *Musician* magazine, http://theband.hiof.no/articles/agg_musician_june_1987.html, accessed September 18, 2014.

31. Interview with the author, September 4, 2014.

32. Interview with the author, May 19, 2011.

33. Interview with the author, September 11, 2014.

34. Frederic Ramsey, "Newport Ho! The Folk Festival," *Saturday Review*, July 25, 1959, 37.

35. Robert Shelton, "Folk Joins Jazz at Newport," *New York Times*, July 19, 1959, http://query.nytimes.com/mem/archive-free/pdf?res=950DEFDB143BEF3BBC4152DFB1668382649EDE, accessed June 19, 2016.

36. Letter from Robert Shelton to Archie Green, August 22, 1959, Archie Green Papers, Southern Folklife Collection, University of North Carolina, Chapel Hill, in Cohen, *A History of Folk Music Festivals in the United States*, 48.

37. "Folk Music Is Called Regional by Nature," *Providence Journal*, July 13, 1959, 13.

38. Interview with the author, September 11, 2014.

39. Interview with the author, September 11, 2014.

40. Judy Collins, *Sweet Judy Blue Eyes: My Life in Music* (New York: Crown Archetype, a division of Random House, 2011), 71.

41. Dave Van Ronk with Elijah Wald, *The Mayor of MacDougal Street* (Cambridge, MA: Da Capo Press, 2005), 125–126.

42. Bob Gibson and Carol Bender, *I Come For to Sing* (Naperville, IL: Kingston Korner, 1999), 37. In David Hajdu, *Positively 4th Street: The Lives and Times of Joan Baez, Bob Dylan, Mimi Baez Fariña and Richard Fariña* (New York: North Point Press, 2001), 37.

43. Eric Tucker, "Newport Folk Festival at 50," http://www.deseretnews.com/article/705320220/Newport-folk-festival-at-50.html?pg=all, accessed June 25, 2016.

44. Joan Baez, *And a Voice to Sing With: A Memoir* (Mono, Ontario, Canada: Summit Books, 1987), 60-61.

45. Baez, *And a Voice to Sing With*, 60–61.

46. John S. Patterson, "The Folksong Revival and Some Sources of the Popular Image of the Folksinger: 1920–1963," MA thesis, Indiana University, 1963, 38, in Cheryl Anne Brauner, "A Study of the Newport Folk Festival and the Newport Folk Foundation," Master's thesis, Memorial University of Newfoundland, 1983, 20–21.

47. Interview with the author, September 11, 2014.

48. Wein and Chinen, *Myself among Others*, 316.

49. All quotes from Bob Shane are from an interview with the author, October 19, 2011.

50. Shirley Jackson, in Cohen, *A History of Folk Music Festivals in the United States*, 49.

51. Interview with the author, May 19, 2011.

52. Gardner Dunton, "Folk Music Draws Throng in Newport," *Providence Sunday Journal*, June 26, 1960, N-14.

53. Robert Shelton, "40 Amateurs Join Hootenanny as Newport Folk Festival Ends," *New York Times*, June 27, 1960, 21.

54. Interview with the author, July 9, 2009.

55. Montgomery, "The Folk Furor," 99, in Cantwell, *When We Were Good*, 298.

56. "Riot Disrupts Newport Jazz Fete; Marines and Guardsmen Sent In," *New York Times*, July 3, 1960, 1.

57. Wein and Chinen, *Myself among Others*, 196.

58. John S. Wilson, "Newport Jazz Fete Closed By Rioting," *New York Times*, July 4, 1960, 9.

59. Wilson, "Newport Jazz," 9.

60. Wilson, "Newport Jazz," 9.

61. Wilson, "Newport Jazz," 9

62. Philip Benjamin, "11,000 in Newport for Jazz Concert," *New York Times*, July 1, 1961. http://query.nytimes.com/gst/abstract.html?res= 9904E0DA1730EE32A25752C0A9619C946091D6CF, accessed October 15, 2014.

63. Interview with the author, July 6, 2009.

64. Wein and Chinen, *Myself among Others*, 214.

3. UTOPIA

1. Theodore Bikel, Pete Seeger and George Wein, "Proposal for the Newport Folk Festival to Be Held in Newport July 1963 on the 26th, 27th and 28th," in the Alan Lomax Collection at the American Folklife Center at the Library of Congress. Following excerpts are from this manifesto.

2. Interview with the author, July 6, 2009.

3. Unpublished interview with Carol Brauner, January 29, 1982.

4. "This first year," the proposal read, "members of the committee will be performers but in future years there is no need for this restriction."

5. Interview with the author, July 6, 2009.

6. Interview with the author, September 4, 2014.

7. David King Dunaway, *How Can I Keep from Singing? The Ballad of Pete Seeger* (New York: Villard 2009), 304.

8. Interview with the author, September 4, 2014.

9. Cantwell, *When We Were Good*, 305.

10. Wein grumbles that the film made the crowd look younger than it was because Lerner's editing focused on the more picturesque shots of earlygoers.

11. Interview with the author, August 20, 2014. Alan Lomax, on the other hand, wrote to the board on August 30, 1966, complaining that Lerner "has put his own artistic ambitions ahead of folk music and the festival, resulting in a movie that completely misrepresents the spirit of the American folk scene—especially the wonderful people in it—in striving for an arty, underground film effort."

12. Interview with the author, July 9, 2009.

13. Jim Rooney and Eric von Schmidt, *Baby Let Me Follow You Down: An Illustrated Story of the Cambridge Folk Years* (Amherst, MA: University of Massachusetts Press, 1979), 249–250.

14. Rooney and von Schmidt, *Baby Let Me Follow You Down*, 189.

15. Robert Shelton, "Folk-Music Fete Called a Success," *New York Times*, July 29, 1963, 15.

16. Interview with the author, July 6, 2009.

17. Cantwell, "When We Were Good," in Rosenberg, *Transforming Tradition*, 58.

18. Interview with the author, September 4, 2014.

19. Interview with the author, September 4, 2014.

20. Unpublished interview with Carol Brauner, January 29, 1982. Spokes Mashiyane, George Wein recalls, was invited to Newport via a letter to his record

company eight months before the event and received no response; the day before the festival, when the Weins were in Newport, they received a call from their New York doorman saying that Mashiyane had shown up at their building, looking for them. He was promptly put on a bus to Newport.

21. Unpublished interview with Carol Brauner, January 29, 1982.

22. Interview with the author, January 14, 2013.

23. Interview with the author, January 14, 2013.

24. In response to complaints that it served as de facto segregation, the concept of a Blues House was eventually discontinued, to the dismay of some observers, black and white alike.

25. Interview with the author, July 14, 2009.

26. Interview with the author, July 14, 2009.

27. Wein and Chinen, *Myself among Others*, 324.

28. Interview with the author, February 17, 2013.

29. Interview with the author, September 12, 2013.

30. Rooney and von Schmidt, *Baby Let Me Follow You Down*, 197.

4. TEXAS WAS THE WORST

1. Wein and Chinen, *Myself among Others*, 323.

2. All of Bob Jones's recollections, unless otherwise noted, are from an interview with the author on January 21, 2010.

3. Bob Jones interview with the author, January 21, 2010.

4. "DeFord Bailey: A Legend Lost," http://www.pbs.org/deford/biography/opry4 .html, accessed March 12, 2016.

5. Interview with Carol Brauner, in Cheryl Anne Brauner, "A Study of the Newport Folk Festival and the Newport Folk Foundation," 185–186.

6. Hamilton and Associates, "Cajuns: Their History and Culture" (National Park Service, 1987), 202. http://archive.org/stream/cajunstheirhistoo2hami /cajunstheirhistoo2hami_djvu.txt, accessed May 22, 2016.

7. "Artist Spotlight—Dewey Balfa, Smithsonian Folkways," http://www.folkways .si.edu/dewey-balfa-master-cajun/music/article/smithsonian, accessed June 12, 2016.

8. Letter from Paul Tate, president of the Louisiana Folk Foundation, to the board, May 19, 1965. In the Alan Lomax Collection at the American Folklife Center in the Library of Congress.

9. The account of Hurt's performance comes from tapes of the 1964 Newport Folk Festival at the American Folklife Center at the Library of Congress.

10. Rooney and von Schmidt, *Baby Let Me Follow You Down*, 148.

11. Interview with the author, October 2, 2014.

12. In Brauner, "A Study of the Newport Folk Festival," 127.

13. Interview with Marjorie Hunt, February 28, 1989, in the Ralph Rinzler Collection at the Smithsonian Institution.

14. Interview with Marjorie Hunt, February 28, 1989.

15. Bob Jones interview with Kate Rinzler, March 16, 1995. In the Ralph Rinzler Collection at the Smithsonian Institution.

5. A REAL FOLK FESTIVAL

1. Interview with the author, July 9, 2009.

2. Filene, *Romancing the Folk*, 3.

3. Simon J. Bronner, "In Search of American Tradition," in Bronner, *Folk Nation: Folklore in the Creation of American Tradition* (Wilmington, DE: Scholarly Resources, 2002), 41.

4. Cohen, *Rainbow Quest*, 136.

5. Rosenberg, *Transforming Tradition*, 12.

6. Filene, *Romancing the Folk*, 46, 49.

7. Charles Seeger, "Reviews," *American Folk Quarterly*, 1948–1949, in Rosenberg, *Transforming Tradition*, 15.

8. Bruce Jackson, "The Folksong Revival," in Rosenberg, *Transforming Tradition*, 73.

9. Cohen, *Rainbow Quest*, 200, 212.

10. Jeff Todd Titon, "Reconstructing the Blues: Reflections on the 1960s Blues Revival," in Rosenberg, *Transforming Tradition*, 221.

11. Ewan MacColl, "The Singer and the Audience," *Folk Music* 1(1), November 1963, 5–6.

12. Oscar Brand, "Winter Meeting of the New York Folklore Society, March 2, 1963," *New York Folklore Quarterly*, June 1963, 92.

13. Alan Lomax, in Brand, "Winter Meeting," 123.

14. Ellen Stekert, in Brand, "Winter Meeting," 124.

15. Irwin Silber, in Brand, "Winter Meeting," 112.

16. Filene, *Romancing the Folk*, 26.

17. Stephen Fiott, "In Defense of Commercial Folksingers," *Sing Out!* December 1962–January 1963, 43–44.

18. Dan Armstrong, "'Commercial' Folksongs—Product of 'Instant Culture,'" *Sing Out!* February-March 1963, 21.

19. Jon Pankake and Paul Nelson, "Tradition Singers," *Sing Out!* February–March 1963, 51.

20. MacColl, "The Singer and the Audience," 4–5.

21. Nathan Joseph, "I Record What I Like," *Folk Music* 1(5), 25–26.

22. Interview with Carol Brauner, January 29, 1982.

23. Susan Montgomery, "The Folk Furor," in Cohen, *Rainbow Quest*, 167.

24. Irwin Silber and David Gahr, "Top Performers Highlight 1st Newport Folk Fest," *Sing Out!* fall 1959, 21–22.

25. Interview with the author, May 17, 2011.

26. Interview with the author, July 9, 2009.

27. Titon, "Reconstructing the Blues," in Rosenberg, *Transforming Tradition*, 230–231.

28. Interview with the author, September 11, 2014.

29. Irwin Silber, in Brand, "Winter Meeting," 113.

30. Josh Dunson, *Freedom in the Air: Song Movements of the Sixties* (New York: International Publishers, 1965), 33.

31. David A. DeTurk and A. Poulin Jr., *The American Folk Scene: Dimensions of the Folksong Revival* (New York: Dell 1967), 13–14.

32. Eileen Stekert, "Cents and Nonsense in the Urban Folksong Movement: 1930–66," in Rosenberg, *Transforming Tradition*, 95–96.

33. Titon, "Reconstructing the Blues," in Rosenberg, *Transforming Tradition*, 229.

34. Interview with the author, September 11, 2014.

35. Cantwell, *When We Were Good*, in Rosenberg, *Transforming Tradition*, 43.

36. Interview with the author, May 17, 2011.

37. Interview with the author, May 20, 2011.

38. Conversation between Bob Weiser and the author, July 27, 2013.

6. KEEP ME COMPANY AND HOLD MY HAND (A PRELUDE)

1. Interview with the author, September 11, 2014.

2. Cohen, *Rainbow Quest*, 238.

3. In Wein and Chinen, *Myself among Others*, 330.

4. Elijah Wald, *Dylan Goes Electric! Newport, Seeger, Dylan, and the Night That Split the Sixties* (New York: Dey St., 2015), 222–223.

5. Joe Boyd interview with the author, December 14, 2011.

6. Barbara Dane, "Newport: Some Questions," *Sing Out!* April–May 1966, inside front cover.

7. Letter from Mary Travers to Archie Green, in Cohen, *A History of Folk Music Festivals in the United States*, 96.

7. A LIMITED AMOUNT OF TIME

1. "In the beginning . . .": Joe Klein, "Wilco: Alt-Country Roads," *New York Times*, June 13, 2004, www.nytimes.com/2004/06/13/books/review/13KLEINOR.html.

2. Cohen, *A History of Folk Music Festivals in the United States*, 96.

3. Wald, *Dylan Goes Electric!* 11–12.

4. Daniel Mark Epstein, *The Ballad of Bob Dylan: A Portrait* (New York: HarperCollins 2011), 159.

5. Joe Boyd, *White Bicycles: Making Music in the 1960s* (London: Serpent's Tail, 2010), 102–103.

6. Unnamed announcer, from the documentary *The Other Side of the Mirror: Bob Dylan at the Newport Folk Festival*, directed by Murray Lerner. BBC Four, 2007.

7. Josh Dunson, *Broadside Magazine* 30, August 1963.

8. Jack A. Smith, *National Guardian*, August 22, 1963.

9. Bob Dylan, in Smith, *National Guardian*.

10. Boyd, *White Bicycles*, 102–103.

11. Johnny Cash, in *The Other Side of the Mirror*.

12. Murray Lerner, in *The Other Side of the Mirror*.

13. Epstein, *The Ballad of Bob Dylan*, 145.

14. "An Open Letter to Bob Dylan," in *Sing Out!* November 1964, 22–23.

15. Boyd, *White Bicycles*, 103.

16. Bob Dylan, in *The Other Side of the Mirror*.

17. Boyd, *White Bicycles*, 97.

18. Epstein, *The Ballad of Bob Dylan*, 111–112.

19. Wein and Chinen, *Myself among Others*, 332.

20. Robert Shelton, *No Direction Home: The Life and Music of Bob Dylan* (New York: Hal Leonard revised edition, 2011), 210.

21. Al Kooper, from the documentary *No Direction Home: Bob Dylan*, directed by Martin Scorsese. PBS and BBC Two, 2005.

22. Shelton, *No Direction Home*, 210.

23. Boyd, *White Bicycles*, 97–98.

24. Wein and Chinen, *Myself among Others*, 332.

25. From the documentary *Festival!* written, produced and directed by Murray Lerner, 1967.

26. Boyd, *White Bicycles*, 98.

27. Shelton, *No Direction Home*, 210.

28. Interview with the author, September 4, 2014.

29. Boyd, *White Bicycles*, 103.

30. Interview with the author, September 4, 2014.

31. Wein and Chinen, *Myself among Others*, 332.

32. Interview with the author, September 4, 2014.

33. Boyd, *White Bicycles*, 103–104.

34. From the recording in the Bruce Jackson/Diane Christian Collection at the Library of Congress' American Folklife Center.

35. From the recording in the Bruce Jackson/Diane Christian Collection.

36. From the recording in the Bruce Jackson/Diane Christian Collection.

37. Boyd, *White Bicycles*, 104.

38. From the recording in the Bruce Jackson/Diane Christian Collection.

39. Epstein, *The Ballad of Bob Dylan*, 159.

40. Boyd, *White Bicycles*, 104.

41. Interview in Blues Power, http://www.bluespower.com/arbn06.htm, accessed September 20, 2014.

42. From the recording in the Bruce Jackson/Diane Christian Collection.

43. From the recording in the Bruce Jackson/Diane Christian Collection.

44. From *The Other Side of the Mirror*.

45. Phil Ochs, "The Newport Fuzz Festival," *Broadside*, February 1966, 17.

46. From the recording in the Bruce Jackson/Diane Christian Collection.

47. Boyd, *White Bicycles*, 104.

48. Shelton, *No Direction Home*, 210.

49. From the documentary *No Direction Home*.

50. From the documentary *No Direction Home*.

51. From the documentary *No Direction Home*.

52. Wein and Chinen, *Myself among Others*, 332–333.

53. From the documentary *No Direction Home*.

54. Boyd, *White Bicycles*, 104.

55. From the recording in the Bruce Jackson/Diane Christian Collection.

56. Boyd, *White Bicycles*, 104.

57. From *The Other Side of the Mirror*.

58. Shelton, *No Direction Home*, 210.

59. Boyd, *White Bicycles*, 104.

60. Wein and Chinen, *Myself among Others*, 333.

61. Shelton, *No Direction Home*, 210.

62. Interview with the author, September 11, 2014.

63. "Newport: The Short Hot Summer," *Broadside* 62, August 15, 1965.

64. Interview with the author, September 4, 2014.

65. Rooney and von Schmidt, *Baby Let Me Follow You Down*, 262.

66. Boyd, *White Bicycles*, 104.

67. Arthur Kretschmer, "Newport: It's All Right, Ma, I'm Only Playin' R&R," the *Village Voice*, August 5, 1965, 6. In Cohen, *A History of Folk Music Festivals in the United States*, 98.

68. "Newport: The Short, Hot Summer."

69. Interview with the author, July 13, 2010.

70. Boyd, *White Bicycles*, 105.

71. Shelton, *No Direction Home*, 210–211.

72. Wein and Chinen, *Myself among Others*, 333.

73. Interview with the author, July 13, 2010.

74. From the documentary *No Direction Home*.

75. Wein and Chinen, *Myself among Others*, 333.

76. From the documentary *No Direction Home*.

77. Dunaway, "How Can I Keep from Singing?" Kindle edition.

78. From the documentary *No Direction Home*.

79. From the documentary *No Direction Home*.

80. Shelton, *No Direction Home*, 210–211.

81. Epstein, *The Ballad of Bob Dylan*, 160.

82. Interview with the author, July 6, 2009.

83. Michael J. Carabetta, "In Defense of Dylan," *Broadside of Boston*, August 18, 1965, 5.

84. Shelton, *No Direction Home*, 210.

85. Rooney and von Schmidt, *Baby Let Me Follow You Down*, 262.

86. From the documentary *No Direction Home*.

87. From the documentary *No Direction Home*.

88. Irwin Silber, "What's Happening," *Sing Out!* November 1965, 5.

89. From *The Other Side of the Mirror*.

90. From the documentary *No Direction Home*.

91. Shelton, *No Direction Home*, 210.

92. Boyd, *White Bicycles*, 103–104.

93. From the recording in the Bruce Jackson/Diane Christian Collection.

94. From *The Other Side of the Mirror*.

95. Paul Nelson, "What's Happening," *Sing Out!* November 1965, 7.

96. Wein and Chinen, *Myself among Others*, 333.

97. From the recording in the Bruce Jackson/Diane Christian Collection.

98. From the documentary *No Direction Home*.

99. In Cohen, *A History of Folk Music Festivals in the United States*," 96–97.

100. Tom Piazza, "Bob Dylan's Unswerving Road Back to Newport," *New York Times*, July 28, 2002. http://www.nytimes.com/2002/07/28/arts/bob-dylan-s -unswerving-road-back-to-newport.html?module=Search&mabReward=relbias %3Ar, accessed October 15, 2014.

101. Wein and Chinen, *Myself among Others*, 333.

102. Interview with the author, September 4, 2014.

103. From the recording in the Bruce Jackson/Diane Christian Collection.

104. Boyd, *White Bicycles*, 105.

105. Shelton, *No Direction Home*, 210.

106. Boyd, *White Bicycles*, 104.

107. From the recording in the Bruce Jackson/Diane Christian Collection.

108. Rooney, "What's Happening," 7–8.

109. Shelton, *No Direction Home*, 210.

110. Boyd, *White Bicycles*, 105.

111. From the recording in the Bruce Jackson/Diane Christian Collection at the Library of Congress' American Folklife Center.

112. From the documentary *No Direction Home*.

113. Nelson, "What's Happening," 8.

114. Interview with the author, July 13, 2010.

115. Boyd, *White Bicycles*, 105.

116. Carabetta, "In Defense of Dylan," 5.

117. Interview with the author, July 13, 2010.

118. Letter to Henry Faulk, in Cohen, *A History of Folk Music Festivals in the United States*, 96.

119. Wein and Chinen, *Myself among Others*, 333.

120. Interview with the author, September 4, 2014.

121. Wein and Chinen, *Myself among Others*, 333.

122. From the Jackson/Christian recording at the Library of Congress.

123. From the documentary *No Direction Home*.

124. Carabetta, "In Defense of Dylan," 5.

125. From the Jackson/Christian recording at the Library of Congress.

126. From the Jackson/Christian recording at the Library of Congress.

127. From the Jackson/Christian recording at the Library of Congress.

128. Wein and Chinen, *Myself among Others*, 333.

129. Silber, "What's Happening, 5.

130. Shelton, *No Direction Home*, 210.

131. From *The Other Side of the Mirror*.

132. Rooney and von Schmidt, *Baby Let Me Follow You Down*, 262.

133. Wein and Chinen, *Myself among Others*, 333.

134. From *The Other Side of the Mirror*.

135. Interview with the author, July 14, 2009.

136. From *The Other Side of the Mirror*.

137. Wein and Chinen, *Myself among Others*, 333.

138. From the Jackson/Christian recording at the Library of Congress.

139. Wein and Chinen, *Myself among Others*, 333.

140. From *The Other Side of the Mirror*.

141. Shelton, *No Direction Home*, 210.

142. From the Jackson/Christian recording at the Library of Congress.

143. Interview with Nat Hentoff, *Playboy*, March 1966, in "Talking Points: A Dylan Mystery," *New York Times*. http://eastvillage.thelocal.nytimes.com/2011/05/27/talking-points-a-dylan-mystery/?pagewanted=print, accessed September 20, 2014.

144. Dunaway, *How Can I Keep from Singing?* Kindle edition.

145. Boyd, *White Bicycles*, 106.

146. Silber, "What's Happening," 5.

147. Boyd, *White Bicycles*, 107.

148. Wein and Chinen, *Myself among Others*, 334.

149. Boyd, *White Bicycles*, 108.

150. Robert J. Lurtsema, "On the Scene," *Broadside of Boston*, August 18, 1965, 11.

151. From the documentary *No Direction Home*.

152. From the documentary *No Direction Home*.

153. Dunaway, *How Can I Keep From Singing?* Kindle edition.

154. Shelton, *No Direction Home*, 211.

155. In Wald, *Dylan Goes Electric!* 277.

156. From the documentary *No Direction Home*.

157. Shelton, *No Direction Home*, 211.

158. Boyd, *White Bicycles*, 108.

159. Nelson, "What's Happening," 8.

160. Shelton, *No Direction Home*, 211.

161. Interview with the author, July 6, 2009.

8. IT IS BEGINNING TO BOG DOWN

1. Letter from the Newport Folk Foundation Board of Directors to performers, volunteers, staff, press and audience, December 1965. In the Alan Lomax Collection.

2. Paul Nelson, "Reviews" column, *Little Sandy Review* 22, 32.

3. Nelson, "Reviews" column, 27, 24.

4. Paul Nelson, "Newport: Down There on a Visit," *Little Sandy Review* 30, 48.

5. Nelson, "Newport," 51.

6. Barbara Dane, "Newport: Some Questions," *Sing Out!* April–May 1966, inside front cover.

7. Ellen Willis, "Newport: You Can't Go Down Home Again," *New Yorker*, August 12, 1968, 86.

8. Interview with the author, September 12, 2013.

9. In Cohen, *A History of Folk Music Festivals in the United States*, 104.

10. Interview with the author, September 12, 2013. Collins surmises that Seeger's attitude toward his own songs, even classics such as "Turn! Turn! Turn!" and "Where Have All the Flowers Gone?" didn't help: "I don't think he always took himself very seriously as a writer." She recalls that someone once called him and said the Kingston Trio had listed themselves as writers of "Where Have All the Flowers Gone?" on one of their albums. He said, "Oh, I must have forgotten to get it copyrighted."

11. This wasn't the first or last time Wein was described as a mere businessman sucking money out of music. In a 2009 interview with the author, he objected to the term, saying that a real businessman figures out how to squeeze every dollar from a venture: "All I knew was, if you spend ten dollars, you have to take in eleven," Wein said. "That was my concept of business."

12. Letter from Ed Badeux to the Newport Folk Festival board of directors, January 12, 1966, in the Ralph Rinzler Collection at the Smithsonian Institution.

13. Dane, "Newport: Some Questions," 64.

14. Interview with the author, October 21,2012.

15. Interview with the author, October 21, 2012.

16. Letter from Alan Lomax to Eliot Hoffman, March 24, 1966, in the Alan Lomax Collection.

17. Letter from Elliot Hoffman to Alan Lomax, April 5, 1966.

18. Letter from George Wein to the Newport Folk Foundation Board of Directors, April 15, 1966, in the Ralph Rinzler Collection. The following quotes are excerpted from this letter.

19. Wein letter to the Board, April 15, 1966.

20. Interview with the author, October 21, 2012.

21. Bruce Jackson, "Newport," *Sing Out!* September 1966, 8.

22. "Report of the Financial Committee to the Board," April 15, 1967, in the Ralph Rinzler Collection.

23. Interview with the author, November 4, 2013.

24. Jackson, "Newport," 11.

25. Interview with the author, July 6, 2009.

26. Wald, "Dylan Goes Electric!" 280.

27. Interview with the author, September 4, 2014.

28. Interview with the author, December 14, 2011.

29. Descriptions of the 1966 festival are derived from tapes of the festival in the American Folklife Center at the Library of Congress.

30. Cantwell, *When We Were Good*, 53.

31. Interview with the author, October 21, 2012.

32. Bruce Jackson, "Newport '66—Good Music, Diabolical Programming," *Sing Out!* October-November 1966, 17.

33. Jackson, "Newport '66," 16.

34. Ted Holmberg, "Blues Open 6th Folk Festival," *Providence Journal*, July 22, 1966, 1.

35. Robert Shelton, "A Fare-Thee-Well for Newport Sing," *New York Times*, July 25, 1966. http://query.nytimes.com/gst/abstract.html?res= 990CEED81231E43BBC4D51DFB166838D679EDE, accessed October 15, 2014.

36. In Cohen, *A History of Folk Music Festivals in the United States*, 104.

37. Mike Seeger, "Recap," undated letter to the Newport Folk Foundation Board of Directors, in the Alan Lomax Collection at the Library of Congress's American Folklife Center.

38. That uptight feeling wasn't just among the staff: late on the Saturday night, police officers roughed up members of SNCC in "a show of blue power." Wein says a lineup was scheduled to identify the offending officers but never actually happened: "It had all been a façade" (Wein and Chinen, *Myself among Others*, 336).

39. Jane Friesen, "Newport—2," *Broadside* 73, August 1966, 15.

40. Undated memo from George Wein to the Newport Folk Foundation Board of Directors and members, in the Ralph Rinzler Collection.

41. Wein memo to board (undated).

42. The 1968 edition was overseen by Judy Collins and Jim Rooney and 1969's was hosted by Oscar Brand and Pete Seeger.

43. Ernie Santosuosso, "Newport Folk Festival Opener Choked By Fog," *Boston*

Globe, July 14, 1967, accessed at http://search.proquest.com/docview/366610937 ?accountid=12084.

44. Interview with the author, December 6, 2013.

45. Bruce Jackson, "The Folksong Revival," in Rosenberg, *Transforming Tradition*, 77.

46. Interview with the author, December 6, 2013.

47. Brian C. Jones, "Folk Concerts Will Start Tonight," *Providence Journal*, July 13, 1967, 1.

48. Irwin Silber (editor), in the "What's Happening" column, *Sing Out!* October–November 1967, inside front cover.

49. Silber, "What's Happening," inside front cover.

50. Silber, "What's Happening," inside front cover.

51. Silber, "What's Happening," inside front cover.

52. *Broadside* had already taken an even darker opinion of the festival a year earlier: "How can there be a time of rejoicing anywhere in this land while the forces of fascism, fattening on the escalating Viet Nam war and the resistance to Negro rights at home, grow more menacing by the day. The mood at Newport only reflected the dark clouds gathering over every American" ("Notes," *Broadside*, August 1966, 16).

53. Barbara Dane, "Newport Folk Fest: Business as Usual," *Village Voice*, July 10, 1969, in *Broadside* 100, July 1969, 8.

54. Interview with the author, October 21, 2012.

55. Interview with the author, September 12, 2013.

56. Interview with the author, September 12, 2013.

57. Mike Seeger, "Recap."

58. Anthony R. Dolan, "Heroes in the Seaweed," *National Review*, October 8, 1968, 1011–1012.

59. Letter from George Lamothe, regional representative, Mid-Atlantic Young Americans for Freedom, to "George Weim," July 28, 1966, in the Ralph Rinzler Collection.

60. Letter from Bruce Jackson to the Newport Folk Foundation Board of Directors, October 5, 1970, in the Ralph Rinzler Collection.

61. Interview with the author, July 6, 2009.

62. John S. Wilson, "Unruly Rock Fans Upset Newport Jazz Festival," *New York Times*, July 7, 1969. http://query.nytimes.com/gst/abstract.html?res= 9F06E6DE1739EF3BBC4F53DFB1668382679EDE, accessed October 15, 2014.

63. Interview with the author, September 12, 2013.

64. Interview with the author, December 8, 2013.

65. Jim Rooney, unpublished memoir.

66. Bruce Pollack, *When the Music Mattered: Rock in the 1960s* (New York: Holt, Rinehart and Winston, 1983), 20–21, 24. In Cohen, *Rainbow Quest*, 261.

67. Jan Hodenfeld, "Newport 1969," *Rolling Stone*, August 23, 1969, 20. In Cohen, *Rainbow Quest*, 284.

68. Happy Traum, "What's Happening" column, *Sing Out!* September–October 1969, 35.

69. Interview with the author, November 4, 2013.

70. Interview with the author, July 6, 2009.

71. "Newport Folk Fete Seeks New Pasture," *New York Times*, March 20, 1970. http://query.nytimes.com/gst/abstract.html?res= 9503E2DB133AE03BBC4851DFB566838B669EDE, accessed October 15, 2014.

72. Interview with the author, December 6, 2013.

73. "Newport's Folk Festival Put Off until Next Year," unsigned AP report in *New York Times*, May 27, 1970. http://query.nytimes.com/gst/abstract.html ?res=980DE4DD1538EE34BC4F51DFB366838B669EDE, accessed October 15, 2014.

74. Interview with the author, July 6, 2009.

75. John S. Wilson, "Newport Closes Festival Early," *New York Times*, July 5, 1969. http://query.nytimes.com/gst/abstract.html?res= 9801E3DD163DEF34BC4D53DFB166838A669EDE, accessed October 15, 2014.

76. Interview with the author, July 6, 2009.

77. Wilson, "Newport Closes Festival Early."

78. Michael Kenney, "Newport Cancels Folk Festival," *Boston Globe*, July 8, 1971. http://search.proquest.com/docview/518709242?accountid=12084, accessed October 15, 2014.

79. Wein and Chinen, *Myself among Others*, 344–346.

80. Wein and Chinen, *Myself among Others*, 348.

9. IT WAS A SWEET TOWN WHEN I FIRST CAME HERE

1. Andy Smith, "The Festival Is Everywhere Now," *Providence Journal*, August 5, 1998.

2. Rick Massimo, "It's a Lively Show of Appreciation," *Providence Sunday Journal*, August 8, 2010, A4.

3. Goldblatt, *Newport Jazz Festival*, xiii.

4. Goldblatt, *Newport Jazz Festival*, xii–xiii.

5. Rick Massimo, "'We Were the Only Founders,' says Elaine Lorillard," *Providence Sunday Journal*, August 8, 2004, K3.

6. Massimo, "'We Were the Only Founders.'"

7. Interview with the author, July 6, 2009.

8. Interview with the author, July 6, 2009.

9. Massimo, "'We Were the Only Founders.'"

10. Eileen Warburton, *In Living Memory: A Chronicle of Newport, Rhode Island, 1888–1988* (Newport Savings and Loan Association, 1988), 139.

11. All Tom Perrotti quotes are from an interview with the author, September 4, 2014.

12. All Peter Lance quotes are from an interview with the author, September 7, 2014.

13. Interview with Rhonda Miller, 2010, furnished to the author by Rhonda Miller.

14. Gene Perrotti's main memory of the festivals, however, was his disappointment of Frank Sinatra at the jazz festival in 1965. The singer helicoptered into Festival Field, sang for less than an hour, and helicoptered out (legendarily so as to hit his favorite New York restaurant before closing time), leaving the elder Perrotti and his fellow Kiwanians with stacks of hot dogs they had cooked up to sell at an expected intermission: "It was a lost proposition, that night!" (from the Rhonda Miller interview).

15. Letter from Elliot Hoffman to Nuala Pell, October 27, 1964, in the Alan Lomax Collection at the American Folklife Center at the Library of Congress.

16. Minutes of the Newport Folk Foundation Board of Directors meeting, November 5, 1964, in the Ralph Rinzler Collection at the Smithsonian Institution.

17. Letter from Oscar Brand to the Newport Folk Foundation Board of Directors, Thanksgiving 1969, in the Rinzler Collection.

18. Letter from George Wein to the Foundation Board of Directors, December 5, 1969, in the Rinzler Collection.

19. Warburton, *In Living Memory*, 145.

20. Interview with the author, August 28, 2014.

21. Warburton, *In Living Memory*, 150.

10. HE WAS AMAZED AND I WAS AMAZED

1. R. E. Reimer, "It Was Nostalgia Time," *Newport Daily News*, August 5, 1985, 12.

2. Interview with the author, July 6, 2009.

3. In 1970, the beleaguered Festival Productions lawyer Eliot Hoffman was writing to Ralph Rinzler with evident frustration: "I think it would be a reasonable idea to have, once and for all, a list of all the recording machinery owned by us, hopefully with details as to serial numbers, accessory equipment and the like. Each one should be accounted for. . . . This has always been a source of irritation to me that I could never get a business-like list out to anybody." Later that year, having evidently received some kind of list, Hoffman asked Rinzler again what exactly the foundation owned, concluding with a seemingly plaintive, "Who has this information?"

4. George Gent, "2 Concerts Sing Folk Festival Blues," July 6, 1972. http://query.nytimes.com/gst/abstract.html?res= 9B02E2DA1F3EE63BBC4E53DFB1668389669EDE, accessed October 15, 2014.

5. Interview with the author, November 15, 2013.

6. Samuel Allis, "No Folk in Newport: Festival Revival Fails for Want of an Audience," *Washington Post*, August 23, 1979, D1, D7.

7. Wein and Chinen, *Myself among Others*, 448. Brown and Williamson allowed Wein to continue to use the Newport name in Newport: "I wasn't asking for sponsorship money, just their permission," he writes. "They had no qualms about me producing a festival in Newport on my own."

8. Rick Massimo, "Golden Age of Jazz," *Providence Sunday Journal*, August 8, 2004, K1.

9. Interview with the author, July 6, 2009.

10. Jeff McLaughlin, "It's Time Again for Folk Revival," *Boston Globe*, April 12, 1985.

11. Rush's fondest Newport memory dates back to the late '60s, eating with some fellow musicians at the Viking: "They set up a separate dining room for the musicians, because they didn't want us upsetting the regular patrons. Bruce Langhorne started playing a little rhythm groove with his spoon on the side of his drinking glass. Then two or three other people picked up on it, and pretty soon there was a rhythm jam going on, using silverware. And the waiters came around and picked up all the silverware and took it away. It was upsetting that the diners weren't just dining." Perhaps predictably, "We just pounded on the table instead."

12. All Tom Rush quotes are from an interview with the author, March 6, 2014.

13. Carolyn Wyman, "Newport Revival Strikes a Less Political Tone," *Christian Science Monitor*, August 9, 1985, 23.

14. Letter from George Wein to Ralph Rinzler, September 17, 1984, in the Ralph Rinzler Collection.

15. Interview with the author, December 6, 2013.

16. Interview with the author, December 6, 2013.

17. Interview with the author, December 6, 2013.

18. Mitchell Zuckoff, Associated Press, "Folk Fest Stages Grand Return," in the Vacaville, California, *Reporter*, August 7, 1985.

19. Jeff McLaughlin, "In the Finest Folk Tradition," *Boston Globe*, August 5, 1985.

20. Unsigned report from UPI, in the *Gloucester Times*, August 5, 1985.

21. Stephen Jones, "Revived Newport Festival Lacks Spirit of Its Former Self," *Detroit Free Press*, August 5, 1985.

22. Jones, "Revived Newport Festival."

23. Jones, "Revived Newport Festival."

24. Judy Rakowsky, "For Folks at Festival, a Fine Day for Nostalgia," *Providence Sunday Journal*, August 4, 1985.

25. McLaughlin, "In the Finest Folk Tradition."

26. Steve Varnum, "The Folk Festival Is Back," *New Bedford Standard-Times*, June 21, 1985, 17.

27. Mike Boehm, "Folk Festival Concludes with Calls for '86 Encore," *Providence Journal-Bulletin*, August 5, 1985.

28. Jon Herman, "Newport News," *Boston Phoenix*, August 13, 1985.

29. UPI report, *Gloucester Times*.

30. McLaughlin, "In the Finest Folk Tradition."

31. Boehm, "Folk Festival Concludes."

32. McLaughlin, "In the Finest Folk Tradition."

33. Interview with the author, July 14, 2009.

34. Interview with the author, November 15, 2013.

35. Interview with the author, July 6, 2009.

36. Interview with the author, November 15, 2013.

37. Interview with the author, December 14, 2010.

38. Interview with the author, December 6, 2013.

39. Interview with the author, February 17, 2013.

40. Interview with the author, February 17, 2013. Among her other memories of her first Newport festival, Williams recalls her mother, evidently unaware of the existence of backstage catering, dropping off a sandwich for her daughter—"so awesome"—and herself talking with her friends in the Nields, "and we all stopped talking when Richard Thompson passed by."

41. Interview with the author, December 6, 2013.

42. Barbara Polichetti, "More Folks at Newport Festival," *Providence Journal*, August 8, 1986, D-3.

43. Mike Boehm, "Newport '86 Crowd Dwindles," *Providence Journal-Bulletin*, August 11, 1986, A-10.

44. Barbara Polichetti, "Newport Fest Draws Fewer than Last Year," *Providence Sunday Journal*, August 10, 1986, A-3.

45. Boehm, "Newport '86 Crowd Dwindles."

46. Ken Franckling, "Newport Folk Festival Needs New Audience," United Press International, 1986. Accessed at http://articles.sun-sentinel.com/1986–08–14 /FEATURES_LIFESTYLE/8602180244_1_wein-newport-folk-festival-folk-talent.

47. Interview with the author, July 14, 2009.

48. Interview with the author, July 14, 2009.

49. Mike Boehm, "Folk Performers Take Chapter from Pop's Book," *Providence Sunday Journal*, August 9, 1987, A-12.

50. All contemporaneous reports regarding the Nestlé sponsorship are in Maria Miro Johnson, "Folk Festival Helps Nestlé Polish Image," *Providence Sunday Journal*, August 9, 1987, A-12.

51. All Jerry Greenfield's reminiscences are from an interview with the author on October 1, 2013.

52. Andy Smith, "The Folk Who Sponsor the Festivals," *Providence Sunday Journal*, August 9, 1992, E-1, E-4.

53. Interview with the author, July 2009.

54. Interview with the author, February 17, 2013.

55. Interview with the author, February 17, 2013.

56. Interview with the author, July 2009.

57. Interview with the author, February 17, 2013.

58. Interview with the author, February 17, 2013.

59. Interview with the author, February 17, 2013.

60. All Nalini Jones's reminiscences are from an interview with the author on October 3, 2013.

61. Interview with the author, July 14, 2010.

62. Interview with the author, July 2009.

63. Interview with the author, July 27, 2013.

64. Interview with the author, January 14, 2013.

65. Interview with the author, February 17, 2013.

66. Interview with the author, January 14, 2013.

67. Interview with the author, September 4, 2014.

68. Mark Johnson, "Folk Festival: 'It's a Laid Back Good Time,'" *Providence Sunday Journal*, August 7, 1994, B-1.

69. Interview with the author, April 2, 2014.

70. Interview with the author, April 2, 2014.

71. Reimer, "It Was Nostalgia Time," 12.

72. I. Sheldon Posen, introduction to "On Folk Festivals and Kitchens: Questions of Authenticity in the Folksong Revival," in Rosenberg, *Transforming Tradition*, 128–129.

73. Jackson, "The Folksong Revival," in Rosenberg, *Transforming Tradition*, 79–80.

74. Interview with the author, May 12, 2014.

75. Stephen Holden, "Philadelphia Tunes Up for its Annual Folkfest," *New York Times*, August 18, 1985.

76. Bryan Rourke, "Newport Folk Festival Won't Fail Fans," *Providence Journal*, April 28, 2002, D-4.

77. Interview with the author, July 27, 2013.

78. Interview with the author, July 2005.

79. Peter Stone Brown, "Dylan at Newport 2002," at http://blog .peterstonebrown.com/dylan-at-newport-2002/, accessed June 2, 2016.

80. George Wein, "A Folk Festival's Idol Returns," *New York Times* August 3, 2002. http://www.nytimes.com/2002/08/03/opinion/a-folk-festival-s-idol-returns .html, accessed October 15, 2014.

81. Francis's reminiscences are in "Bob Dylan at the Newport Folk Festival 2002," at http://www.strangefamousrecords.com/forum/viewtopic.php?t=710&sid= ea256749e7ad302e5ed3f6dfe7a9bce0, accessed on June 2, 2016.

82. Brown, "Dylan at Newport 2002."

83. Karen Ziner, "Dylan Back in Newport," *Providence Sunday Journal*, August 4, 2002, A-1, A-8.

84. Brown, "Dylan at Newport 2002."

85. Vaughn Watson, "Festival Ends on a Personal, Mellow Note," *Providence Journal*, August 5, 2002, A-4.

86. Interview with the author, February 17, 2013.

87. Interview with the author, July 27, 2013.

11. SHE WAS MY GIRL

1. The account of the Weins' courtship and marriage is from Wein and Chinen, *Myself among Others*, 63–73.

2. Wein and Chinen, *Myself among Others*, 47.

3. This passage comes from an interview with the author on July 6, 2009; the story of the bus is retold in Wein and Chinen, *Myself among Others*.

4. The process of interviewing Wein, one quickly learns, entails asking your questions, enjoying his answers, and reconciling the inevitable discrepancies later.

5. It would, however, be wrong to think they never needed any help along the way. John Dunson, the former *Broadside* editor, wrote to Theo Bikel in 1964 about separate onstage placements for black and white groups, as well as accommodations for most black players in a communal "Blues House" while pop performers stayed at the ritzy Hotel Viking. According to Wein's book, the closure of the Blues House the next year was met with mixed reactions from white and black performers and observers alike.

6. Lyndon B. Johnson, "Speech before Congress on Voting Rights March 15, 1965," http://millercenter.org/president/speeches/speech-3386, accessed June 30, 2016.

7. Rick Massimo, "Joyce Wein Worked Tirelessly on Details for Folk and Jazz Festivals," *Providence Journal*, August 17, 2005, G-7, G-8.

12. IN THE WOODS THEY GOT ELECTRONIC INSTRUMENTS

1. Interview with the author, June 23, 2014.

2. Ben Ratliff, "George Wein Sells Company That Produces Music Festivals," *New York Times*, January 25, 2007.

3. The account of Jay Sweet's early life and early experiences with the Newport Folk Festival is taken from an interview with the author on May 7, 2014.

4. Strasburg now runs the iconic Colorado venue Red Rocks; Thomas has worked at AEG and Live Nation and runs the Aspen Jazz Festival.

5. Interview with the author, June 23, 2014.

6. Interview with the author, August 5, 2015.

7. It was also the year that beer and wine were sold at the Newport festivals for

the first time in decades, though the alcohol was (and is) dispensed from tents on the end of a pier, far from the stage. There were no alcohol-related incidents.

8. The birth name of the artist Cat Power.

9. Interview with the author, July 10, 2014.

10. Interview with the author, July 6, 2009.

11. Joan Anderman, "New Folks at Newport Rock Festival's Traditions," *Boston Globe*, April 17, 2008, A-1.

12. Anderman, "New Folks at Newport Rock."

13. Anderman, "New Folks at Newport Rock."

14. Rick Massimo, "Buffett Brings Heat to Newport, but Everybody's Cool," *Providence Journal*, August 4, 2008, A-4. Today, Sweet says that he booked "about 10 percent" of the 2008 festival and quickly adds that "I had nothing to do with Jimmy Buffett." He claims that the Buffett camp likes to needle him about the fact that the Newport show is the only Buffett concert in more than twenty years not to sell out, but that he considers the distinction a badge of honor.

15. Interview with the author, July 10, 2014.

16. All Larry Mouradjian's accounts are taken from an interview with the author on July 25, 2014.

17. Interview with the author, July 31, 2014.

18. Interview with the author, October 3, 2013.

19. Interview with the author, May 7, 2014.

20. Davidson's accounts are taken from an interview with the author on July 26, 2014.

21. Interview with the author, June 23, 2014.

22. E-mail to the author, July 14, 2014.

23. Interview with the author, June 23, 2014.

24. James Reed, "Founder Pitches to Again Lead Newport Fests," *Boston Globe*, March 4, 2009. http://web.archive.org/web/20090311044953/http://www.boston .com/business/articles/2009/03/04/founder_pitches_to_again_lead_newport _fests/.

25. Interview with the author, June 23, 2014.

26. Interview with the author, July 6, 2009.

27. Reed, "Founder Pitches to Again Lead Newport Fests."

28. Interview with the author, July 6, 2009.

29. Interview with Jay Sweet, August 6, 2014. Similarly, that year's jazz festival in Newport was called George Wein's Jazz Festival 50.

30. Interview with the author, August 6, 2014.

31. Interview with the author, July 27, 2013.

32. Rick Massimo, "George Wein Is Back in Charge," *Providence Sunday Journal*, August 2, 2009, F-1, F-8.

33. Interview with the author, July 9, 2009.

34. Both bands had rags-to-riches journeys to Newport: the three then members of Low Anthem—Ben Knox Miller, Jeff Prystowsky and Jocie Adams—had worked as recycling volunteers for Clean Water Action, Miller's girlfriend's organization, the previous year, but resolutely passed out demo tapes as they worked, eventually reaching Sweet's ears; meanwhile, Deer Tick's Andrew Tobiassen was an usher at the backstage tent, "checking to make sure everyone had the right pass. Now I've got the right pass."

35. Rick Massimo, "Newport Folk Fest Was a Day for the Young—and Pete Seeger, Too," *Providence Sunday Journal*, August 2, 2009, A-1.

36. Interview with the author, July 27, 2013.

37. Interview with the author, May 20, 2011.

38. Interview with the author, May 20, 2011.

39. Sweet's recollection of the 2009 festival is taken from an interview with the author, May 7, 2014.

40. Interview with the author, July 10, 2014.

13. LET THEM KNOW THAT YOU KNOW WHERE YOU ARE

1. Interview with the author, May 7, 2014.

2. Detailed in "Newport Folk Festival Sold Out," August 1, 2011. http://www.capecodacoustics.com/acoustic-guitar-blog/newport-folk-festival-sold-out.

3. James Reed, "Newport Folk: Singular Sensations," *Boston Globe*, July 28, 2014. http://www.bostonglobe.com/arts/music/2014/07/27/singular-sensations-newport-folk-festival/5J9uvbFbViZQ8LaFC4nOxl/story.html.

4. Interview with the author, July 27, 2014.

5. Interview with the author, July 30, 2014.

6. Interview with the author, July 27, 2013.

7. Interview with the author, July 27, 2013.

8. Interview with the author, August 14, 2014.

9. Interview with the author, May 7, 2014.

10. Interview with the author, May 7, 2014.

11. Interview with the author, May 7, 2014.

12. Interview with the author, May 7, 2014.

13. Filene, *Romancing the Folk*, 131.

14. Filene, *Romancing the Folk*, 55.

15. Filene, *Romancing the Folk*, 75.

16. Filene, *Romancing the Folk*, 124.

17. Filene, *Romancing the Folk*, 127.

18. Filene, *Romancing the Folk*, 131.

19. Interview with the author, July 27, 2014.

20. Interview with the author, August 6, 2014.

21. Interview with the author, July 26, 2015.

22. Interview with the author, June 23, 2014.

23. Interview with the author, July 27, 2014.

24. Interview with the author, July 27, 2014.

25. Interview with the author, August 6, 2014.

26. Interview with the author, July 26, 2014.

27. Interview with the author, July 27, 2013.

28. Quote provided by Johnette Rodriguez.

29. Interview with the author, July 27, 2013.

30. Interview with the author, July 27, 2013.

31. Interview with the author, May 7, 2014.

32. James Reed, "Sweet Gives Newport Folk Festival a Distinct Flavor," *Boston Globe*, July 26, 2012. http://www.bostonglobe.com/arts/music/2012/07/26/sweet-gives-newport-folk-festival-distinct-flavor/OYcR9NZW5eAYky6jtAycKJ/story.html?camp=pm.

33. Interview with the author, July 27, 2013.

34. Interview with the author, July 27, 2013.

35. Interview with the author, September 4, 2014.

36. Cantwell, *When We Were Good*, 54.

37. Cantwell, *When We Were Good*, 170.

38. Cantwell, *When We Were Good*, 53.

39. Cantwell, *When We Were Good*, 285.

40. Cantwell, *When We Were Good*, 14.

41. Cantwell, *When We Were Good*, 22.

42. Cantwell, *When We Were Good*, 29.

43. Nate Chinen, "Newport Folk Festival, with Arlo Guthrie and Jackson Browne," *New York Times*, July 30, 2012. http://www.nytimes.com/2012/07/31/arts/music/newport-folk-festival-with-arlo-guthrie-and-jackson-browne.html?pagewanted=all&_r=1&.

44. Interview with the author, July 27, 2013.

45. Interview with the author, February 15, 2013.

46. Interview with the author, July 31, 2013.

47. Interview with the author, August 7, 2013.

48. Interview with the author, August 7, 2013.

49. Interview with the author, July 2010.

50. Interview with the author, July 26, 2014.

51. Interview with the author, July 30, 2014.

52. Interview with the author, July 27, 2014.

53. In Reed, "Sweet Gives Newport Folk Festival a Distinct Flavor."

54. Interview with the author, September 6, 2013.

55. Interview with the author, July 10, 2014.

56. Gene Youngblood, "Change in Contemporary Folk Music Chronicled on Film," *Los Angeles Free Press*, November 17, 1967, 13. In Cohen, *Rainbow Quest*, 290.

57. The mission statement is at http://www.newportfestivalsfoundation.org /about-us/mission-statement/, accessed June 25, 2016.

58. Interview with the author, August 14, 2014.

59. Interview with the author, August 6, 2014.

60. Interview with the author, July 27, 2014.

61. Interview with the author, August 14, 2014.

62. Cantwell, *When We Were Good*, 306.

63. Patrick Doyle, "Levon Helm, Edward Sharpe Rock Newport Folk Festival," www.rollingstone.com, August 2, 2010. http://www.rollingstone.com/music /news/levon-helm-edward-sharpe-rock-newport-folk-festival-20100802 #ixzz36dMgs6Hs.

14. #DONTLOOKBACK

1. Cantwell, *When We Were Good*, 38–39.

BIBLIOGRAPHY

BOOKS AND ESSAYS

Baez, Joan. *And a Voice to Sing With*. New York: Summit Books, 1987.

Boyd, Joe. *White Bicycles: Making Music In the '60s*. London: Serpent's Tail, 2010.

Bronner, Simon. "In Search of American Tradition." In Bronner, *Folk Nation: Folklore in the Creation of American Tradition*, 3–70. Wilmington, DE: Scholarly Resources, 2002.

Cantwell, Robert. "When We Were Good: Class and Culture In the Folk Revival." In *Transforming Tradition: Folk Music Revivals Examined*, edited by Neil V. Rosenberg, 35–60. Urbana: University of Illinois Press, 1993.

———. *When We Were Good: The Folk Revival*. Cambridge, MA, and London: Harvard University Press, 1996.

Cohen, Ronald. *A History of Folk Music Festivals in the United States: Feasts of Musical Celebration*. Lanham, MD: Scarecrow Press, 2008.

———. *Rainbow Quest: The Folk Music Revival & American Society, 1940–1970*. Amherst, MA: University of Massachusetts Press, 2002.

Collins, Judy. *Sweet Judy Blue Eyes: My Life in Music*. New York: Crown Archetype, a division of Random House, 2011.

DeTurk, David A., and A. Poulin Jr., eds. *The American Folk Scene: Dimensions of the Folksong Revival*. New York: Dell 1967.

Dunaway, David King. *How Can I Keep from Singing?: The Ballad of Pete Seeger*. New York: Vilard, 2008.

Dunson, Josh. *Freedom in the Air: Song Movements of the Sixties*. New York: International Publishers, 1965.

Epstein, Daniel Mark. *The Ballad of Bob Dylan: A Portrait*. New York: HarperCollins, 2011.

Filene, Benjamin. *Romancing the Folk: Public Memory & American Roots Music*. Chapel Hill and London: University of North Carolina Press, 2000.

Goldblatt, Burt. *Newport Jazz Festival: The Illustrated History*. New York: Dial Press, 1977.

Hamilton and Associates. "Cajuns: Their History and Culture." National Park Service, 1987. http://archive.org/stream/cajunstheirhistoo2hami /cajunstheirhistoo2hami_djvu.txt. Accessed May 22, 2016.

Hajdu, David. *Positively 4th Street: The Lives and Times of Joan Baez, Bob Dylan, Mimi Baez Fariña and Richard Fariña*. New York: North Point Press, 2001.

Jackson, Bruce. "The Folksong Revival." In *Transforming Tradition*, edited by Neil V. Rosenberg, 73–83. Urbana: University of Illinois Press, 1993.

Rooney, Jim, and Eric von Schmidt. *Baby Let Me Follow You Down: An Illustrated Story of the Cambridge Folk Years*. Amherst: University of Massachusetts Press, 1979.

Rosenberg, Neil V., ed. *Transforming Tradition: Folk Music Revivals Examined*. Urbana: University of Illinois Press, 1993.

Shelton, Robert. *No Direction Home: The Life and Music of Bob Dylan*. New York: Hal Leonard revised edition, 2011.

Stekert, Ellen. "Cents and Nonsense in the Urban Folksong Movement." In *Transforming Tradition*, edited by Neil V. Rosenberg, 84–106. Urbana: University of Illinois Press, 1993.

Titon, Jeff Todd. "Reconstructing the Blues: Reflections on the 1960s Blues Revival." In *Transforming Tradition*, edited by Neil V. Rosenberg, 220–240. Urbana: University of Illinois Press, 1993.

Van Ronk, Dave, with Elijah Wald. *The Mayor of MacDougal Street*. Cambridge, MA: Da Capo Press, 2005.

Wald, Elijah. *Dylan Goes Electric! Newport, Seeger, Dylan, and the Night That Split the Sixties*. New York: Dey Street Books, 2015.

Warburton, Eileen. *In Living Memory: A Chronicle of Newport, Rhode Island, 1888–1988*. Newport: Newport Savings and Loan Association, 1988.

Wein, George, and Nate Chinen. *Myself among Others: A Life in Music*. Cambridge, MA: Da Capo Press, 2003.

JOURNALS AND MAGAZINES

Armstrong, Dan. "'Commercial' Folksongs—Product of 'Instant Culture.'" *Sing Out!* February–March 1963.

Dane, Barbara. "Newport Folk Fest: Business as Usual." *Village Voice*, July 10, 1969, in *Broadside* 100 (July 1969).

Dolan, Anthony R. "Heroes in the Seaweed." *National Review*, October 8, 1968.

Fiott, Stephen. "In Defense of Commercial Folksingers." *Sing Out!* December 1962–January 1963.

Jackson, Bruce. "Newport." *Sing Out!* September 1966.

———. "Newport '66—Good Music, Diabolical Programming." *Sing Out!* October–November 1966.

Joseph, Nathan. "I Record What I Like." *Folk Music* 1(5), March 1964.

MacColl, Ewan. "The Singer and the Audience." *Folk Music* 1(1), November 1963.

Nelson, Paul. "Newport: Down There on a Visit." *Little Sandy Review* 30, 1965.

Pankake, Jon, and Paul Nelson. "Tradition Singers." *Sing Out!* February–March 1963.

Silber, Irwin. "What's Happening" column. *Sing Out!* October–November 1967.
Silber, Irwin, and David Gahr. "Top Performers Highlight 1st Newport Folk Fest."
     Sing Out! fall 1959.
"Winter Meeting of the New York Folklore Society, 2 March 1963." *New York
     Folklore Quarterly*, June 1963.

FILMS

Festival! Written, produced and directed by Murray Lerner, 1967.
No Direction Home: Bob Dylan. Directed by Martin Scorcese. PBS and BBC Two,
     2005.
The Other Side of the Mirror: Bob Dylan at the Newport Folk Festival. Directed by
     Murray Lerner. BBC Four, 2007.
Pete Seeger: The Power of Song. Genius Products DVD, 2008.

SOUND RECORDINGS

The Newport Folk Festival 1959, Not Now Records, 2011.
Tapes of the Newport Folk Festivals between 1963 and 1968 are at the American
     Folklife Center at the Library of Congress.

OTHER DOCUMENTS

Cheryl Anne Brauner. "A Study of the Newport Folk Festival and the Newport Folk
     Foundation." Master's thesis, Memorial University of Newfoundland, 1983.
Unpublished interview with Joyce Wein by Carol Brauner. Provided by George
     Wein.

CREDITS

INDEX

Sainte-Marie, Buffy, 101, 127

Saletan, Tony, 34–35

Saliers, Emily, 141, 144

Santana, 146

Sardella, Richard, 123

Savoy-Doucet Band, 136

Scalzi, Leonard, 27

Schmidt, Eric von, 34, 61–62

scouting, 96, 46–47, 106. *See also* Lomax, Alan; Jones, Bob

Scruggs, Earl, 23–24, 101

Scruggs, Lester, 184

Sebastian, John, 136

Second Beach, 35

Secor, Ketch (Old Crow Medicine Show), 191

Seeger, Charles, 56, 70, 96

Seeger, Mike, 42–44, 101, 103, 108, 137, 146

Seeger, Peggy, 25

Seeger, Pete, 64, 95–97, 107, 138, 159–60, 176; at 1959 Festival, 1–2, 21, 25; at 1965 Festival, 67–68; at 1966 Festival, 103; at 1986 Festival, 135; at 2009 Festival, 2–3, 171–72; in the Almanac Singers, 13; attitude towards own songs, 212n10; blacklist of, 37; death in 2014, 194–96; discontent with mainstream society, 125; early career of, 29–30; exclusion from ABC, 57; fundraiser, 126; gets lost, 173; helps make other music venues possible, 150–51; "If I Had a Hammer," 6; letter to George Wein after the first Festival, 55; letter to performers in 1965, 93; manifesto of Festival written by, 34, 179; as the past of folk music after Dylan, 100; planned on being featured in Jazz Festival "Folk Afternoon," 11; reaction to Dylan's 1965 electric performance, 60, 76–80, 82, 87–90, 174; remembers boats in Newport harbor, 148; and revival of Newport Folk Festival in 1963, 31–32, 63; schism between Bob Dylan and, 184; Sweet respecting model of Festival originated by, 178; as the touchstone of the folk movement, 199; Utopia of, 66; visual tribute at 2014 Festival to, 188; as Wein's first native guide, 29–30; winning battle with courts, 63; "You Playboys and Playgirls Ain't Gonna Run My World," 35

Seeger, Tao Rodriguez, 2, 64, 171–72, 187, 195

Seeger, Toshi, 5, 25, 134–35

Shane, Bob, 23–24

Sharp, Cecil, 59, 180

Shearing, George, 28

Shelton, Robert, 18, 20, 24–26, 35, 103

Shepherd, Dewey, 40

Shields, Chris, 162–63, 165, 169–70, 179

Shocked, Michelle, 128, 137, 145, 147–48, 151, 188

Shoreline Media, 163

Siggins, Betsy, 38, 90, 145–46, 167

Silber, Irwin, 58, 63, 67, 96–97, 106–7

Silverman, Jerry, 60, 64

Sinatra, Frank, 216n14

singer-songwriter, 3, 39, 62, 66, 95, 128, 144, 149, 166–67, 171, 190

Sing Out!, 17, 59–60, 67, 96–97, 102, 130, 149

Slim, Langhorne, 176

Smashing Pumpkins, 146

Smith, Andy, 117

Smith, Harry, 15, 35

Smith, Willie "the Lion," 26

Smither, Chris, 164, 166

Smithsonian Folklife Festival, 53

Smithsonian Institution, 53

Music:Interview

A SERIES FROM WESLEYAN UNIVERSITY PRESS

Edited by Daniel Cavicchi

The Music/Interview series features conversations with musicians, producers, and other significant figures in the world of music, past and present. The focus is on people who have not only made good music but have had insightful and profound things to say about creativity, politics, and culture. Each Music/Interview book presents an original approach to music-making, showing music as a vehicle for inspiration, identity, comment, and engagement. The interview format provides conversations between knowledgeable insiders. By foregrounding individual voices, the series gives readers the opportunity to better appreciate the sounds and music around us, through the voices of those who have experienced music most directly.

Yip Harburg
Legendary Lyricist and Human
Rights Activist
    Harriet Hyman Alonso

Fela
Kalakuta Notes
    John Collins

Words of Our Mouth, Meditations of
Our Heart
Pioneering Musicians of Ska, Rocksteady,
Reggae, and Dancehall
    Kenneth Bilby

Reel History
The Lost Archive of Juma Sultan and the
Aboriginal Music Society
    Stephen Farina

Producing Country
The Inside Story of the Great Recordings
    Michael Jarrett

Always in Trouble
An Oral History of ESP-Disk, the Most
Outrageous Record Label in America
    Jason Weiss

ABOUT THE AUTHOR

RICK MASSIMO grew up in Providence, Rhode Island, and covered the Newport Folk Festival for nine years for the *Providence Journal.* He is also the author of the book *A Walking Tour of the Georgetown Set*, and he and his wife live in Washington, D.C.